SATAN,
SOCIALITES,
and SOLLY GOLD
Three New Plays from England

# SATAN, SOCIALITES, and SOLLY GOLD

*Three New Plays from England*

*Coward-McCann, Inc.*
*New York*

*Questo misero modo*
*tengon l'anime triste di coloro*
*che visser sanza infamia e sanza lodo.*

*Mischiate sono a quel cattivo coro*
*delli angeli che non furon ribelli*
*ne fur fedeli a Dio, ma per se foro.*

*Caccliani i ciel per non esser men belli,*
*ne lo profondo inferno li riceve,*
*ch'alcuna gloria i rei avrebber d'elli.*

# THE DEATH OF SATAN
## by Ronald Duncan

# THE SOCIALITES
## by Kenneth Jupp

# ENTER SOLLY GOLD
## by Bernard Kops

# THE DEATH OF SATAN

*A Comedy*

*by*

RONALD DUNCAN

# CHARACTERS

DON JUAN

SATAN

CATALION

OSCAR WILDE

LORD BYRON

BERNARD SHAW

A BISHOP

ANTHONY LISSENDEN, an English novelist

MARCIA LISSENDEN, his wife

LIONEL, an American businessman

EVELYN, his wife

LADY MORETON

HENRIETTA, her companion

A RECEPTIONIST

*Period:* Contemporary

## ACT ONE

Scene One: Hell
Scene Two: The Don Juan Hotel
Scene Three: Evelyn's bedroom

## ACT TWO

Scene One: As Scene 2, Act One
Scene Two: In the garden of the hotel
Scene Three: Hell

The action of the play is confined to one night.

# Act One

*The Present.*

*The scene suggests something between the shabbiness of a railway waiting room and the comfortable but dingy atmosphere of the Reading Room at a London club.*

*It is a late winter afternoon. The room is unlit except by reading lamps. A tea tray stands on a small table (FS) surrounded by three leather club chairs, the occupants of which are hidden behind their newspapers with only their legs visible. One wears kneebreeches, another is clothed in the narrow trousers of the Edwardian period, while the third, as far as one can see, is attired in the style of the late eighteenth century.*

*A large table in the centre is neatly arranged with periodicals. At the back of the room a man is seated at a small writing desk. Only his face is lit.*

*Two heavily curtained windows (BS) with a horsehair sofa between them. A door (BSR) and a fireplace surrounded by a club fender. The only people who are entirely visible are a parson who stands gazing moodily into the fire, and a servant who moves silently about the room picking up newspapers which he arranges fussily on the table.*

*Nobody speaks when the curtain rises, and from the way the servant moves, it is apparent that nothing is allowed*

11

*to break the atmosphere—sepulchral yet very comfortable gloom.*

THE PERSON AT THE WRITING DESK. Damn and blast! And may the devil . . .

*He throws his pen down on the desk. The* PARSON *standing at the fireplace turns slowly and smiles indulgently in his direction. The three newspapers are lowered one inch and then raised again. Only the* SERVANT *fails to react at the interruption.*

FIRST NEWSPAPER (*Motioning to* SERVANT *but not lowering his paper*). Take this ball pen to the writing desk, will you?

SERVANT. Yes, Sir.

SECOND NEWSPAPER. I suppose all his ink's dried up again?

THIRD NEWSPAPER. Yes, that's the worst of this central heating.

SECOND NEWSPAPER. Personally, I like it. It reminds me of New York
And being reminded of New York makes me
Appreciate the comfort we have here.

*The* PARSON *again turns from the fire and now scowls in the direction of the three armchairs. He continues to do so with mounting displeasure.*

FIRST NEWSPAPER (*Lowering newspaper to reveal* GEORGE BERNARD SHAW). Nothing much in the newspapers, is there?

THIRD NEWSPAPER (*Revealing* BYRON). Nothing. The usual murders, robberies
With violence, rapes with acquiescence,
War in China and riots in Teheran.
Nothing unusual.

SHAW. That's what I notice.
It's certainly becoming difficult
To know whether one is reading
Today's papers, the day before yesterday's
Or even last year's.

BYRON. Quite. The press is not what it was.
I can't think why I read it.

SECOND NEWSPAPER (*Revealing* OSCAR WILDE). I can. I read these rags because of their salacious detail

Which remind me of both London and Paris
And the more I'm reminded of those two cities
The more I appreciate the peace we all have here.

SHAW. Of course in my day, I used to write for the *Gazette*.
The *Whitehall Gazette*.

BYRON. Did you? Who would have guessed it?

SHAW. And I may say my occasional letter to *The Times*
On the subject of phonetics or some aspect
Of dialectics enlivened that journal considerably.

BYRON. Remember your promise. Spare us an example.

SHAW. And I may add the *Sunday Observer* was always grateful
Whenever I sent them a poem; I used a nom-de-plume, of
course.

BYRON. Of course.

SHAW. Did I ever read you my last?

WILDE. You did.

BYRON. I seldom wrote for the papers. They continually wrote
about me.

WILDE. Yes, you showed us your cuttings yesterday.

SHAW. You know, it wouldn't surprise me if even I
Didn't become a typical club bore.

WILDE. What a metamorphosis.

BYRON. Well, let's brighten ourselves up a bit
With another cup of tea.
       *He beckons the* SERVANT.
D'you think you could find
Some more hot water, Catalion?

CATALION. There should be no difficulty there, Sir.

SHAW. Quite, I was forgetting.

CATALION. As we all do.

BYRON. And bring some crumpets.

WILDE. And some cucumber sandwiches.

SHAW. I often wondered why you didn't repeat
The success you had with Lady Bracknell.

WILDE. I left it to you.

BYRON. Now you two. No Missolonghi here!
> *The* SERVANT *enters with a tray. The* PARSON *beckons him towards the fireplace.*

PARSON (*Whispers to him*). The next time they ask for hot water, bring ice
And see that their crumpets are burned.

SERVANT. Yes, Sir.
> *The* PARSON *stoops and flings a scuttleful of coal on the already blazing fire.*

BYRON. There he goes again.

SHAW. In Russia, of course, nobody's allowed to burn coal
That is, in open grates.

WILDE. What do they do? Burn books?

BYRON. I would have thought they'd have found it
More profitable to burn bores.

SHAW. And they are also exploiting the thermal potential
Between the different levels of the Earth's crust.

WILDE. You mean to say it's hotter lower down?

BYRON. Surely we all know that.

SHAW. All gases expand as you raise their temperature.
But what Rudvodkin has demonstrated is
If you bury a cylinder of carbon dioxide only fifty feet
You can produce sufficient pressure, that is, power
To drive a turbine on the surface. You should read him.
> *He hands* BYRON *the book.*

WILDE. I thought you two were friends. Didn't we make a pact
That if you three stop talking about Russia, I'd stop coining epigrams?

BYRON. Thanks, but I won't have time to read it. I'm still stuck in Wordsworth's *Prelude*!
And there's the whole of *The Excursion* waiting. . . .

WILDE. May I borrow it? There's no indulgence quite so sweet
As reading about the Soviets, for reading about the Soviets
Makes me appreciate the luxury and the warmth we all have here
> *The* PARSON *scowls again.*

BYRON. Yes, there's nothing so pleasant as an open fire, is there? And the buttered crumpets are quite delicious, aren't they?

SHAW. Are they? Yes, we've got everything here but equality.

BYRON. One could say our only discomfort was in our conscience.

WILDE. I never felt more at home in all my life.

SHAW. Well, what about a rubber of bridge before dinner?

WILDE. All right.

BYRON (*Turning towards the desk*). Shall I ask Don Juan to join us?

WILDE. You can but try.

BYRON (*Going over to* DON JUAN). Will you join us in a rubber, senor?

DON JUAN. I haven't any money.

BYRON. Nor have I. That's why I'm going to play.

DON JUAN (*Rising*). I'm sorry. I have a letter to write.

BYRON. No hurry. We'll wait while you finish it.

DON JUAN. No, please don't. When I've written it once, I only tear it up
Then write it again. Shall I read it to you?

WILDE (*To* SHAW). He asked for it.

SHAW. The poor fellow certainly suffers.
An example to us all.
   *The* PARSON *smiles.*

DON JUAN (*Reading*). 'Let me ask you one question
And I will never ask another:
Do I walk through your dreams
As you . . .'

SHAW and WILDE. '. . . now run through mine.'

DON JUAN (*Oblivious of them*). '. . . Answer this question
I will not ask another.'
   *He breaks down and sits again at the desk.*

WILDE. It's a pity Byron didn't make his tutor eat him.

SHAW. And to think I put him here!

WILDE. For taking such an obvious course, you deserved to join him.

DON JUAN. Well, what d'you think? Will Dona Ana ever get it?

BYRON. Who? Get what?
    *BYRON saunters back to the armchair.*

DON JUAN (*To* PARSON). You see he wasn't listening, nobody ever listens.

PARSON (*Comforting him at the desk*). There, there, it's a pleasure for me to see your pain.

BYRON. He's hopeless.

WILDE. Anyway I prefer three-handed poker.

DON JUAN. They're indifferent to my suffering. I detest their smugness,
And their comfort.

PARSON. So do I, my son.

SHAW. Yes, cut throat makes a good game among friends.
(*To* SERVANT) The cards, please.

CATALION. Certainly, Sir.
    *He removes the tea tray then crosses the room to fetch the cards. The PARSON intercepts him, takes the pack, removes six cards and replaces them by six others which he takes from his pocket. Then he returns the pack to the SERVANT.*

PARSON. That should ruin their evening.
    *The SERVANT hands the cards to WILDE.*

WILDE. What are the stakes, the usual?

BYRON. No. What's the point in playing for money?

SHAW. What else?

WILDE (*Dealing*). Our reputations.

SHAW. You've nothing to lose.

BYRON. All right. We'll dispense with the kitty.

SHAW. Three.

BYRON. Give me five.

WILDE. Dealer takes two, being honest. I never could bluff. It's you to bet.

SHAW. I'll wager *Mrs. Warren's Profession.*

BYRON. I'll raise you: *Childe Harold.*

WILDE. So? *Lady Windermere's Fan.*
And I'll raise with *The Importance of Being Earnest.*

SHAW. Strange. The cards usually take some time to warm up.
Are you sure you shuffled? You can't have done.
Anyhow I won't be bluffed out. *Saint Joan* to equal.

WILDE. Question.

SHAW. And I'll raise with *Caesar and Cleopatra.*

BYRON. So? Here's *English Bards and Scotch Reviewers*
And *Werther* to top you both.

WILDE and SHAW. It doesn't.

BYRON. Perhaps you're right. Then *Don Juan* too.
    DON JUAN *stands.*
No, not you . . .

WILDE. Very well. My name as a wit.

SHAW. I'll see you. Mine as a playwright.

BYRON. Mine as a poet. We're all in. You're seen.

WILDE (*Laying cards down*). I'm sorry, gentlemen. A full house.
Two aces, two kings
And a joker.

SHAW (*Putting cards down*). Is that all! I was never impressed by
those epigrams.
Three jacks and a joker.

WILDE. Two jokers?

BYRON. No, four! I've a royal flush—ten, joker, queen, joker, ace,
And all in hearts.
    *They all look at the* PARSON.

SHAW. Quite ruined our game. Can't rely on anything here.
This place is going to hell.
    *The* PARSON *beams.*

BYRON (*Indicating the desk*). I suppose there's nothing we can do
now
But sit and listen to Don Juan's adventures.

WILDE. Nonsense. We'll play poker. Whoever monkeyed with this pack
Has only succeeded in enlivening our game. Five jokers
Make it really exciting. It's your deal.

SHAW. I quite agree. It's the same for all of us
Now we know. . . .

DON JUAN. You see. . . .

PARSON. This is the last straw.
*He marches over to the players.*

BYRON. What will you drink?

WILDE. Whisky. Shouldn't this be a jackpot?

BYRON. Ace pot after fours. Two whiskies and a glass of milk. Two please.

WILDE. Three.

SHAW. Dealer takes four.
*The* PARSON *paces up and down.*

BYRON. He doesn't seem to approve.

SHAW. Shouldn't we offer him a hand?

WILDE. No. He'd sure to cheat.

BYRON. Anything to stop him marching up and down.
Would you care to cut in, Sir?

PARSON. I would not.

WILDE. I should have thought you would have approved of poker.

PARSON. I do not.

SHAW. Why? It's a harmless enough game in all conscience.

WILDE. Ssh . . . He means of course, Sir, that it's a good game
Because it's ruined so many. Are you sure you won't join us?

PARSON. I am.

WILDE. Then d'you mind sitting down, Sir,
So that we may concentrate on our cards?

PARSON. I do. Furthermore, I forbid you to play poker this evening.

WILDE (*Dealing*). Why? It's not Ladies' Night, is it?

PARSON. D'you hear what I say? I forbid it.

BYRON. Let's get on with the game and ignore him.
You to open.

WILDE. Sorry I can't open an ace pot.

PARSON (*Overturning table*). Where the devil do you think you
are—
The card room at White's?
*They bow their heads at the word devil.*

WILDE (*Looking round and then glancing at* SHAW). At least it
might pass for the R.A.C.
Or with Shaw, here, the Reform.

PARSON. Well you are not. This is Hell. And I am Satan.
And I'd have you three remember it.
You're supposed to be suffering
Like my good friend, Don Juan, over there,
Not sitting around in garrulous smug comfort.

BYRON (*Picking cards up*). Strange. I'd have sworn that Satan
would have been
A gentleman.

SATAN. Why don't you suffer?
Have you no sins weighing on your immortal souls?
Where's your conscience? And where is your remorse?
How is it your spirits are not crying to Christ for mercy,
Can you not realize you are damned eternally?
You should be now telling your rosary of sins
With tears of contrition and begging forgiveness
Or at least showing some signs of inconvenience.
Have none of you not loved? Have none of you
Not lost someone whom you had loved and
Then finding yourself separated for ever
Know you must suffer alone for ever
Like my good friend Don Juan over there?
DON JUAN *tears up another letter and groans again.*

BYRON. E quella a me 'Nessun maggior dolore
Che ricordarsi del tempo felice
Nella miseria . . .'

WILDE. '. . . E cio sa 'l tuo dottore.

SATAN. Canto 5. But, sir, let me again remind you this is Hell
And English alone is spoken here . . .

Yes, his groans are most gratifying
And I wouldn't complain if you were half as miserable
But instead, those who now arrive here
Sit around as smug and comfortable
As though they were still in St. James's or Pall Mall.

WILDE. He knows his way around.

BYRON. But surely he must see our mistake is understandable
Any man might take this place for the Garrick.

SHAW. No, the evening papers would be delivered there by now.

WILDE. True, this is sufficiently like a club
For me to wonder how I got into it.
Tell us just why did you design Hell so?

SATAN. Because in my innocence I thought
There was no surer way of making men suffer
For their sins than to give them the surroundings
In which they could remember them and
Where they had no diversion to forget them either,
And so I damped down the fires of Hell
And turned it into this club, believing
That as man suffers most when he remembers most,
And here his punishment is the boredom of listening
To those who've committed similar sins
As his own. But it's plain I was mistaken
And those who arrive in Hell now
Are merely relieved to get here. I've lost my touch
I must be getting old.

BYRON. Come, it's not as bad as that.

WILDE. Cheer up, old chap. Have a drink. A drop of whisky
Will pull you together.

SATAN. Thank you, but I don't approve of drink
Unless taken to excess.
       SATAN *returns to the fire.*

WILDE. Plagiarist!

BYRON. I doubt it. He was your original. And in his day
He was an inspiration to us all.
       *Noise off.*

SHAW. There goes that damned lift again. Now in Russia
They would have installed an escalator.
I wonder who it is?

BYRON. Nobody I know.

WILDE. Or who'll know me.
> *Enter a* BISHOP *carrying a gladstone bag.* SATAN *greets him.*
> *The three writers prepare to play cards again, they've heard*
> *most of the following before.*

CATALION. Good evening, Sir.

SATAN. Catalion, take His Lordship's bag to his room.
The left wing.

BYRON. It's not the Dean, is it?

SHAW. No, a bishop.

BYRON. What shall we play for? I don't think any of us wants
each other's reputation.

BISHOP (*Looking round*). Dear me, just a minute there, bring my
bag back.
I fear I've wandered into the wrong club.
Thought I didn't recognize your face, Sir,
But didn't say anything as I'm never sure.
Mine's the Athenaeum, of course, this will be the Scribblers I
presume.
I hope my cab's not gone yet. Please take my bag outside.

SATAN (*To* CATALION). Leave it here.

BISHOP. I beg your pardon, Sir.

SATAN. Your taxi won't be there
Because you did not come by one.

BISHOP. Don't be silly, man. If I didn't come by cab
How d'you think I got here?

SATAN. How did you get here?

BISHOP. Yes, tell me that.

SATAN. D'you know where you are?

BISHOP. Well, seeing that well-known face over there
I naturally assumed that this was the Scribblers . . .

(*Whispering to* SATAN)
But d'you know I was under the impression Shaw was dead.

SATAN. He is. So are you. And you are late.

BISHOP. Ah, the traffic.

SATAN. You did not come by cab. It was Coronary Thrombosis.
Don't you remember your funeral? Now can't you guess where
you are?

BISHOP. My dear Saint Peter! Why of course.
How can you forgive me! And to think I've kept you waiting.
Boy, take my bag right up. I do apologize for not recognizing
you at first
Though I knew I'd seen your face often enough before.

SATAN. Quite. Now perhaps you'll allow me to introduce you
To your fellow members. This, your lordship, is one of our
oldest members.
May I present Don Juan Tenorio.

BISHOP. How d'you do.
        DON JUAN *ignores him.*

BISHOP (*To* SATAN). A foreigner?

SATAN. You must make allowances. He suffers considerably.
A most gratifying case.

BISHOP. A late conversion?

SATAN. Hardly.

BISHOP. Death bed repentance?

SATAN. Oh no. He fell in love with Dona Ana,
But her father, Don Gonzalo, would not let her marry.
Don Juan always had the reputation of a rake.
Dona Ana tried to forget Juan one way; and Juan
Tried to forget her in another. He became
An inveterate amorist.

BISHOP. Dear me.

SATAN. And she became a novice.

BISHOP. And later converted him?

SATAN. Who's telling this story?
As I was saying, Don Juan went to the Devil.

DON JUAN. Sometimes we are more faithful than we know.

SATAN. Would you prefer to tell your story?

DON JUAN. I beg your pardon. Please go on.

SATAN. Eventually Don Juan broke into her convent
Intending to abduct her. But she, believing
It was better for her to break her vows
Than his heart, went with him willingly.

BISHOP. What an anticlimax.

SATAN. But Juan didn't seduce her.
Indeed he again begged her father to give her to him as his wife.
Don Gonzalo again refused. Juan killed him and escaped.
And Dona Ana died of grief. And ever since then
Don Juan has tried to reach Dona Ana from this pit of his
remorse.

BISHOP. And where is she?

SATAN. In the other place.

BISHOP. Yes, the fault is generally with the fairer sex.
  *They move across the room.*

SATAN. And these gentlemen you know, being fellow countrymen
Of yours.

BISHOP. I must say it's gratifying to find
So many Englishmen here. But odd that all are poets.
What! D'you allow them to play cards here?

SATAN. I don't encourage it, of course, far from it.
But there's a place for tolerance even here.
The stakes aren't high—they play for the Ten Commandments.

BISHOP. How very odd. But then I suppose you don't need such
precepts here.

SATAN. I see you need no introduction.
  SHAW *rises without taking his eyes from his cards and
  perfunctorily takes the* BISHOP's *hand.*

BISHOP. Don't think me rude but I must admit
I'm quite surprised to see you here.

SHAW. It's all publicity.

BISHOP. But it's a real pleasure,
And I dare say you now withdraw

Some of those unkind remarks you used to make
About the C. of E.

SHAW. I'll see you, here's 'Do not steal'
And I'll raise you with 'Adultery.'

WILDE. You're very cautious.

BYRON. I throw in.

SATAN. You know these two, of course?
     *BYRON rises.*

BISHOP. Yes, indeed, I've always wanted to thank you
For those lines
'Oh to be in England now that April's here.'
I don't know how you wrote them.

BYRON. Ask Browning.
He'll be back any moment.
     *WILDE rises.*

SATAN. And of course . . .

BISHOP. Well, if you've forgiven him, who am I . . . ?

WILDE. A whisky, Sir?

BISHOP. Thank you, that is, if you've no objection.

SATAN. None at all.

BISHOP. Your health, Sir. Well, I must say I'm surprised
It's one thing to believe in Heaven, but quite another
To find one's faith was fact, and, indeed, discover
That the comfort here surpasses our most pious hopes.

WILDE. I can't open a jackpot.

BYRON. Nor can I.

BISHOP. And I don't mind admitting to you gentlemen here
That the prospect of spending an eternity in heaven
Without any of the comforts of the body
Appeared to me a trifle dim.

WILDE. Two.

BYRON. Three.

SHAW. I'll play these.

BISHOP. But it is good to be back here again.
     *The card players turn towards him.*

*To* BYRON.
As you yourself said, Sir, 'Heaven lies about us
In our infancy.

BYRON. I throw in!

BISHOP. The pity is, that now we have passed over 'to that bourne
From which no traveller returns,' as you'd say
And, as a reward for our devotions, have at last reached heaven,
We have no means of letting those on earth
Know where we are, or that heaven does exist
Though such news would do so much
To encourage those who waver . . .

WILDE (*Whispering to* BYRON). Shouldn't one of us tell him where
he is?

BYRON. I think His Nibs anticipates that pleasure.

BISHOP. I suppose you gentlemen have tried to get through?

WILDE. That bluffs me out as well.

SHAW (*Taking stakes*). And that makes this a queen pot.

BISHOP (*To* SHAW). But surely you should have had at least a pair
To open? Or are the rules different here?

BYRON. Not at all.

WILDE. If anything they're stricter.

SHAW. Don't you trust me?

WILDE. No.

BYRON. Let's see your openers.

SHAW. I never did like the C. of E. But this makes me a Jesuit.
*He goes in a huff.*

BISHOP (*To* SHAW). Ah, 'If you can keep your head while those
about you . . .'

BYRON. Quick, before he attributes that to me.
*They go over to the fire. The* BISHOP *picks up the cards
and starts to play Patience.* SATAN *approaches him.*

SATAN. I hope your lordship is quite comfortable.

BISHOP. Thank you, I am.

SATAN. Good. I do hope you won't be bored
Sitting here with your own thoughts for eternity.

BISHOP. No, don't worry about me.

SATAN. Eternity is a long time.

BISHOP. I shall need all of that if I'm to get this game out
And as a matter of fact I have some burden
Weighing on my conscience . . .

SATAN. Ah . . .
*The* POETS *too are interested.*

BISHOP. Not something I have done, but something I always meant
to do,
And never did.

SATAN. Tell me what it was. Does the omission
Make you suffer?

BISHOP. I've always meant to settle down
And read those books I've never read.

SATAN. And is that all you meant by something on your conscience?

BISHOP. It's quite a load. And d'you know I must confess . . .

SATAN. Yes, to what?

BISHOP. That I've not even read all the Epistles
Let alone Saint Thomas Aquinas. I suppose you've got
A good library here?

SATAN. Valuable signed editions mostly presentation copies.

BISHOP. Good. Now I can settle down and read *Paradise Regained*
And dip into *Pilgrim's Progress.*
*The* POETS *show some disappointment in his choice of
books.*

SATAN. And can you face eternity with equanimity
Won't you be lonely?

BISHOP. I've always enjoyed my own company;
And this comfortable chair, that fire and a book
Is my idea of heaven.

SATAN. Heaven, Sir? This is Hell. And I am Satan.
*The* BISHOP *stands.*

BISHOP. There must be some mistake.

SATAN. Precisely.
And it was you who made it.

BISHOP. But what have I done to deserve . . . ?

SATAN. My hospitality?

BISHOP. And what are you laughing at?

SATAN. Most men know what sins they've committed and such
people I prefer.
But you don't even know why you're here. I'll tell you.
You are in Hell because you were charitable, chaste,
Temperate and honest.

BISHOP. But these are accounted virtues . . .

SATAN. It's not I who balance the account.
You see, by being honest you never felt the thief's temptation.
By being temperate and chaste, you knew nothing
Of the drunkard's misery or the philanderer's brief remorse.
Your frugality and caution deprived you
Of experiencing the prodigal's repentance.
These virtues of yours kept you from sorrow
And a man who knows no sorrow, knows no God.

WILDE. And sometimes sorrow leads only to bitterness
As I remarked in De Profundis.

SATAN. You keep out of this.

BISHOP. Are you suggesting that evil is an attribute to good
And that it's necessary to sin in order to go to heaven?
You make yourself out to be an angel indispensable to God.

SATAN. I was. And I still am indispensable to Him.
Nobody gets to heaven unless they come here first.
Nobody finds his God unless I introduce him.

BISHOP. But what have I done to deserve damnation?

SATAN. There's only one sin which gets a man to Hell: self-love.
And there's nothing like virtue to make a man
Love himself. The pit is pride, smugness is its smoke.

BISHOP (To BYRON). Does this fellow always rant on like this?

BYRON. Yes, he is a trifle evangelical.

SATAN. Do you not acknowledge who I am?

BISHOP (Picking up paper). You look like one of my curates and
what's worse
You talk like one of 'em.

SATAN. I am Satan.

BISHOP. Yes, yes, of course.

SATAN. You don't believe it?

BISHOP. Yes, I do. . . . (*To* WILDE) I suppose one has to humour him!

SATAN. You don't take me seriously?

BISHOP. My dear fellow, you should try a new line.
Satan is a mythological figure,
A mere Old Testament allusion.

SATAN. I've never been so insulted in my life!
It's bad enough to be ignored. It's the last straw
When I'm told to my face that I don't exist.
And I suppose Hell to you is no more than . . .

BISHOP. A mild expletive.

SATAN. So I notice. I designed this place to be a Hell of boredom,
A waiting room between one memory and another regret,
A reading room in which you'd read nothing but your misery.
Yet you all seem comfortable enough and only
My dear friend Don Juan over there
Appreciates the terrors of this place.
In the good old days, people knew why they were in Hell
And I could walk these halls and hear
The unending echoes of remorse and rub my hands
As soul upon soul suffered till each was transformed
Into an attitude of eternal sorrow.
> *The* BISHOP *reads the paper. The* POETS *yawn at first then
> watch* SATAN's *growing excitement with concern for his
> health.*
But that I see is no more, and why?
Are appetites no longer tempted,
And noble aspirations rubbed away with compromise?
Does the tongue no longer thirst
Does the grape no longer ripen?
Do men no longer yearn and women yield?
Does the sun not shine up there? Has man's leisure
Lost its indolence and indolence its opportunity?
Has lust been quite eclipsed and greed and usury put out?
Have you or you no God whom you've betrayed

And need no rope with which to hang yourself?
Or tell me, can it be
His simple word has taken gentle root
And the heap of ash that was the martyrs' fire
Not burned in vain? Has His Church triumphed?
Have men's natures been restrained and forgiveness—
Has it flooded over all? . .
No, no, that catastrophe cannot be
Yet something must have put sorrow to flight
What can it be? Tell me. I command you to speak!

BISHOP (*As though not having heard the above*). Have you got
a light? No? Then I must get one.
> *Exit* BISHOP.
> SATAN *now appears almost broken and physically ailing.*

SATAN. Don Juan Tenorio, come here.
> JUAN *approaches.*
How long have you been in Hell?

JUAN. To time and sorrow there is no end.

SATAN. And have you suffered here, my friend?

JUAN. A man needs no other punishment than memory.

SATAN (*Turning to others*). You hear? What would you give
To be able to return to the Earth for one year?

JUAN. For that I'd give my soul. . . .

SATAN. You have not got.

JUAN. . . . I have not got.

SATAN. Then you shall return to that place in Spain
Where you died three hundred years ago.
For one year you shall walk the earth again
> *The others listen attentively.*
Before returning here to make your report to me. . . .

BYRON. That's an idea that would have made another Canto.

SHAW. It might have made a play.

WILDE. I doubt it!

SATAN. . . . For I wish to know why people don't suffer
Here in Hell any more.
And why the damned appear so unrepentant, comfortable and
smug.

JUAN. And will she be there?
Will I find Dona Ana once again?

SATAN. Didn't she go to that other place?

JUAN. Heaven was where she was.

SATAN. If she is there I cannot answer.
Liaison between the two establishments is not what it was.

SHAW. As a playwright I insist.

BYRON. Oh, surely you could stretch a point?

WILDE. And exercise a poet's licence?

SATAN. God is not a poet.

WILDE. That explains why I'm here.

JUAN. If I cannot find her, I do not wish to go.
Earth will be only another Hell if she's not there.

BYRON. You see?

SATAN. Then I promise you that you shall find her.
Her eyes, her lips, will be as you last saw them
Only one thing she'll lack and that's beyond my call.

JUAN. Her love?

SATAN. No, her soul. But you'll not notice that.
She'll appear like any modern woman.

JUAN. Will she love me?

SATAN. With her body.

JUAN. That will be enough for me.

SATAN. I wonder . . .

JUAN. Can I go now?

SATAN. This instant.

JUAN. And may Catalion go with me?
After all, I'm a Tenorio and need my servant.
            SATAN *rings*. CATALION *appears*.

CATALION. You rang, Sir?

SATAN. Catalion, you may return to Earth with Don Juan for one
year.

CATALION. Thank you, Sir. Will there be only four for dinner?

BYRON. This isn't such a good idea. If Catalion goes too
Who's to wait on us?

WILDE. This place will be like a cafeteria.
Self help indeed? Oh hell!

SATAN. Precisely. And I hope you'll find these arrangements
Most inconvenient. I should have thought of them before.
You can each be servant to one another.

SHAW. Damme if Socialism hasn't followed me to hell.

JUAN. Will I return to Seville?

SATAN. Yes, where you died
At the foot of the statue of the man you killed.

BYRON. But aren't you going to give him a mission,
Certain precise sins to perform?

SATAN. No, just be yourself. That'll do.

WILDE (*To* JUAN). I hope you bring a good report back. He needs
some encouraging.
One more shock like His Lordship just gave him,
And we'll be without a host.

SHAW. But you can't let him go dressed like that
People will wonder where he's come from.

SATAN (*Taking* BISHOP's *cloak*). Wear this meanwhile. When
you arrive just steal
If I can't make other arrangements for you.
Now stand back to back. Breathe deeply
In, out, in, out . .

CURTAIN


SCENE TWO


*The same evening.*
*The courtyard of the* DON JUAN HOTEL, *Seville. It is very*
*modern and most de luxe. There is nothing Spanish about*
*it except its situation; it is as international as an Airway*

*Terminal and as clinical as an American bathroom. The
statue of the Commandant Don Gonzalo can be seen in the
background.*
*When the curtain rises, the receptionist is at her desk and
the guests are enduring each other's company and taking a
cocktail before dinner.*
*There are three small tables, a couple sits at the first and
second: and a woman at the third. A musician plays the
guitar but nothing relieves the atmosphere of comfortable
boredom and one is reminded of the opening of the pre-
ceding scene.*

### First Table

EVELYN.  Did you say anything?

LIONEL.  No.

EVELYN.  I'm sorry.
   I thought you spoke.

LIONEL.  No, I was thinking.

EVELYN.  What were you thinking?

LIONEL.  Of something to say.

### Second Table

ANTHONY.  Will you have another drink?

MARCIA.  Thank you.

ANTHONY.  A gin and lime or a gin and orange?

MARCIA.  I hate having to make a decision.
   I think I'll have a gin and lime,
   It makes a change from a gin and orange.

ANTHONY.  But you've just had a gin and lime.

MARCIA.  Have I? Then I'll have a gin and orange.

ANTHONY.  Waiter. Bring two large martinis, please.
         *Enter* LADY MORETON. *She pauses at the first table before
         sitting at the third.*

LADY MORETON.  Good evening.

LIONEL.  Good evening, Lady Moreton.

LADY MORETON (*To* EVELYN). How pretty you look. And have you seen
Any interesting ruins today?

EVELYN. Several.

LADY MORETON. Isn't it thrilling?
Don't you find it thrilling?

EVELYN. Not exactly.

LADY MORETON. What, here on the very place
Where the Palace of the Tenorios stood
One can almost imagine Don Juan himself
Walking in here, can't you? Such a romantic figure, don't you think?

LIONEL. Definitely.

LADY MORETON. And to think the Commandant's statue
Still stands there! Fascinating, I call it.
Don't you think the past is fascinating?

LIONEL. It sure is.

EVELYN. Still, I can't think why we
Find old buildings so beautiful whereas . . .

LADY MORETON. . . . Age in people is merely ugly? Don't be embarrassed.
I shan't feel like a monument
Till I've got an inscription!
*She goes to the third table with a friendly nod to the couple at the second.*
Ah, there you are, dear Henrietta?
Did you have a good lie down? It must have been the fish
You ate at luncheon at the Waldorf which upset you.

HENRIETTA. Yes, it's a mistake to fly on fish.

LADY MORETON. I think you may have got something there,
Something that every woman might remember.
*She beckons the* WAITER *who approaches her table.*

### First Table

EVELYN. Don't look now. But d'you see what I see?

LIONEL. What d'you see?

EVELYN. I see somebody who thinks she's a cherry stone clam,
  For she's certainly dressed up in a lot of Ketchup.
  How she thinks she can wear that colour
  With her complexion, I don't know.

LIONEL. Don't you? I think she looks very pretty.

EVELYN. You would. She looks like a flag looking for an old bull.

### Second Table

MARCIA. I suppose we'd better ask them to join us.

ANTHONY. I suppose so. That's the worst of Spain.
  One has either to go to the cheap hotels
  And put up with inadequate sanitation,
  Or come to a vulgar place like this
  And tolerate Americans.

MARCIA (To first table). Won't you bring your drinks over and
  join us?

LIONEL. Thank you.

EVELYN. My! what a lovely robe. The colour suits you.
  A model, of course?

MARCIA. No, I picked it up here in Seville.

EVELYN. I don't believe it!

LIONEL. No, this round is mine.
  *The attention is directed to the third table.*

### Third Table

LADY MORETON. Well, Henrietta,
  I hope you haven't wasted your entire evening
  And that in spite of your indisposition
  You've been able to glean some news for me.
  No? How disappointing. I had hoped you'd have discovered
  Precisely what those Lissendens are doing here.
  It can't be their honeymoon, they've been married years
  And this place is far too expensive
  For a gentleman. Well, if you can't tell me
  Anything about the Lissendens, perhaps you can be
  More informative about the other people?

HENRIETTA. I'm afraid not.

LADY MORETON. Come, Henrietta, your flagrant lack of interest
In other people's affairs is nothing less
Than self importance concerning your own,
Which is quite inexcusable since you have not any
Except with fish. What's the use of a companion
Who doesn't keep both ears to the ground?
It is as well that I fend for myself. I haven't been so idle.

HENRIETTA. I believe that they're Americans.

LADY MORETON. How did you guess? She is his second, he's her
third,
The money's hers. Her father started as a lift boy
And rose to the top. I must say, they look
Very friendly together. I suspect they're discussing us.
Nothing makes people so animated
As mutual animosity.

### Second Table

MARCIA. It's getting quite chilly. Excuse me, I must get my wrap.
The climate's most deceptive once the sun's gone down.

EVELYN. But that dress looks so warm.

MARCIA. Does it? You must be frozen.
*Goes across courtyard and exits.*

### Third Table

LADY MORETON. Ah, I wish I were young again. Those two girls
Have certainly got their past before them.
Henrietta, did you hear what I said?
Now what are you staring at?

HENRIETTA. A man. Two men, in fact.
They're standing outside by the statue.

LADY MORETON. Are they indeed? Why didn't you say so?
You're becoming both secretive and mean.
Now where are my glasses?
> DON JUAN *and* CATALION *can be seen by the statue in the
> garden.* JUAN *wears a dinner suit.* CATALION *is dressed as
> his valet. The others continue talking.*

DON JUAN. The sculptor was right: the stone has weathered three
centuries

CATALION. Standing here, don't you feel any remorse?

DON JUAN. None. My conscience is even tougher.
But where's Don Luis' effigy? Didn't my father
Break up the Palace and turn the whole garden
Into a pantheon as a memorial to those I'd killed?

CATALION. Yes. One statue doesn't do you justice.
They've even moved Dona Ana's sepulchre.

DON JUAN. I did not kill her. She died of grief.

CATALION. But it was you she mourned.

DON JUAN. But where's the lake?

CATALION. It was here. Your father drained it to build the Pantheon
Which someone's converted into this: *The Don Juan Hotel.*
*They enter.*
I must say I prefer the place we've come from.

RECEPTIONIST. Would you mind signing the register, senor?

DON JUAN. Not at all. Have rooms been reserved for me?

RECEPTIONIST. Yes, senor. We received your cable.

DON JUAN. Where was it sent from?

RECEPTIONIST. New York, senor.

DON JUAN. That sounds appropriate
From what I hear.

RECEPTIONIST. Will you be staying long, senor?

DON JUAN. Precisely one year. One year to the day, I fear.
Has Dona Ana arrived?

RECEPTIONIST. No one of that name has registered.

DON JUAN. You may expect her. See that her room is close to mine.

RECEPTIONIST. Certainly, senor. Your luggage has already been
taken up.

DON JUAN. Has it indeed? One must give the devil his due.

RECEPTIONIST. I hope you'll be quite comfortable here.

DON JUAN. Thank you. I always was.

RECEPTIONIST. If there's anything you need . . .
*Others rise from the second table.*

DON JUAN (*As if to himself*). No, my tastes are simple. Four
    things I love
And any man may find them: the sun for its warmth,
Night for its coolness, horses for their grace
And women for their. . . .

CATALION. Senor, quick.

DON JUAN. What is it?

CATALION (*Indicating* EVELYN *who wears a backless dress*). A lady
    naked! Some villain must have torn the clothes off her back.

DON JUAN (*Placing his cloak around her*). Senorita, allow me.

EVELYN. Just what d'you think you are doing?

DON JUAN. Chivalry could do no less for modesty
In such distress.

LIONEL. I'd have you know, Sir, that's my wife.

DON JUAN. Then why strip her in public?

EVELYN (*Brazenly removing cloak*). Don't you like my dress?

DON JUAN. Indeed I do. Don't you, Catalion? (*Whispering*)
There's nothing like the sight of the small of a woman's back
To lend character to her face, is there?

CATALION (*Whispering*). Perhaps this is a brothel?

DON JUAN. My apologies, senora.
Where I come from fashions are different.
Certain proprieties are observed there . . .
    *He notices his own evening clothes.*
But here, I see, women wear less, men wear more.
Catalion, you look like a donkey
Peering over a whitewashed wall. . . .

ANTHONY. Have you travelled far?

DON JUAN. Yes, but the journey seemed so quick
I feel somewhat disembodied; it's as though my body were here
But my mind was still elsewhere. Such speed requires some
    adjustment.

ANTHONY. You flew, of course?

DON JUAN. So fast the wind in front of us
Hadn't time to close behind us.

LIONEL. From your remark about what people wear
  I presume you come from the East?

DON JUAN. That depends where you are.

ANTHONY. Have you ever been in Selancor?
  I often wish I were back in Selancor.
  The Sultan was a good chap. I was at Oxford with him.
      *Enter* MARCIA *unobserved by all except* DON JUAN.
  And his wife, she was a pretty little thing.

DON JUAN. Ana . . .

ANTHONY. No, that wasn't her name.

DON JUAN. Ana . . .

ANTHONY. No, my dear fellow, she was called Sunita.
  Yes, she was a pretty little thing. . . .

DON JUAN. I have not dared to close my eyes for fear of seeing
  her
  Nor open them to know she was not there.

ANTHONY. Really, well, I didn't get it quite like that.

DON JUAN. Our souls are entwined round one another.
      *He greets* MARCIA *and embraces her passionately.*
  Ana, Ana.
      *She breaks away as soon as she has overcome her surprise.*

ANTHONY. You know each other?

MARCIA. How dare you?

DON JUAN. Ana.

MARCIA. My name is Marcia.

DON JUAN. Names can alter, eyes do not.

MARCIA. I've never seen you in my life.

DON JUAN. In my death I've kept your face ever before my
  eyes . . .

ANTHONY. I must ask you, Sir . . .

DON JUAN. It was my suffering in hell which gave life to you.

ANTHONY. . . . To leave my wife alone.

DON JUAN. Ana, who is this man?

MARCIA. My husband.

DON JUAN. Ah, of course, marriages are made in heaven . . .
But though you made me jealous once
I was never jealous of a man.

MARCIA. What are you talking about! I've never seen you before,
And I'm sure I don't wish to see you again.

DON JUAN. Ana.

MARCIA. For the last time, my name is Marcia.

ANTHONY. Since it's plain you've made some mistake,
Perhaps you'll have the grace to apologize.

DON JUAN. Certainly, but there's been no mistake . . .
Men may err, Satan never. . . .

MARCIA. Don't argue with him, Anthony.
There's nothing so embarrassing as a scene.
Let's go in to dinner.
          ANTHONY, MARCIA, EVELYN *and* LIONEL *exit.*

LADY MORETON. Come, Henrietta, if we can't have a good brawl
We may as well get a hot dinner. But remember
We fly to Rome tomorrow but not on lobsters.
          *They exit.*

CATALION. It looks as if Satan's made a mistake.

DON JUAN. Nonsense. It is she. Not only my eyes
Recognize her eyes, but my hands
Know her hands, my blood . . .

CATALION. Quite so, senor.
The mistake I meant was Satan giving you a year up here.
At this rate that will be too long. We've only been here ten
minutes
And already you've got two women on your hands
And their husbands at your throat.
Yes, it's certain that she's Dona Ana,
The hair's the same, the eyes are too,
But there must be something missing.

DON JUAN. Nothing. It is she.

CATALION. Then how is it that she doesn't remember you?

DON JUAN. Perhaps heaven is to forget. It is we in hell
　Who remember. For memory is all our hell.
　　*He sits.*

CATALION. But how do you account for her husband?
　Dona Ana was never married.

DON JUAN. How do you account for these clothes we wear?
　And a beautiful woman is improperly dressed
　Unless chaperoned by a lover, or failing that
　Supported by a husband.

CATALION. I think you'll find there's little magic in him.

DON JUAN. It's that which I supply.
　　*Enter* EVELYN. DON JUAN *stands.* CATALION *exits.*

EVELYN. Please . . .
　Do sit down. I was only going up to my room.
　Well, if you won't, then I suppose, I must.
　　*She sits.*
　I see you make amends for our introduction.
　Back home a man only gets to his feet when a woman
　Enters a room if he's already got another
　Sitting on his knee.

DON JUAN. Where do you come from, senora?

EVELYN. No kidding, can't you tell? Why, America of course.
　San Francisco to be precise.

DON JUAN. Ah, the colonies.

EVELYN. The what? Just where have you been?
　Didn't they teach you any history at school?
　Don't you read the newspapers?

DON JUAN. As a matter of fact, where I come from
　There's little else to do.

EVELYN. And where's that?

DON JUAN. Hell. I came from Hell. I shall return to Hell.

EVELYN. Don't we all? I see you don't intend to tell me.
　Most mysterious, quite intriguing.
　I suppose you're on some mission? What's your line?

DON JUAN. I don't understand.

EVELYN. They never do.
Let me guess. I'd like to bet you're doing some research.
And travelling on account of it.

DON JUAN. How very shrewd of you.

EVELYN. I knew it. You're in atoms, aren't you?

DON JUAN. No. Sin.

EVELYN. How disappointing. But you must show me sometime.

DON JUAN. What?

EVELYN. Sin, or whatever you call it.

DON JUAN. But we scarcely know each other.

EVELYN. What's that to do with it,
If you've got something to sell and I want to buy?
Though, I daresay, it's too expensive for me.

DON JUAN. Senora, I am or was a gentleman.

EVELYN. Why be offended? I don't mind paying high
For something that's exclusive. Though no woman wants
To find that every other girl in town has it as well.

DON JUAN. Whatever my indiscretions were, senora,
They were never indiscriminate.

EVELYN. No fault of yours. Fashion is all of taste
And price is all there is to fashion.
My advice to you is to keep your price
So high that it will hurt.

DON JUAN. Senora!
EVELYN. And if you do
I think your new brand of perfume
Is bound to be a great success.
What did you say the name was?
Sin? Yes, I think you've got something there.
The name alone should sell the goods.
But what is yours? I mean your name.

DON JUAN. Don Juan Tenorio, at your service.

EVELYN. Well, that's fine. I'm Mary Queen of Scots.
My, you are secretive . . .
You forget, Senor Don Juan, I can easily

Discover who you really are
Merely by looking at the register.
> *She goes to the desk.*

How strange, your signature's been burned out.
Look, how did that happen? Do you fill your pen with nitric
acid?

DON JUAN. I must have left a cigarette burning there.

EVELYN. No, that might have singed the page
But this has picked out the letters of your name. How's that?

DON JUAN. The devil only knows.

EVELYN. My, you must be passionate!

DON JUAN (*Playing up*). You mean my heart transferred
Its feeling to my hand. . . .

EVELYN. Yes.

DON JUAN. . . . and my urgent blood transformed
The nature of the ink?

EVELYN. Yes, now let our lips sign again
I'll keep your signature a secret
And this kiss shall be anonymous.
> CATALION *returns.* JUAN *kisses her abstractedly then sud-*
> *denly with passion.*

DON JUAN. Ana . . .

EVELYN. No, that is not my name. But I will be whoever you wish
If I can have whoever you are.
> *She turns to go.*

And don't forget—that's my window there.
> *Exit.*

DON JUAN (*Calling after her*). Whatever your name is, I shall
call you Isabella.

CATALION. Did you hear, senor?

DON JUAN. What?

CATALION. The senora was sufficiently indiscreet,
To inform you which was her window.

DON JUAN. I did.

CATALION. I suppose that places you under the usual
Obligation?

DON JUAN. It does.

CATALION. Then I'd better get the ladder?

DON JUAN. Do.

CATALION (*Placing it to window*). I suppose this calls for a serenade at least?

DON JUAN (*Picking up guitar*). I suppose so. Give the usual signal, if you see the husband.
 *He begins to mount.*
That's the worst of being a gentleman, you have to behave
Like a cad out of sheer good manners.

CATALION. A couple of verses should satisfy her.

DON JUAN (*Half way up*). I wonder . . .

CATALION. Though I can't see how this furthers our mission.

DON JUAN. Can't you? Personally I'm beginning to suspect
That the reason people don't suffer in hell any more
Is because they know this drudgery that is heaven.
 *He mounts to the window which is closed and twangs his
 guitar and sings.*
  If I were to sing of my love
  You would not listen to my song.
  If I were to open my heart
  You would not open your window.
 *The window opens.* DON JUAN *shakes his head, the house
 curtain begins to lower,* JUAN *observes it falling.*
Ah well, at least some of the proprieties are still observed.

CURTAIN

SCENE THREE

*Immediately following.*
EVELYN's *bedroom. She's dressed in négligé and is waiting
impatiently by the open window while* DON JUAN *continues
his song.*

DON JUAN. If you have felt a flood
       Bursting the banks of a river
       Then you have held my love
       No, you could never.
       *She anticipates his entry and is disappointed as he goes on.*
       If you have felt the fire
       Burning the gorse and the heather
       Then you have known my love
       No, you would never.
       *She waits a moment expectantly then goes to the window
       and looks out.*

EVELYN. Where are you going? Oh no, you don't!
       *She hauls* DON JUAN *in.*
D'you always approach a lady's bedroom from the window?

DON JUAN. There is a sort of tradition for it.

EVELYN. What's wrong with the door?

DON JUAN. They're usually locked.

EVELYN. Mine wasn't.

DON JUAN. One can hardly stand in a corridor
And sing through a piece of oak.

EVELYN. Nobody asked you to sing.
       *Pause.*
Well, what else is—traditional—?
       DON JUAN *remembers his reputation. He takes her hand.*

DON JUAN. Give me your hand
       So that your hand shall know
       That intimacy your eyes desire
       But dare not show.

       Look in my eyes
       So that in yours I'll see
       Myself in prison, so cruel is your
       Lips' tyranny.

       Give me your lips
       So that my tongue can teach
       Your tongue that language in which my blood
       And silence speaks.

EVELYN. My, who wrote that?

DON JUAN. I do not gain my ends, senora, by quoting others.

EVELYN. You mean to say you made it up yourself?
You must be a poet.

DON JUAN. No, any gentleman should be able
To break in a horse or improvise a compliment
To a lady.

EVELYN. Ah, you mean it wasn't sincere?

DON JUAN (*Offended*). I trust I did not show that.

EVELYN. Or true, which is more important.

DON JUAN. There's something more important than the truth.

EVELYN. What?

DON JUAN. Good manners. Now goodnight.
*He goes to climb out of the window.*

EVELYN. I will not let you go until you've said
Goodnight properly.

DON JUAN. Were I to say goodnight properly
It would be good morning.

EVELYN. Then stay.
*He relents.*

DON JUAN. For were I . . .

EVELYN. Yes?

DON JUAN. . . . to describe your beauty
Night which veils your modesty
Would blush and all this darkness would dissolve
And we would think it dawn.

EVELYN. Modesty? You get me wrong . . .
I only slipped this thing on because it's a little cool
After the sun goes down.
*She removes the gown.*

DON JUAN. The whiteness of your shoulders puts the moon to
flight
And cleaves this abyss of darkness
With the miracle of light.
Cover yourself again and do not tease my eyes
Or tempt my lips.

EVELYN. Well, I'm waiting . . .
Or do you make love with words?

DON JUAN. It's words that make us love.
From these alone you must interpret my heart's tense
Or make meaning of my mind's metaphor . . .

EVELYN. You mean?

DON JUAN. I love another.
*He again tries to leave.*

EVELYN. Oh yes? That's all the better.
I hate an emotional tangle—such a waste of time.

DON JUAN. Then what do you want?

EVELYN. You. Why do you look so shocked?

DON JUAN. I, shocked!

EVELYN. Yes. Or is it that I'm not attractive?

DON JUAN. No.

EVELYN. Then what are you waiting for?
*She leads him to the divan.*

DON JUAN. My breath.
*They embrace and, during the following duet, each—un-
noticed by the other—idly turns the pages of a coloured
magazine which lies behind the other's shoulder on the
divan, this action belying the intensity of their speech.*

EVELYN. My lips were not lips till your lips
Kissed them.

DON JUAN. My hands were not hands till your hands
Touched them.

EVELYN. Oh my beloved, what is love?

DON JUAN. The river that's lost in the ocean is love.

EVELYN. Oh my beloved, what is love?

DON JUAN. The river that flows to the sea is love.

EVELYN. Oh my beloved, what is love?

DON JUAN. The water that falls in the river is love.

EVELYN. Oh my beloved, what is love?

DON JUAN. The swimmer who drowns in this river is love.
  *Enter* LIONEL.

LIONEL. I'm sorry, dear, I had no idea
  You weren't alone . . .
    *He goes to the wardrobe, then turns.*
  But really, Evelyn, I protest . . . !
    DON JUAN *leaps to his feet, and snatches an antique sword*
    *which hangs on the wall.* EVELYN *and her husband watch*
    *him with bewilderment.*

DON JUAN (*Drawing*). Have no fear, I'll defend you and my
  honour!

LIONEL (*Ignoring him completely*). . . . As I say, I protest, here
  you are again
  With a man in your room and you haven't learned yet
  To lock the door. You really might show some
  Consideration and save me from such
  Embarrassment. After all, I am your husband . . .

DON JUAN. And I'm her lover!

LIONEL. And I'm sure you will agree it's most remiss of her not to
  assure
  Your privacy. It's difficult to concentrate without it.
    *He observes the magazines.*
  That's a most interesting number, isn't it, dear?

EVELYN (*Piqued as she notices the magazine* DON JUAN *has been*
  *looking at, as well as her own*). Which?
  (*To* DON JUAN) Just what are you holding that sword for?

DON JUAN (*Straight*). One of us must die!
    *Both* LIONEL *and* EVELYN *take his line as conscious parody*
    *of the situation. They smile.*

LIONEL. I quite agree with you! Let's be civilized. . . .
  And remember we're adults. . . .
  Perhaps you'll both forgive my intrusion
  By letting me get you a drink.
    *He pours one and hands it to* DON JUAN.

DON JUAN (*Throwing sword down angrily*). I don't understand. I
  seduce your wife
  And you merely offer me a gin and orange.

LIONEL. Nonsense, my dear fellow, she seduced you and that's a
gin and lime.
Shall I change it for you? Perhaps you'd prefer sherry?

DON JUAN (*Recovering*). Ah, which is poison?

LIONEL. All if you ask me.
Well, here's to us then!
*He drinks.*
I hope your headache's better?

EVELYN. Yes, that and this is most refreshing.

DON JUAN. As though I were an aspirin!

LIONEL. Aren't you drinking?

DON JUAN. No, I'm not drinking.

LIONEL. Is it too warm? Some more ice?

DON JUAN. It's too cold already.

LIONEL. A drop more gin then?

DON JUAN (*Putting glass down violently*). I protest!

EVELYN. What, you too? What bores men are.

DON JUAN. This will not do! This isn't good enough!

LIONEL. You want me to go?

DON JUAN. I do not! I've got a grudge.
And you're going to hear it. Stay where you are.

LIONEL. Sir, I hope you're not casting aspersions
Against my wife. I've had no complaints before.

DON JUAN. It's you I complain of!

LIONEL. Me?

EVELYN. Surely that's my prerogative?

LIONEL. I can't think what I've done to give offence.

DON JUAN. Fool, it's what I've done that's caused you no offence.
It's that which angers me.
Not in all my unhallowed past
Can I recall one escapade so utterly unrewarding.
Damnation is a sack of guilt my shoulders
Were designed to carry, but your indifference

Breaks me. What evil can I do
If there's nothing you forbid?

LIONEL. What do you mean?

DON JUAN. This is what I mean—how can I who am
A man proud of the evil that is man,
Enjoy anything any more if nothing is now a sin?

EVELYN. Ah, the stuff you travel in.

DON JUAN. Yes, and it seems that the distribution has outrun
The production of that object.

LIONEL. Come, my dear fellow,
Is there anything I can do for you?

DON JUAN. For me? It's against me you should act
Forget your manners, man, and be a gentleman
And show such violence to me that gentleness
Can follow.

LIONEL. Do you expect me to wail and rant
Like a cuckold?

DON JUAN. You might at least squeal.
What pleasure d'you think can be obtained
By seducing your wife, if it only leads
To your gratitude? Had she no vows
That she has broken? And you, had you
No trust that I have trespassed?

LIONEL. I don't know where you come from, bud,
But in America we look on these things
In quite a different way. In our democracy
All men are free and free of inhibitions
And that goes for all bodily functions.

DON JUAN. Speaking as a confirmed libertine
I can assure you free love's not worth half the price.

EVELYN. Would you have us all return to the restraint
Of the eighteenth century . . . ?

DON JUAN. Oh to be a child again!

EVELYN. . . . When desire was inarticulate? . . .

DON JUAN. Oh come!

EVELYN. . . . When men's and women's natural appetites
Were secret, corseted and repressed?
You should know your D. H. Lawrence.

DON JUAN. I do.
That's why I haven't read him.

LIONEL. Nor have I.

EVELYN. . . . restraint's unnatural . . .

DON JUAN. So is music.

LIONEL. That's a point. One up to you.

EVELYN. Such repression's harmful. . . .

DON JUAN. Self expression's evil.

EVELYN. . . . All those emotions and desires without fulfillment
Of sexual gratification is quite obscene.

DON JUAN. And sex without emotion and even without desire
Is even more obscene. You should read Dante.

EVELYN. Who?

DON JUAN. The unresponsive women whom I knew
Were at least able to quote their betters
And what they didn't feel themselves, they had
The decency to feign.

EVELYN. But we need not feign, we're free from that.

DON JUAN. I suspect that this freedom which you mention is too
arduous
To attract a gentleman of leisure.
Madam, I apologize for my deficiencies.
Sir, forgive me for my excess.
        *He bows and makes to go.*

LIONEL. Don't carry on, bud. Just forget it.

DON JUAN. No, I shall never forgive myself for this,
In future I must remember this principle:
Never commit a sin unless adequately tempted.
For tonight's folly I deserve hell's damnation
Including bridge and poker.

LIONEL. My advice to you is to forget all about it.
Self reproach is self-destructive.

And might give rise to the most morbid
Physical manifestations such as
A rash on your leg, paralysis of your feet
Or even impotency. Now, you wouldn't want that, would you?
So, take my advice, rationalize your sense of guilt
Or failing that forget it. Come, let's be friends.
Most men have made the same mistake.

EVELYN. D'you refer to me?

LIONEL. We've much in common.

EVELYN. Now I protest!

LIONEL. I bear you no grudge.

DON JUAN. It was not my intention
To be regarded as a good neighbour.

LIONEL. Come, nobody's blaming you.

DON JUAN. Oh, more's the pity.

LIONEL. Your guilt complex amounts to an obsession.
It's as though you had an appetite for sin.

DON JUAN. So I have and consequently I now find myself
As you would say, most frustrated.
For since there are no virtues now, how can there be sin?
And to sin was both my purpose and my pleasure.

LIONEL. I say, that sounds pretty pagan to me.

DON JUAN. No, Satan's the best evangelist of all.
It's my knowledge of him that almost convinces me
That there's a God. One can't exist without the other.

EVELYN. You sound more like John Bunyan than Don Juan
Or whoever it is you say you are.

DON JUAN. And I resent being turned into a Moralist.
But how can I be profligate if there are
No proprieties? Indeed your lack of them
Not only deprives me of my purpose
But my identity as well. I'll say goodnight.
*He goes to window.*

EVELYN. What's wrong with the door?

DON JUAN (*On the ladder outside*). Surely you wouldn't deprive
me
Of even my habitual exit?

EVELYN. You've forgotten something. Don't look so nervous.
I meant this guitar.
*He disappears.*

LIONEL (*Sitting on sofa and picking up one of the magazines*).
You do go in for the oddest types
What d'you say his name was?

EVELYN (*Also turning over a magazine*). Don Juan.

LIONEL. That explains it.
He's probably employed by this Hotel.
It's part of their service, quite a stunt.

EVELYN (*Still reading*). You make me feel rather cheap.

LIONEL (*Also reading*). Wait till I get the bill!

### CURTAIN

# Act Two

*A few minutes later.*
*Set as Scene Two, Act One.*

DON JUAN (*Descending ladder*). Yes, I know . . .
There's no tyranny like a good habit.
Catalion! Where are you?
   CATALION *runs in.*

CATALION. Here, senor.

DON JUAN. Where have you been? For hell's sake what have you
been doing?

CATALION. Just that.

DON JUAN. You too? You surprise me.
You always used to be a woman hater.

CATALION. The senor does me an injustice: I still am.

DON JUAN. Then d'you mind telling me what you have been doing?

CATALION. Doing what Satan instructed, trying
To fulfil his mission of discovering
Why people don't suffer in hell any more.

DON JUAN. Which only proves a man can't serve two masters.
I'd have you know that because of your sense of duty—
I was discovered in mine.

CATALION. Not by her husband?

DON JUAN. Yes. A case almost without precedent.
Hell has not improved you.

CATALION. But I kept my eye
On both the ladder and the stairs.

DON JUAN. Yes, but there's been some progress on the earth
Since we were here. Now there are not only two ways to a
girl's room
But three!

CATALION. He surprised you from the roof?

DON JUAN. No, Catalion, he came up by that lift.

CATALION. And to think I saw him enter! I thought he was quite
safe—there.
Locking himself in and being so unusually self-effacing.
I shall never be able to lift my head
In Seville again.

DON JUAN. Don't take it to heart.
But you might in future keep up to date
And read your subject up in some of those technical magazines
One sees in hell. I understand now why
Satan subscribes to each.

CATALION. I will; it's a relief to see the senor is unscathed.
I presume that the husband is . . .

DON JUAN. No, Catalion, duels too are out of date.
He was a cuckold by consent.

CATALION. And the senora? At least there's one more
Who's known happiness, at least one who'll suffer in hell?

DON JUAN. I doubt it; she showed so much emotion
It's plain she had none left to feel.

CATALION. The senor seems most depressed.

DON JUAN. So I am. I'm tired of desire which is sad
Desire which is desperate and all the angry acrobatics
Of passionate indifference.
It's not that literature imitates life now
But life is all a pastiche of literature
They're like bull-frogs quoting bull-frogs.

CATALION. If you feel like that
Why doesn't the senor take a vow of chastity?

DON JUAN. I would, if I didn't suspect that I
Should endure it only too easily.

CATALION (*Taking ladder down*). I suspect the senor's depression
Is tinged with remorse.

DON JUAN. For what?

CATALION. Being unfaithful to Dona Ana.

DON JUAN. Nonsense, Catalion, women seem so alike nowadays
That it's quite impossible for a man to recapture
The relish of being unfaithful
To any one. Besides, as you know,
It was never so. I wish it were. Other women merely gave me the petals
Of the flower I pinned in her hair.

CATALION. What shall we do now, senor?

DON JUAN. What can we do, Catalion? Get me a drink.
It seems to me that all we can report
Is that people don't suffer in hell any more—fill it up, man!—
Because they're so bored on earth they don't notice
That ennui which is eternity.
Tell me, isn't that what you find too?

CATALION. More or less and I've questioned several
While you were up there.

DON JUAN. Let's forget that episode.
Tell me where you've been.

CATALION. All over this hotel, even down in the kitchen,
Quite a city by itself;
With reading rooms, writing rooms, waiting rooms and bathrooms.
The only thing it lacks is a cathedral.
Indeed it's a world in miniature and as far as I can discover
From talking to the chef and the porter,
It's both guiltless and godless,
A world in which universal comfort covers all.

DON JUAN. You mean they're all upholstered atheists?

CATALION. Not quite. It's not that they've no gods
But strange gods. Whereas we—or rather I—
Worshipped God—nowadays they are very pleased with man.

DON JUAN. But surely science has succeeded—

CATALION. It has
In multiplying human needs.

DON JUAN. Even so
I daresay they have their consolations.
No doubt their government has improved,
Whereas we lived under tyrants . . .

CATALION. Democracy has now made each man his own.
Even charity has dried up.

DON JUAN. You exaggerate. I must make a few enquiries for myself.

CATALION. Why don't you question that girl over there?

DON JUAN. Yes, she will do. Though I admit
She appears to be so bored with her life on earth
That hell might well be an improvement for her.
        JUAN *approaches the* RECEPTIONIST. CATALION *produces pad
        and writes.*

DON JUAN. Good evening, senorita. What's your name?

RECEPTIONIST. Baptista, senor.

DON JUAN. How pretty and appropriate.
Now, Baptista, d'you mind if I ask you a few questions?

BAPTISTA. No, senor. As you see, this is the enquiry desk.

DON JUAN. A place for everything, I see.

BAPTISTA. Can I help you?

DON JUAN. Yes, tell me why you look so bored?
Are you unwell?

BAPTISTA. No, I'm full of vitamins.

DON JUAN. Then tell me why you choose to sit up all night
Within this little box. Surely it's a trifle dull?

BAPTISTA. It is, it's as dull as death.

DON JUAN. Then why do it?

BAPTISTA. When I got married, I took this job
In order to earn enough money
To buy a refrigerator and a vacuum cleaner
And a washing machine.

DON JUAN. Why?

BAPTISTA. In order to free me
From the drudgery of housework.

DON JUAN. And did they?

BAPTISTA. Yes, they're so wonderful that I had to get this job back
In order to give me something to do.

DON JUAN. D'you understand this, Catalion?
*He shakes his head.*
But where's your husband?

BAPTISTA. He's one of the porters here.

DON JUAN. Have you no family?

BAPTISTA. No, we've no trouble there.
He works the day shift and as you see at night I'm here.
We get on very well together.

DON JUAN. Indeed? Well, you'll have more room in hell, my
dear—
Besides other consolations—
*He leaves the reception desk and joins* CATALION. ANTHONY
*enters and goes to it.*

CATALION. Isn't that man Dona Ana's husband?

DON JUAN. Yes.

CATALION. Aren't you jealous?

DON JUAN. No, of course I'm not. Why should I be?
That's an emotion other men feel towards me.

CATALION. In this case the situation's different.
He has what you've waited three centuries for.

DON JUAN. Even so I'm not jealous; jealousy
Isn't love of another but love of oneself,
And that's not a love that's everlasting.
Are rivers jealous because they flow

Into the same sea? Does each parched tree resent
The summer shower because the gentle fingers of the rain
Fall over the entire forest? . . .

CATALION. Yes, I expect so.

DON JUAN. . . . Love's not a coin which, given to one beggar,
Cannot be given to another.
Love's not like wine which, because it flows
Down one throat, cannot slake the thirst
Of another. Love's paradox is this:
The more it gives the more it has
To spend, and in profligate philanthropy
It does increase, and yield without usury.
The woman who cannot love two men
Is hardly likely to love one, either.

CATALION. So you're not jealous?

DON JUAN. Isn't that what I've been telling you?
But what are you questioning me for?
The devil knows I suffer in hell. Don't torture
The inquisitor. Let's ask him some questions.
He should be happy enough on earth to suffer
When he's in hell. . . . Get your pad.

CATALION. Yes, he certainly looks pleased with himself.
*He goes over to the desk.* ANTHONY *returns with him.*
BAPTISTA *begins to read a magazine.*

DON JUAN. Good evening, senor, I was wondering
Whether you'd care to take a glass of wine with me?

ANTHONY. Thank you. Mine's a whisky sour. They mix it well
here.
I recommend it.

DON JUAN. Catalion, get two whisky sours.
*He does so.*

ANTHONY. Aren't you the man who mistook my wife
For somebody whom you knew—?

DON JUAN. Yes.

ANTHONY. Well, we've all done the same thing sometime.
I remember once when I was walking down Piccadilly
I saw a man coming towards me.

I knew his face, but couldn't think who he was
But I knew every contour of his features intimately.
But there was no avoiding him. We approached;
And as I took his hand I had a moment of
Inspired recognition. 'Good morning, Father,' I said . . .
And d'you know who it was? Laurence Crossfield.
I see you don't know Laurence Crossfield.

DON JUAN. No.

ANTHONY. The film star.
And I don't suppose you know my father, either?

DON JUAN. No.

ANTHONY. No wonder the joke went rather flat.
Mine usually do.

DON JUAN. As a matter of fact
I would like to ask you a few questions.

ANTHONY. Are you a journalist, too?

DON JUAN. In a manner of speaking.

ANTHONY. You should get to know my wife.
She's European editor of View. And don't tell me
You don't know View, nor that you read it.
What d'you want then? The usual stuff. What am I working
on?
What do I think of Spanish women, eh?
Is that your line? Right-ho, fire away,
But I warn you it'll cost you three more of these.

DON JUAN. First of all, your name?

ANTHONY. That's very funny.

DON JUAN. I promise I won't laugh.

ANTHONY. I didn't mean my name is humorous,
The joke is you don't know it. I spend my life
Avoiding interviews from people who know all about me.
And here I am giving one to somebody
Who doesn't know who I am.

DON JUAN. But if I knew the answers I would
Have no need to ask the questions.

ANTHONY. You've got something there.
Well, I'm Anthony Lissenden.

CATALION (*Writing*). How d'you spell it?

ANTHONY. L I S S E N D E N.

DON JUAN. And what's your profession?

ANTHONY. I say, this is good for one's pride! I write novels,
Plays, essays and poems—not to mention
An occasional film script
Though at the moment I'm busy on television.

DON JUAN. Why d'you do so many different things
Don't you excel at any one in particular?

ANTHONY. Income Tax must be very low where you come from.

DON JUAN. It is.

ANTHONY. I must settle there.

DON JUAN. You will.

ANTHONY. Are you fellows doing this for some Gallup Poll?

CATALION. No, just for devilment.

ANTHONY. Well, what d'you want to know? The title of my next
book?

DON JUAN. My questions are more important.

ANTHONY. Well, what are they?

DON JUAN. D'you think you will suffer in hell when you get there?

ANTHONY. I beg your pardon?

DON JUAN. Or find it comfortable by comparison
As so many nowadays seem to do?

CATALION. Especially of your profession.

ANTHONY. You're not seriously asking me that?

DON JUAN. I've come some considerable distance to do so.

ANTHONY. It's very difficult for me to answer.

DON JUAN. Why?

ANTHONY. Because your question's meaningless. It's couched
In terms which no longer have any reference.

If hell is where we are, your question means: 'am I suffering
now?'
And before I could answer that
I would have to ask you:
What d'you mean by suffering? I suppose all men suffer
Who remember their teddy bear when they see it
Abandoned in a boxroom with one eye missing
And a wound that bleeds with straw . . .
I suppose all men suffer who dare to remember
Where they were going and then look at their destination.
Take me for instance. . . .

DON JUAN. That's what I wanted to do.

ANTHONY. I'm a writer—but don't let me bore you—

DON JUAN. You won't. I'm used to them.

ANTHONY. All I ever wanted to do was to compose one or two
poems which were to be
As melodic as Schubert, as tough as Villon,
And with something I thought I could add. But what am I
doing?
I am writing a script for television about the beauty of old Spain.
Is that what you meant?

DON JUAN. Hardly. Men must eat.

ANTHONY. But not necessarily as well as I do.
Or d'you mean the terrible tedium each of us finds,
Pacing up and down this prison of our personality,
Or the loneliness we know as each embrace
Fails to release us, since we are
Judge, jailor and prisoner too. Or d'you mean
The vacancy we feel when we look up into
What used to be called God's sky
And see nothing but the grin of our own reflection?
Is that what you mean?

DON JUAN. No. But you are getting very close
I was thinking of suffering which is sorrow
And sorrow which is remorse
And remorse that is the realization of a sin.

ANTHONY. Oh, there you go again. It's all a question of termi-
nology.

Sin's a word quite out of currency with no contemporary meaning . .

CATALION (*To* JUAN). It looks as if you taught
Far better than you knew.

ANTHONY. Today we believe in . . .

DON JUAN. Ah?

CATALION. In what?

ANTHONY. Toleration.
Whereas other generations have carried a load
Of personal guilt, we've learned to tolerate
Our own weaknesses and find a modus vivendi
With our own natures. I don't think you or I seriously believe
in sin
In the old sense, for that postulates an absolute moral code . . .

DON JUAN. Catalion, mind my wallet. . . .

ANTHONY. . . . Which presupposes of course a divine authority.

DON JUAN. Then you are not a Christian?

ANTHONY. Certainly I was baptized one.
And I'm not going to steal your change,
If that's what you mean.
But there's no doubt to my mind
That Christianity was a necessary development
In human consciousness and that Christ was one of the world's
great men
As Gandhi was . .

DON JUAN. I frequently play chess with him.

ANTHONY. You mean you did . . . But I certainly can't believe
That Jesus Christ was unique or was the Son of God
In any sense that you or I are not . . .

DON JUAN. Oh, I'm the Devil's son.
But what does your wife think of your disbelief?

ANTHONY. I don't think we've ever mentioned it.
She's a very busy woman; as I told you she's European editor
of *View*.
But tell me, d'you believe in an immortal soul?

DON JUAN. I believe in Hell.

ANTHONY. And d'you think you will suffer there?

DON JUAN. For ever and ever, amen.

ANTHONY. For what?

DON JUAN. For love.

ANTHONY. Of whom?

CATALION. You're supposed to be answering the questions not
asking them.

DON JUAN. A woman.

ANTHONY. No? Tell me about her.
I'm interested.

CATALION. So you should be.

ANTHONY. As a novelist, of course.
I thought romantic passion
Was a thing of the past.

DON JUAN. I suppose it is. Love never had a future . . .

ANTHONY. Tell me what she's like. Here, let this round be on me.
    CATALION *goes off to bar again.*

DON JUAN. As I'm no poet I cannot describe her.
And if I were, what use are words to me?
For they are all so logical and the heart's reasons
Are irrational.

ANTHONY. Well, is she fair or dark?

DON JUAN. Her skin is white, her hair is black and her lips—
Her lips are red for that's where beauty bleeds away.

ANTHONY. From your description I'm sure I'd know her anywhere.

DON JUAN. When we take a rose apart we hold petals in our
hands
It is the same with beauty except we're left with words
And each word is a metaphor for a thing
And of itself, is nothing, as meaningless as the wind.
There's no way to translate the language of her looks,
For each of her features is a platitude
And like any other woman's—else were she deformed.
No, what I love is not her lips,
Though I once crawled across this continent for them;

Nor is it in her hair or on her breasts
Though once I knew no quietus unless I lay upon them.
Appearance is like passion, as ephemeral
As our thoughts. Yet the thing we love remains.
Age cannot alter it. Time never took
Any loveliness from woman. For a woman's beauty
Lies behind her eyes, it's in the tenderness of her look or no-
where

ANTHONY. My wife always wears sun glasses. I must get her to
take them off.
But have you known this woman long?

DON JUAN. I didn't live before I knew her;
Therefore I can say, I've known her ever since I was,
Which seems for ever, since time without her
Doesn't move at all.

ANTHONY. Yes, it's a common delusion among lovers that they've
known each other a long time.
It's some compensation for the brevity of these affairs.
And is this girl of yours married?

DON JUAN. Yes, to a writer.

ANTHONY. I wonder if I know him?

DON JUAN. No, that's most unlikely.

ANTHONY. But tell me something of her personality.

DON JUAN. You mean her character?

ANTHONY. Yes, I suppose I do.

DON JUAN. She knows without the knowledge, and in all things
Is kind. She's modest too, and chaste
And so pious that all her life is an unspoken prayer.

ANTHONY. She sounds like a nun.

DON JUAN. She was a novice. She was the nearest thing to God
I knew.
And in loving her I might in time have loved Him too.

ANTHONY. Funny you should have mistaken my wife for her.
Quite a romantic figure, aren't you?

DON JUAN. You know how easy it is
To get a reputation.

ANTHONY. And I presume this affair of yours is quite unfulfilled.
Only love that's unfulfilled can be a tragedy, it's a mere comedy
when it is
You haven't met for some time?

DON JUAN. Those who can be separated, never loved.
*Enter* MARCIA. *She puts her hand on* ANTHONY's *shoulder.*

ANTHONY. You gave me quite a start.

MARCIA. Did I, darling? I'm sorry.
I hear there's a cable for me, so I came downstairs to get it.
They generally need an answer and it'll save time
If I write it here.
*She goes to the desk.*
This must be in code. I can't make head or tail of it.
*Reads.*
        'Let me ask you one question
         And I will never ask another
         Do I walk through your dreams . . .'

DON JUAN.  '. . . As you now run through mine
         Answer this question
         I will not ask another.'

MARCIA. How did you know what was in it?

DON JUAN. I sent it.

MARCIA. How amusing. I always wanted to meet one of those odd
people.
Who send anonymous letters to people they don't even know.

DON JUAN (*To* ANTHONY). You may go.

ANTHONY. What did you say?

DON JUAN. You may go.
The interview is finished. Leave me with your wife.

CATALION. There speaks Don Juan Tenorio!

ANTHONY. I've as much right here as you have.
This is an hotel.

DON JUAN. Show him round my gardens, Catalion—
Especially the pantheon.

CATALION. Yes, senor. I'm sure you'll be interested in the pantheon
It contains statues of all those Don Juan killed . . .

MARCIA. This cable is signed Don Juan too.

DON JUAN. I admitted that I sent it.

ANTHONY (*Pushing* CATALION *off*). This is a damn silly joke! Get the hell out of here.

MARCIA. No, darling, leave me alone with him.
I've a hunch there's a story here. 'Interview with Maniac.'
If it's good I may make the next number with it.

ANTHONY. Are you quite sure you'll be all right?

MARCIA. Yes, darling, but don't be too far away.
    *Exit* CATALION *and* ANTHONY.

CATALION (*Off by statue*). And this was Don Meija . . .
    JUAN *kneels to* DONA ANA.

MARCIA. What are you doing?

DON JUAN. Kneeling for forgiveness.

MARCIA. For what? Sending this cablegram?

DON JUAN. For killing your father. My remorse weighs more heavily on me,
Than the statue does on him.

MARCIA. I don't know what you're talking about.
My father is alive.

DON JUAN. Yes, of course, you always had two fathers.
And one of them was beyond my reach: Indeed I never met Him
Though in time you might have led me to Him.

MARCIA. I think we must be talking at cross purposes.
You're not one of those odd people, are you,
Who believe in transmigration of souls?
I don't know whom you're mistaking me for
But I'm not particularly flattered. Let's get this straight:
My name is Marcia . . .

DON JUAN. I shall call you Ana.

MARCIA. I live in London—though I shan't give you my address,
I'm thirty-two . .

DON JUAN. Yes, I know—European editor of *View* . . . and I'm wearing clothes I've never worn before
We could hardly stand here naked, could we? . . .

MARCIA. That's some relief to hear!

DON JUAN. . . . without a name and background.
But you're taking yours too seriously.

MARCIA. Am I indeed?

DON JUAN. It's only for appearance' sake. Both Heaven and Hell
provide.

MARCIA. I'd have you know
I like being editor of *View* . . . it's a position of some influence
And responsibility too. . . .

DON JUAN. Yes, darling, of course it is.
You always had a strong sense of duty, didn't you?
And loyalty too. But, Ana, let us forget this life we're living,
And remember that death we have not died.

MARCIA. Completely non sequitur! They'd say I was turning *View*
Into a surrealist rag if I reported this.

DON JUAN. Don't you remember—after I'd killed your father—
That one (*Pointing to the statue*) I escaped and left you to die
of grief?
But they did not say for whom.

MARCIA. Though I have died many times, as any woman's done,
I've never died of grief—though that I suppose must come.

DON JUAN. You remember nothing of what I am saying?

MARCIA. Nothing.

DON JUAN. But of course! Of course!
Hell is to remember. Heaven is to forget.

MARCIA. And I'm sorry to disappoint you, I'm very much alive.

DON JUAN. It's my desire in hell which gives this life to you.
You move as I move you and when you rest
It is because my desire is sleeping.

MARCIA. Sit down. Though I am not the person whom you think
I am
There is something in you that makes me want to listen.
Now please do sit down. I did not say so close. And tell me
What makes you so unhappy?

DON JUAN. Love.

MARCIA. Where do you come from?

DON JUAN. Hell.

MARCIA. It will not always seem so. It will pass.
But tell me what you do?

DON JUAN. Nothing. I'm condemned to idleness,
The punishment of my own thoughts.
But I do understand why you don't remember.

MARCIA. I should have realized it before,
It's odd how we fail to recognize a situation.
You think you are in love with me—
And please don't look at me like that—
I'm trying to help you. What has happened to you is this:
Somehow in your childhood, or in your adolescence,
You formed an image of your ideal woman.
And by some accident I fit this fantasy.
Don't worry, your trouble is in no way unique.
I read somewhere how frequent it is
For a young man to be attracted by a photo,
And quite unconsciously he then seeks the woman who fits the image.
But I assure you we've not met before. And please don't
Stare at me like that. Please. Remember your manners.

DON JUAN. I wish I could forget them. When we look into
Each other's eyes, our souls recognize,
And all your words are wasted.

MARCIA. Give me a cigarette.

DON JUAN. You're smoking one.
*He goes to take her hand.*

MARCIA. One thing is obvious, your name's appropriate.
I can see you're an incorrigible flirt.

DON JUAN. To hear you say that proves you do remember me!
*He takes her hand.*
And you still love me?

MARCIA. Haven't we missed a page or two?
I admit I find you quite attractive. You're my type.

DON JUAN (*Shocked*). That I can never be. I'm unique and
damned for it as well.

MARCIA. Don't tell me you don't do this to every girl.

DON JUAN. Ah, that's the tone I used to hear from you.

MARCIA. Well, isn't it true?

DON JUAN. Women deceive themselves if they are pleased
When men do not deceive them.
For women are so alike, and have so much tenderness
In common, that the man who does not find five or six to love
Is unlikely to find one either. Therefore when a man says
He loves only you, you should know he loves not you.

MARCIA. You seem to have that speech off pat!

DON JUAN. In each woman whom I knew burned some part of you.
Thus did I seek you before I knew you,
Thus did I know you before I'd found you.
My God, I wish there were some release
From this tyranny of your tender eyes.
My whole life's been a pilgrimage to those eyes,
And hell has been because you closed those eyes.
For you it was different, for your love was always given to
another. . .

MARCIA. Was it?

DON JUAN. You know I did not mean a man.

MARCIA. This is instructive! (*Recovering*)
But you admit that you are faithless?

DON JUAN. Yes, faithless as the world knows faith.
It doesn't matter how faithless we are to one another,
So long as we are never faithful to ourselves.

MARCIA. It seems you've lived up to your name—and his reputation.

DON JUAN. And the only part of my reputation I resent,
Is that suggestion I enjoyed women without loving them.
And when they used to ask, as all women rightly do,
Whether I loved them, I used to look away,
For I too was fool enough to think
That if love was given to another, there was less of it left for
you

MARCIA. And isn't there?

DON JUAN. No, the more we love, the more we're able to.
It is a thing which increases as we spend it.

If men were honest they should all admit
That first they loved their mother, nurse and then the girl
next door.

MARCIA. You're talking of affection—

DON JUAN. So do we lisp before we learn the language.
I did too—well enough to talk, but not well enough to sing.

MARCIA. What do you mean by that?

DON JUAN. Oh, it is easy to love beautiful women,
But what I hoped was that I'd learn to love ugly women too,
And by loving them make them more beautiful.

MARCIA. How generous of you!

DON JUAN. Now you are jealous.

MARCIA. I . . .

DON JUAN. What could they take from you?
Can't you see, you of all people,
That it's only by learning to love each other
That we can learn to love God too.
Don't you think that's true?

MARCIA. Why ask me, you seem to have all the answers.
Though yours sound like an apologia for promiscuity.

DON JUAN. Now you're hurt. Ana, I'm sorry.

MARCIA. You have no need.
Although I'm a woman of the world I know little
Of this world of love, and perhaps even less of passion.
But from what I've seen of it, I am glad.
The ability to love is as rare
As talent is for other things. Perhaps there is a genius
For love. Perhaps that's what genius is?
At any rate, great love is not for me.

DON JUAN. If not by love how were your eyelids formed?
If not for love why are your lips so red?
If not because of love, why do you look away?

MARCIA (*Towards him again*). Not because I'm falling in love
with you
If that is what you mean. Never in all my life
Have I met a man like you before.

DON JUAN. That I do not doubt.

MARCIA. Or found such insufferable male arrogance before.
Women exist for more than
The crumbs men throw them.
The modern woman's made for more than love.

DON JUAN. What?

MARCIA. A woman can be a person in her own right too.
She need not be a detached shadow,
Waiting for the image of a man,
Before her life is given validity or meaning.
We've got other things besides now.

DON JUAN. What?

MARCIA. Emancipation for one thing . . .

DON JUAN. Like that girl who works in that desk?
Slavery without even the awareness of the shackles.

MARCIA. She's independent. Try and take it away from her.
Independence is the most precious thing there is.

DON JUAN. It's certainly rare, for it doesn't exist.
Not even Satan's independent.

MARCIA. You make me speechless with indignation.
I'd have you know women are free now,
Free in a way they've never been before.
In a sense the modern woman is the first woman,
For up till now a woman's been, not what she was
But what men thought she should be.
Not only did you men tell us what our duties were
And of course all of them were to you;
But worse. You even told us what our feelings were
So that when you embraced us you heard
Only what you'd taught us to say.
You did not even let us love you
As we could have loved you. . . .

DON JUAN. Oh, that's unfair, I did.

MARCIA. I'm talking in general terms, you dolt!
And d'you think you're the only man that ever was?
As I was saying, you, that is mankind in general—
Told us what we women were: women were passive,

Women were tender, women were this and women were that.
And once we'd given birth to a replica of you
We were fulfilled and finished.
All that's as true as to say: man's proper function
Is to climb trees. I tell you we are free now
And don't you dare tell me: liberty's not worth having.

DON JUAN. It's the tyranny, we accept; that's all.
A woman's made for man: you, for me.

MARCIA. You're insufferable. You're quite mad.
Or have you forgotten
As you keep saying I forget?

DON JUAN. Forgotten what?

MARCIA. That I am married.

DON JUAN. No. I realize that. Once there was your father between us,
Now it's a husband. No matter. There's no separating us.

MARCIA. Let's try and get this straight. I'm not only married;
I am happily married. I admit it's rare.
True, I may not have experienced
The sort of passion you seem to have surrendered yourself to,
But I'm very fond of my husband, as he is of me.
Our marriage is a refuge and a consolation.

DON JUAN. It should be a risk and a consecration.

MARCIA. What it is or is not: I am content.

DON JUAN. I notice only this: that when you are gay
There is desperation in your gaiety;
And when you are sad,
Your sadness is not sorrow.

MARCIA. You're so conceited you believe
A woman can't be happy unless with you.

DON JUAN. We're using happiness in a different sense.
You're talking about a level of feeling
Which is lack of feeling,
And I'm thinking of an emotion which is like pain.
The world you're talking about is safe;
Mine was cruel, but its cruelty contained gentleness.

Your world may have a high standard of living,
Mine has a high standard of feeling.

MARCIA. I wonder. Anyhow you misjudge us
If you think we're superficial, though I admit
We must all appear superficial. We tend to understate;
Today we don't believe in articulating
All the emotions we may feel.

DON JUAN. The danger is if you don't express your feelings
You may in time cease to feel them.
 *He goes to her.*
I don't understand this change in you.

MARCIA (*Moving away*). I won't have you dismiss all I stand for.
And though I say it myself, being editor of *View*
Is a really responsible and influential position. . . .

DON JUAN (*Ignoring her gesture—deaf to what she says*). I'm
sure it is.
What pretty hands you have.

MARCIA. . . . You may not realize it but our circulation
Is over two millions . . .

DON JUAN. D'you remember when you mended
My cloak?

MARCIA. . . . With one like that of course
We can't always print what we'd like to print.
One has to compromise.
But nevertheless the work is most rewarding. . . .

DON JUAN. That pulse still beats there on your neck.

MARCIA. . . . And I'm able to see that some culture
Gets into our readers' lives. And surely that's a good thing,
isn't it?

DON JUAN. What, darling?

MARCIA. That some culture should get into our readers' lives.

DON JUAN. Is it? I thought culture was how man lived . . .
I agree you get into their lives.

MARCIA. I mean we're able to bring art to the people.

DON JUAN. Surely that's bad for their indigestion?

MARCIA. Oh, you're hopeless—I'll have to educate you.

DON JUAN. Ah, that's what I like to hear: when a woman promises
To ruin me completely!

MARCIA. You think I sound like a prig.
And a bit evangelical?

DON JUAN. I wouldn't have you change—any part.

MARCIA. But I do believe what I'm doing and trying to do
Is worth doing. I know I may sound like a handbook.
It's easy to ridicule anybody
With good intentions. But one has to believe in something:
I believe in education. And the best way
Of educating anybody is not to let them know
That they are being educated. That's what I try in *View*.
And so you see, I'm something more than a mere woman.
        *Pause. He kisses her.*

DON JUAN. Well? Aren't you going to slap my face?

MARCIA. Why?

DON JUAN. Why not? I kissed you.

MARCIA. Yes, it was very pleasant.

DON JUAN. Pleasant? It was passionate.

MARCIA. Well? You did it to shock me but it's you who's shocked.

DON JUAN. How can you be so unfaithful and not turn a hair?

MARCIA. Unfaithful? Nonsense, it was a moment of attraction,
Purely physical.

DON JUAN. There's no such thing as physical love.
Our bodies are statues unless our spirit moves them.

MARCIA. You surprise me.

DON JUAN. I surprise myself.

MARCIA. You boast of your unfaithfulness, then turn on me for mine.
But I've told you women are just as free as men.

DON JUAN. Are they? What would you say if I asked you
To come to me tonight?

MARCIA. Where?

DON JUAN. You mean you will?

MARCIA. Where? Or did you ask because you thought
I would refuse?

DON JUAN. By that statue of Don Gonzalo. At three.
You will? . . . But what of your husband?

MARCIA. Leave him to me.

DON JUAN. Ana, what are you going to do?

MARCIA. He'll not wake.

DON JUAN. You wouldn't dare. Not while he sleeps.

MARCIA. Why not? Leave Anthony to me . . . ssh, here he
comes
At three.
> JUAN *goes to the side. Enter* ANTHONY *and* CATALION.

ANTHONY. Well, darling, have you finished? Got your interview?
Mind he doesn't sue you.

MARCIA. I will. It's been sweet of you to wait.
I hope you've not been too bored?

ANTHONY. No, this fellow seems to know the way around.
Those statues are quite interesting,
Though a bit naturalistic for my taste.

MARCIA. Then let's go up. It must be getting late.

ANTHONY. No, it's only twelve. But sightseeing is so exhausting
I think I could sleep till Doomsday.
> MARCIA *and* ANTHONY *exit.*

JUAN. So he will. Catalion, did you mark how affectionate she
was,
Taking his hand in her hand.

CATALION. He is her husband after all.

JUAN. Such duplicity. To think the same hand . . .

CATALION. What, senor?

JUAN. She's changed, Catalion.

CATALION. Satan warned you she'd be different.

JUAN. But this is more than I understand.
The modern woman's more than a match for me.

CURTAIN


# SCENE TWO


*Later the same night.*
*By the statue of Don Gonzalo in the garden of the hotel.*
*Enter* DON JUAN *followed by* CATALION *carrying a basket*
*which contains a bottle of wine and glasses.*

DON JUAN. Not so much noise, Catalion,
Tread softly, man, for if this is a dream
I do not wish to wake. This is the hour I love
When night like a young Empress walks the broad valley
And drags an endless train of planets, moons and stars.
Look how the river shows her naked feet
And there, where those white swans which were her toys of
state
Follow her slowly as the royal cortege goes
To the callous executioner of dawn. And here, Catalion,
through these trees
The great cathedral stands sentinel to sleep;
And the whole city: brothels, shops, convents and taverns
Nestle like chicks beside her. It was there
Dona Ana and I were confirmed. It was there
I made my first confession. . . .

CATALION. It looks just the same to me.

DON JUAN. Yes, it's odd how His house is unaltered
While no trace of mine remains.

CATALION. Except for these statues.

DON JUAN. The sculptor told me
That the stone would weather three centuries.
I didn't know my remorse would last as long . . .

     A *noise off.*
But what was that?

CATALION. Don't you remember
How those rusty figures above the cathedral clock
Used to parade just as the hand reached up . . .

DON JUAN. May hers not—

CATALION. . . . And as the hour struck—
Time would lift his scythe and the gilded figure
Of a girl would turn round slowly,
To show the features of a crone?

DON JUAN. Remorse could do as much. May she find
More pity for her husband than I had for her father.

CATALION. Listen, now it strikes.

DON JUAN. I would that that clock could unwind itself
And time not budge from here.

CATALION. Shall I uncork the wine?

DON JUAN. No.

CATALION. You think she will not come?

DON JUAN. I fear she will. That wine will taste bitter.

CATALION. It shouldn't. You chose it yourself.
    *He draws the cork.*
It looks all right to me. Try it, the sun itself
Has bled into that glass.
    JUAN *drinks.*

DON JUAN. And thus goes my conscience too.
Satan should canonize the grape. For now my blood
Leaps back into the sun. This is the moment I was born for.
Now is. And all the past has purpose
Only in so far as it led this minute in.
Tell me what consolation have humans got
But human love? None, but imagination.
Better to clutch what we have than seek
What we can never find. . . .
Why is she late, Catalion? See if she comes, d'you hear?
    CATALION *looks.*

Well? Tell me.

CATALION. There is someone.

DON JUAN. Someone! Is it she?

CATALION. Yes, walking across the lawn.

DON JUAN. Why doesn't she run? Her feet must know the way.
How often in my dreams have they brought her towards me!

CATALION. Now she's passing the lake.

DON JUAN. Doesn't she hesitate or falter?

CATALION. No, she comes straight here.

DON JUAN. What? Without even a glance over shoulder?
I was never so resolute.

CATALION. None.

DON JUAN. Think of it, Catalion. She who was a novice
Has now undone her soul for me,
And doubled her first sacrifice.
May God Himself be jealous, for she shows
What human love can do.
     *Enter* MARCIA. *Pause.*

MARCIA. Well? Are you not pleased I've come?
I must say I expected a different welcome.

DON JUAN. First let me see you. My eyes have much to do
Before they convince my hopes. I couldn't live that last hour
over again.
Nothing I have ever done myself
Has been so frightening as this hour, waiting.

MARCIA. How typical of a man!
Whatever sacrifices we make for them,
They manage to demand our sympathy
Even when they've nothing to do but wait
Till we come to them.

DON JUAN. Now I begin to see you; and know that you are here.
This moment slams the past behind us
And whatever the future is, it is our future.
Nothing shall take you from me or me from you.
This, for your lips that told me you would come . . .

MARCIA. Mind my lipstick.

DON JUAN. This, for your eyes that showed you where I waited . . .

MARCIA. And my mascara.

DON JUAN. And this for your hand. Why must this glove conceal
That part of you I now love most? Take it off.

MARCIA (*Removing her gloves*). Why, don't you like them?
I think they go very prettily with this dress, don't you?

DON JUAN (*To* CATALION). Prettily. Did you hear that, Catalion?

CATALION. It's hard to tell where courage ends
And callousness begins. I think our sex divides them . . .
Where will you take your wine, senor? Here?

MARCIA. No, let's have it over here, on this stone.
*She sits by the sepulchre beneath the statue of Don Gonzalo.*

CATALION (*To himself*). As I say . . .

DON JUAN. That stone's a tomb.

MARCIA. Not if you're above it. It makes a good flat table.

DON JUAN. Yes, it was used for that once before.

CATALION (*To* JUAN). Shall I?

DON JUAN. Yes, Catalion.
*He sits beside* MARCIA *while* CATALION *places glasses, etc.*
And bring another glass for him.
This will make him walk.
No better bait was ever laid for a ghost of a father
Than I should breakfast with his daughter upon his very tomb!
He is sure to come; go and watch for him, Catalion.

MARCIA. Are we going to see a ghost? How exciting.
I've always wanted to see a ghost.

CATALION. You will.
*He goes to watch.*

DON JUAN (*Toasting* MARCIA). Let us drink to each other
For now we are equal in the violence done for love.

MARCIA. I simply don't know what you mean.

DON JUAN. Of course not. Once there was a novice
Who was about to be professed;

She broke her vows rather than break my heart.
Hers was one sacrifice—
    MARCIA *puts her glass down and moves off.*
Yours another . . .
Is anything wrong?

MARCIA. It's not exactly flattering to me
To sit here while you do nothing but talk about some other
woman

DON JUAN. Could you be jealous even of yourself?

MARCIA. Yes. I thought you were supposed to know something
about women.
Let me tell you a woman resents even hearing
How she looked two years ago,
Let alone having to listen to you talking about somebody she's
never heard of.

DON JUAN. I'm sorry.

MARCIA. Perhaps this ghost of yours will prove better company.

DON JUAN. Some more wine?

MARCIA. Thank you. I wish I'd brought a camera,
If only to show you the picture of your imagination.
    CATALION *turns back.*

DON JUAN. Well, Catalion? I thought I told
You to watch for the ghost.

CATALION. There's nothing there.

DON JUAN. No? In that case you won't mind going back, will you?
And tell us what nothing looks like?
    CATALION *returns.* JUAN *goes to the statue.*
You thought you'd part us for ever
But see! Now come back, undo your revenge
And give us your blessing.

MARCIA. Surely one shouldn't shout at a ghost?

DON JUAN. I've often noticed those in heaven
Were rather hard of hearing.
Now, Catalion, tell us what you see.

CATALION. A shadow, though nothing casts it.

DON JUAN. Now do the dead haunt the dead.
Has it no form?

CATALION. Like a man.

MARCIA. Let me see.

DON JUAN. Don Gonzalo.

CATALION. It draws closer.

DON JUAN. Does it limp—where I lamed him?

CATALION. No, it seems to stride.

DON JUAN. He's been a ghost long enough to get his balance.

CATALION. And walks as though it had a purpose.

DON JUAN. So it has. (*To* MARCIA) Give me your hand.
Let us be like this when he enters
And he will surely bless us.

CATALION. Senor, it is not her father, Don Gonzalo—but her
husband!

DON JUAN. Oh God, can men haunt us even before
Their blood is cold?
   *He looks at* MARCIA's *hand which he holds then drops it
   violently and joins* CATALION, *who still watches, and whis-
   pers to him.*
Not even allowed a brief sleep at death, Catalion,
But has to return, as I've done too,
To where his heart is tethered

CATALION. And he's no doubt where that is.
Look, he comes straight towards us.
   JUAN *returns to* MARCIA *at the tomb.*

DON JUAN. It is your husband. What horrible revenge will he
require?

MARCIA. Anthony? Revenge? Why d'you look so frightened?
My husband's not a jealous man—as I told you,
I know how to handle him

DON JUAN. Oh, I wish you had not.

MARCIA. Well, I like that! Anyhow, what's he to be jealous
about?

DON JUAN. A man's sometimes jealous of his life
When his wife has taken it away from him.
*Enter* ANTHONY, *carrying a wrap.*
Look, he carries his shroud, poor ghost.
JUAN *approaches* ANTHONY.

MARCIA. I see! You thought . . .
*She collapses across the tomb in silent, hysterical laughter.*

ANTHONY. I hope I don't intrude?

DON JUAN. No, I have a glass for you, here.
*He pours and hands him a drink.*
Let me take your shroud.

ANTHONY (*Sitting at tomb*). I thought she might like to have it
round her shoulders.
The temperature's dropped considerably.
Has she passed out? I must apologize for her.

DON JUAN (*Noticing* MARCIA *for first time*). A vision never has a
witness.
She will wake when you have gone.

ANTHONY. I've never known her find my company
So intoxicating before. She should bite the dog which bit her.

DON JUAN. Well, how's everybody this evening?

ANTHONY. Who?

DON JUAN. Wilde, Byron and Bernard Shaw.

ANTHONY. My dear fellow—are you trying to make conversation?
Although I'm a writer—you know I do other things but read.
*He drinks.*
Well, don't let me spoil your gay little party.
*He rises.*
The water looked so tempting with the moon on it,
I thought I'd take a last dip. She has to go back tomorrow.

DON JUAN (*With command*). No.

ANTHONY (*Going*). And I too. Don't worry about her. She'll be
all right.
I'll pick her up and take her back to bed in an hour.

DON JUAN. There's still that much life in you?

ANTHONY. You're so bloody rude. I like you.
Well, cheerio, and thanks for the drink.
   *He turns.*
By the way, by suffering you didn't mean
Anything spiritual, did you? No, I thought not. . . .
   *Exit* ANTHONY. MARCIA *looks up still laughing hysterically.*

MARCIA. Admit you thought he was a ghost . . .

DON JUAN. Yes.

MARCIA. And that I'd killed him. . . .

DON JUAN. Yes.

MARCIA. Nobody will believe it—

DON JUAN. No.

MARCIA. No wonder you were frightened,
Talking of his revenge! . . .

DON JUAN. Stop laughing.

MARCIA. You thought I'd killed him! . . .

DON JUAN. Ana, stop it!
   *He slaps her face.*

MARCIA. How dare you! What did you do that for?

DON JUAN. Because I am angry.

MARCIA. I can't be angry with you.
You're too ridiculous. You thought—
   *She begins to laugh again.*

DON JUAN. Ana, why didn't you kill him?

MARCIA. Why should I? Are you mad?
What makes you think I would?

DON JUAN. I asked you to come to me here.
You said you would.

MARCIA. Well?

DON JUAN. I didn't ask you here merely to offer you a drink
But to offer you my life; if I may call it that.
And when I asked you what you were going to do with your
husband
You replied, 'I'll deal with him. Leave him to me.'
What did you mean by that?

MARCIA. What I said. I didn't think he'd wake.
But as a matter of fact he did. So I just told him
That I was meeting you here in the garden.
He knew I was interested in you. . . .

DON JUAN. Interested?

MARCIA. Anthony and I are two adults. We don't try and keep
Each other in one another's pockets.

DON JUAN. Then you did come here—only for a drink?

MARCIA. I'd hoped for a little more than that.

DON JUAN. What is a little?

MARCIA. Not much, I admit. I thought you'd only asked me
Because I was safely married. I agreed because
You thought I wouldn't come.

DON JUAN. I see. You came because I thought you wouldn't.
And you came merely for a drink. But what if there'd been
more?

MARCIA. You mean if I'd lost my head?

DON JUAN. Or found it. You can see I love you.

MARCIA. Yes, I believe you do. Well, if it had come to that—

DON JUAN. As it might have done.

MARCIA. As it might have done.
Yes, I admit that.

DON JUAN. Then tell me what you would have done.
I don't believe you hadn't considered it.
        *He goes to her.*
And might have to do yet. Would you . . . ?

MARCIA. I'd do nothing violent if that's what you mean.
What do you think I am? I suppose I'd put it down
To the credit of experience and the debit of self control—
And in time forgotten you. There's no experience one can't
forget
If on puts one's mind to it. You're hurting my arm.

DON JUAN. Ana, be serious. Don't profane our love,
I'm not a mere experience, as you call it.
I am your destiny and your damnation too.
Our souls are confused

Like vines entwined round one another.
And that you know . . .
. . . and that you can't deny, can you?
Be as honest with yourself, as I am with you.
And don't hurt me—or yourself any more
With such levity with our emotions.
Besides our time is brief.

MARCIA (*Putting her face to his*). It's you who's wasting it.
 *He kisses her.*

DON JUAN. Yes, brief. Even eternity will seem brief.

MARCIA. Be practical. We've only an hour.

DON JUAN. Nonsense. You must tell him. What will you tell
him?

MARCIA. About us? Nothing tonight, that's certain.
I might find myself saying things I didn't mean.

DON JUAN. Then tomorrow?

MARCIA. That all depends
How fond I am of him tomorrow.
It's nothing less than most unkind to tell
Somebody we love that we've been unfaithful to them,
Only to halve our conscience of the burden of deceit.
Deception can be a kind of protection. And I daresay
Anthony protects me many times that way.
Those who've never lied, have never loved.

DON JUAN. But if you find you are not so fond?

MARCIA. Then I may tell him.

DON JUAN. And what will he do then?

MARCIA. Forgive what he can and what he can't
Forget.

DON JUAN. He may forgive nothing.

MARCIA. I think he would in time. Why are you so shocked?—
Our marriage is more than a mere physical relationship.
It's a sort of partnership to which we both contribute
And in which each of us respects the other's individuality
And feelings. You can't live with a man as I've lived with
Anthony

Without getting fond of him. Fondness is not passion.
It's something more precious. A woman becomes fond of a man
Not because of his strength but because of his weaknesses,
And I suppose that's why women find so much to love.
And there are other things too, they may sound small:
He can remember people's faces, I can recall their names.
I'm the only person who knows his diffidence
Masks his sincerity and that he's shy.
He knows I appear so energetic because I'm really lazy.
In a way marriage is like a music hall turn,
Feeding each other's stories, not only when one's dining out
But when one is alone. Knowing when to laugh, and more important,
When not to. The best thing about our marriage is:
It produces that kind of intimacy
Which allows either of us to relax
Even in moments of passion without giving the other
Cause for offence. Perhaps that's why falling in love with a stranger
Is such a strain, though it seems I can talk to you.

DON JUAN. But you haven't answered my question.

MARCIA. If Anthony couldn't forgive? Then I suppose we'd come to
What others seem to—separation or divorce.

DON JUAN. But of course you couldn't do that.

MARCIA. Why?

DON JUAN. As you know, those who can divorce, were never married.
Or as you'd say: your vows are sacred. . . .

MARCIA. First you talk to me as though I were a murderess
Now as though I were a nun. . . .

DON JUAN. Or a novice. . . .

MARCIA. I'd hardly be married if I were either!
I simply don't understand your values.

DON JUAN. Or I yours.

MARCIA. You're all extremes. Obviously romantic
And quite obviously immature . . .

DON JUAN. That can't be through lack of years.

MARCIA. . . . And naive too.
First you're surprised that I didn't kill my husband
Because you want me;
Then you are shocked because I say I might divorce him
Because I want you. I don't know how old you are
But you're very young.

DON JUAN. Am I?

MARCIA. Very clumsy and—

DON JUAN. Yes?

MARCIA. Very funny.
*She laughs at him. He goes to the sepulchre, picks up a
glass and crushes it with his hand.*

MARCIA. Did you hear what I said?

DON JUAN. Yes.

MARCIA. You're very funny.

DON JUAN. Am I? Well, good night.

MARCIA. You can't go like that.

DON JUAN. Why not? Doesn't such violence fit your opinion of
me?
You say I'm all extremes, so is my heart.
Now allow me to be consistent even in my immaturity.
Let me go back to where I came from.
I shall not suffer there so much
Now I have suffered here with you.

MARCIA. I'm sorry. I did not mean to hurt you.
Come and sit down again. You've cut your hand.
We seem to have lived in different worlds.
I've told you something of mine. Tell me
Something of yours. I will try to understand.
Much separates us, but something more draws us together.
Look at me. I've said I'm sorry.

DON JUAN. No, that I dare not do, for I have loved you
So that there was nothing but you.
Now I suppose I must learn to look beyond you,

Though there's nothing there. Perhaps the purpose of love like mine
Is that it inevitably leads to sorrow,
And perhaps it's sorrow alone that leads to . . .

MARCIA. To what?

DON JUAN. Something you know—and I've never known.

MARCIA. Resignation?

DON JUAN. No; and you know I did not mean that!

MARCIA. It seems that our solution lies in silence,
And only our eyes should speak. Your hand is bleeding.
Kiss me.

DON JUAN. No; what's the use? You do not love me
As I've loved you. It is finished.

MARCIA. No, it begins.
When you looked at me, I was not moved;
Now you've looked beyond me, I am.
And I know now that I love you
As I did not know I could love.

DON JUAN. You're crying.

MARCIA. Yes, and do not dry these tears.
For I can see through them so much better
Than when my eyes were dry.
The trouble with you is: you love women
Till they behave like women.
Have you no pity? Look at me.
Must I now woo you? Then so I will, and simply: I want you.

DON JUAN. On your terms?

MARCIA. No; on yours. Oh, look at me.

DON JUAN. I don't believe you.

MARCIA. Tell me what they are.

DON JUAN. For ever or never.

MARCIA. For ever.

DON JUAN. Completely or not at all.

MARCIA. Completely.

DON JUAN. I can't believe you.

MARCIA. Now it's you who are being cruel.

DON JUAN. Would you give up your precious independence . . . ?

MARCIA. Darling, don't tease me.

DON JUAN. Your important position, your influence, your . . . ?

MARCIA. Those were toys, I had to have something to play with
While I waited. I was a child, you've made me a woman.
Now take me away.

DON JUAN. And your husband?

MARCIA. Poor Anthony

DON JUAN. You mean you will break your vows again for me?

MARCIA. Rather than break *my* heart.

DON JUAN. Even so, He will always be between us.

MARCIA. No, I'll never see him again or think of him again.
There'll be no shadow.

DON JUAN. I did not mean your husband.

MARCIA. Then who? Ah yes, you mentioned him before.
You seem to think I've got a lover.

DON JUAN. Yes, as you said:
　　　Whose love is greater than my love,
　　　Whose love is more durable than my love,
　　　Whose passion is more peaceful than my passion,
　　　A lover whose tears are as wine.
I shall not believe you, until you take off that Cross
Which hangs about your neck. Now d'you remember?

MARCIA (*Removing it*). What, this?

DON JUAN. Give it to me.
　　　*She does so.*

MARCIA. It's nothing. It's not very valuable. I picked it up here
in Seville.
But I think it's pretty.

DON JUAN. That word again. Doesn't it mean anything to you?

MARCIA. Should it? I don't know what gave you the impression
that it would.

I'm not superstitious. Why d'you look at me like that?
What have I said? What have I done?

DON JUAN. You mean: you don't love Him any more?

MARCIA. But I can love you.

DON JUAN. It is not enough. Now I know what I always knew.
If we don't love something greater than ourselves
We are incapable of loving one another.

MARCIA. What I am is yours.

DON JUAN. It is not enough. Now I see that He Who was be-
tween us,
Was the One Who drew us together.
Now there is nothing between us, we are forever apart.
For it was that in you I loved.
It was your chastity that made me desire you.
It was your piety that made me protect you.
It was your love for Him that made me love you.

MARCIA. And now?

DON JUAN. You leave me nothing to look up to,
Nothing to overcome. Flesh of my flesh.
A man does not love his own flesh.
     *He laughs.*
And the last twist of the knife is:
When a profligate atheist like me,
Finds that the only thing he loved was the soul which he
denied.
You look bewildered; there's irony in that too.
One woman today made a moralist out of me; you'll turn me
Into an evangelist. It's time I went . . .

MARCIA. I can love you as a woman
What human love is, I can give to you.

DON JUAN. It is not enough. Human love's inadequate.
Human love is this: a squalid scene
Of passionate predatory emotions
I laughing, you crying; I crying, you laughing.
Think of the last half hour, that is what it is;
Human love's all self-love, even tenderness is a disguise.
And that is not enough.
     *He goes to the statue.*

Quick, quick, give me your hand again.
Better to die with an illusion
Than live with a reality one cannot face.
Quick, quick, for pity's sake release me.
Let me fly back to Hell for there's no damnation there, in Hell,
So terrible as being granted what one desires here on earth.

> *He dies.* MARCIA *goes to the body and takes a small mirror
> from her bag and places it in front of* JUAN's *lips. She
> turns the mirror to see if it is clouded and unconsciously
> adjusts her hair. Then laughs hysterically again. Enter*
> ANTHONY.

ANTHONY. What? Has he passed out too, now?
Come, darling, you'll make yourself ill with laughing.

MARCIA. But do not ask me why.

CURTAIN

# SCENE THREE

*Hell again.*
*The same night.*
*The inmates are reading the evening papers.*
*A screen conceals a sofa which is drawn up to the fire.*

SHAW. Nothing much in the papers is there?

BYRON. Nothing.

BISHOP (*Playing patience*). But at least we have leisure to read
them.

WILDE. Quite.

BYRON. I may say the *Standard*'s dramatic critic
Has fallen off badly . . .

SHAW. Did I ever tell you . . . ?

BYRON. You did. But that was music, and anybody
Can write unintelligently about music.

This notice of A *Woman of No Importance* is poor,
Very poor.
    *Passing the paper to* WILDE.
Have you read it?

WILDE. No. To read one's notices here would be
Too obvious. Besides, I can find it quite sufficient
To relish the fact that I am constantly being revived.

SHAW. Don't let it go to your head. It's only because
You're out of copyright.

WILDE. I know. That's why each production now
Gives me so much satisfaction, as I sit here
Adding up all those royalties I shall never receive
Nor have to pay in supertax—

BYRON. Yes, that's a consolation
Worth waiting for!

SHAW. More; it's something worth dying for!

BISHOP (*Going to the bell*). What would you gentlemen say to a
drink?
One for the road? . . . Well, a night-cap? . . .

WILDE. It's no use ringing that bell. Catalion
Isn't here to answer it.

BISHOP. Of course. I was forgetting.
    *He returns and picks up an empty tray and collects the*
    *empty glasses.*
But one would have thought that there would have been
Plenty of poor people here who'd be only too pleased
To take his job.

SHAW. The poor are not always with us.

BYRON. And for that, you've only yourself to blame.
Didn't you preach that poverty was a virtue?

WILDE. And service too?

BISHOP. Service is one thing,
But self-help's another!
    *He stalks off to the pantry carrying the tray.*

BYRON. That's putting it mildly.
I doubt if my digestion will recover

From that Nature salad Shaw gave us for dinner.
Red cabbage and beetroot, both grated, both raw . . .

SHAW. Full of vitamins!

BYRON. I don't believe in vitamins.

SHAW. Very good for you.

WILDE. That damns it completely.

BYRON. Thank God, it's my turn tomorrow.
I've got a surprise in store for you.

WILDE. I bet it's Spaghetti à la Bolognese.

BYRON. How did you know? But mine's with a difference.

WILDE. That's what I feared.
          *The* BISHOP *returns with the drinks.*

BISHOP. Here we are: two whiskies and soda and a gin and tonic.
I'm sorry, but I can't find any ice.

SHAW. Hardly surprising.

BISHOP. Still, it's nice to get genuine Scotch isn't it?
          *A groan comes from behind the screen. The poets try in
          vain to stop the* BISHOP *from his tactless appreciation of
          the comforts.*
This is the only place I know where the whisky's really reliable
It's a considerable comfort to know that he's got crates of the
stuff in there . .
          *Another groan is heard.*
I see what you mean. Well, let's drink to his recovery.

WILDE (*Whispering*). I don't like the look of him at all. It's all
your fault.
First mistaking him for Saint Peter; then
Adding insult to injury by dismissing him
As a mythological figure. That was a cruel blow.

SHAW. A shock like that may well prove fatal.

BISHOP (*Sitting down and picking up a paper*). My mistake was
understandable, if not pardonable.
The comforts and the consolations of this place
Might deceive both saints and martyrs.
          SATAN *groans again.*

WILDE. Ssh! . .

BYRON. Don't rub it in, you fool. You'll make him worse.

SHAW. Tactless ass, the Church was always tactless.
And where would the Church be, may I ask,
If anything serious should happen to him?

WILDE. Don't even mention it. We would have no refuge.
While there's temptation, there is hope.

BYRON. While there's damnation, there is warmth.

WILDE. Precisely. Let's try and cheer him up.

BISHOP. How?

WILDE. By looking miserable, failing that, look bored.
First, put that paper down; that's right.
Now try and recall something of which you are ashamed.
No, that won't do at all. I said miserable,
Not pious or smug. Try and look like Don Juan
Did. But if you've never loved or lost, then cast your mind
Back to how you felt when merit was rewarded
And preferred before you. Think of the time you waited
While your juniors were appointed to their dioceses.
There, that's perfect; that will do. Lust sometimes fails;
But envy, never.

> WILDE *removes the screen.* SATAN *is revealed lying on the
> sofa. He is propped up with pillows and covered in a
> scarlet velvet rug. He looks frail. A sidetable is cluttered
> with bottles of medicine.*

Your Eminence is looking better.

SATAN (*With hand mirror*). I'm not.

WILDE. I trust you managed to snatch a few hours' sleep?

SATAN. I did not.

WILDE. Didn't the doctor's draught help?

SATAN. It did not . . . that damned Faustus with his ridiculous
potions
And penicillin! I must find another quack.

WILDE. There should be plenty to choose from here.
As a matter of fact, I'm not feeling too good myself . . .

SATAN. So? That's better. But I suppose it's nothing but your
liver?

WILDE. No, nothing physical. Worse than that—
I must have been sitting in the draught of time,
For I feel all the signs of an attack of regret.
And if I don't nurse it, I fear
I'll be laid up with a bout of conscience.

SATAN (*Sitting up*). Indeed? That's a real tonic to hear.
*He notices the unhappy expressions which the others are
feigning.*
And it seems that it's contagious. This is encouraging.
I've never seen Lord Byron looking
So genuinely miserable before . . .

WILDE (*Returning to the others*). See? Now keep it up.

SATAN (*Cheerfully*). What? No cards this evening? Has the
Bishop
Cleaned you out and cornered the Ten Commandments?

SHAW. We thought it only proper to refrain this evening.

BISHOP. . . . Out of deference to your indisposition.

BYRON. Knowing nothing annoys Your Eminence so much
As when we are enjoying ourselves.

SATAN. Naturally. I'm touched. I must say you look
Deliciously bored. What have you been doing?
Reading one another?
*He picks up a book and turns to the fire and picks at a
bunch of grapes while he reads.*

WILDE (*Whispering*). There, you see, he's better already.

BISHOP. Isn't there anything else we can do?

BYRON. Of course, there's nothing like a really good confession
To set him up.

WILDE. Yes, that would have him on his feet
In no time. (*To* SHAW). You start. Tell him of your *affaire*
With Mrs. Patrick Campbell.

SHAW. He knows that off by heart.

WILDE. Well, try Ellen Terry.

SHAW. No, that was quite platonic.

WILDE. He'll think that twice the sin. And surely you can
  Remember others?

SHAW. None.

WILDE (*To* BISHOP). Then you try.
  It's your job anyhow.

BYRON. Be brazen, there's a good fellow.
  And if you can't recall anything you're ashamed of
  Then invent it . . .

BISHOP. Anything to oblige the sick.
  *He goes to the sofa.*

SATAN. Go away. I don't want your prayers.

BISHOP. I haven't come to pray.

SATAN. Then what do you want?

BISHOP. To confess.

SATAN. A sin? Now, that's different.
  Well, I'm waiting. Make it brief. It's venial, no doubt?

BISHOP. No, mortal.

SATAN. That's for me to judge. Who was she? And when?

BISHOP. The Secretary of the Cathedral Guild . . .
  But I was not Bishop then.

SATAN. The mitre doesn't exonerate
  Or insulate. How old was she?

BISHOP. Forty-two. The Guild had held
  A Jumble Sale. The receipts were most disappointing.
  The Secretary had worked so hard. . . . It was my intention
  To console her.

SATAN. Well?

BISHOP. I did.

SATAN. Don't waste my time, that's not a sin.
  But charity. This damned Samaritan
  Leads my world astray. . . .
      *He sinks back exhausted. The* BISHOP *returns to the others
      and continues his game of patience.*
  Oh, I wish I had not sent Juan away.
  This place without him is Hell indeed.

BISHOP. I can't do any more. (*To* BYRON). You have a try.

WILDE. No, let me. His were not sins, but mere excesses.

BYRON. Don't be offensive! Besides, he's heard all yours **before**.

WILDE. I doubt it. And he's desperate. Now's the time.
It is a pity Don Juan's not here.
*He goes to the sofa.*
Your Excellency. . . . Your Eminence, I have a confession to make.

SATAN. Oh, it's you. Don't bore me.

WILDE. A sin you do not know.

SATAN. Don't be presumptuous.

WILDE. I mean it's one I've not admitted before.

SATAN. That's different. But don't waste my time.
Sins which are physical are also trivial.
It'll take more than one of those to cheer me up.

WILDE. Mine will do that.

SATAN. I wonder. What was it? One of those so-called deadly sins, I suppose?

WILDE. No, vital and therefore spiritual.

SATAN. Pride?

WILDE. No, more . . .

SATAN. Self-love?

WILDE. Worse than that . . .

SATAN. Indeed. This sounds quite promising.

WILDE. Something more than immoral . . .

SATAN. That goes without saying.

WILDE. More than criminal. . . .

SATAN. Of course, of course.

WILDE. Beyond the condemnation of the Laws of Man. . . .

SATAN. Ah, tell me what it is.

WILDE. Beyond the Edicts of the Holy Church . . .

SATAN (*Raising himself a little*). A sin against Him Himself?

WILDE. Yes.

SATAN. Let me hear it!

WILDE. After I had walked up and down the streets of human
   sorrow,
   And stood in the gutters of despair, I found that sin
   Which once tasted devours the soul itself,
   Leaving no possibility of repentance,
   For it dries up that spring from which flows all remorse.
   It is the sin of indifference;
   Indifference to good, indifference to evil,
   Indifference to man, indifference to . . .

SATAN. Say no more, I feel better now.
      *He sits up.*
   But do not repeat what you have just confessed to me.
   Yours is not only a sin against Him, but against me too.
   I hesitate to think what would happen
   If others followed your example.
   There are some things I can tolerate in the individual
   But not, were they to become general.
      *Enter* DON JUAN *and* CATALION. *The former nods to the
      poets and goes straight to the desk he sat at in Scene One,
      Act One.*

WILDE. There, and his return should complete the recovery.
      SATAN *beams in* DON JUAN'S *direction.*

BISHOP. This game of patience couldn't have taken
   A whole year.
      JUAN *sits staring at something he holds in his hand.*
      CATALION *picks up the empty glasses and puts them on the
      tray.*

BYRON. A pity; I was looking forward to making
   Spaghetti à la Bolognese.

CATALION. For that, you need Parmesan.

BYRON. I know.

CATALION. And we have no Parmesan.
      *Exit* CATALION. SATAN *regards* JUAN *with mounting con-
      cern.*

SATAN. Well? Haven't you got anything to say to me?
   You might at least ask me how I am.

I'm ill, though nobody seems to notice it—
Or is that why you've returned before your time?
Come here, my son, and tell me what devilment
You've been up to and omit no detail.
Come, I'm waiting.
>            JUAN *goes to the sofa.*
What's wrong with you?
You don't look your usual dejected self at all.
Don't tell me that even you are glad to be here?

DON JUAN. Yes.

SATAN. That was most unkind.
Is that why you've come back so early?
Tell me, do not spare me. Is it?

DON JUAN. There is no place for me but here—Hell.

SATAN. And did you not find Dona Ana?

DON JUAN. Yes.

SATAN. Then what have you lost, my son,
To bring you back so soon?

DON JUAN. My love for Dona Ana.

SATAN. Why? Did she not look as you remembered her?

DON JUAN. Yes.

SATAN. Was she not beautiful?

DON JUAN. The mask of her beauty was like an unwritten book,
A hideous blank page, vacant with lack of suffering.

BYRON. Were her lips not as you had known them?

DON JUAN. Like a crimson rose which bled into the night.

WILDE. And her eyes?

DON JUAN. As opals or emeralds are: hard. Sorrow had not softened them
Nor tenderness touched them.

SHAW. Was she not passionate?

DON JUAN. Yes, that was there;
But the only thing I'd loved, she lacked.

SATAN. And what was that?

DON JUAN. Her soul.

SATAN. I warned you that was beyond my recall.

DON JUAN. Yes; but I did not know that that was all I'd loved.

SATAN. And now you'll yearn no more for her?
I see I've made a mistake. What else did you discover?

WILDE. Have you nothing to confess to?

DON JUAN. Nothing much—unless a sin is doubled
When it lacked adequate temptation . . .
I met two girls, both were married.
One treated me as a cure for insomnia;
The other, Dona Ana, as an experience.
The first almost made a moralist out of me;
The second an evangelist. Both were passionate
Without emotion; both were amorous
Without affection—though what they lacked, they feigned;
And were most articulate, of course.

BISHOP. Strange how a man complains when women
Follow his example.

DON JUAN. Not mine.
It was their modesty which I enjoyed.

SATAN. And tell me, what did the husbands do?

DON JUAN. Showed either gratitude or resignation.

SATAN. But didn't Dona Ana love you?

DON JUAN. Yes; but for me, it was not enough.
She lacked what I had admired.
Only those women who know the spiritual side of life
Are capable of great physical passion.
The rest rehearse what they can't perform and take
What they cannot give. The paradox is
I, who was an amorist, now know
There's nothing in the flesh to love. I, who was an atheist,
Discovered it was her soul which I'd adored.

SATAN. This is appalling!
        *He gets out of bed and approaches* DON JUAN.
But what of my mission?
Why don't people suffer in Hell any more?
That's what I want to know.

DON JUAN. As I say: because they no longer love, as I have loved.
Because they no longer believe, as she believed.
Their heaven is comfort; their hell is lack of comfort.
And universal comfort is the aim for all.

SATAN. But have they no god?

DON JUAN. Yes, their god is Man.

SHAW. What an absurd generalization. . . .

SATAN. Have they no spiritual aspirations?

DON JUAN. They have material ambitions.

SATAN. Do they not experience remorse
Or sorrow?

DON JUAN. Some are frustrated, some are inhibited,
All are disappointed, but none know sorrow.

SATAN. This is worse than I had feared;
Worse than I had planned. . . .

WILDE. Don't let him upset you.

BISHOP. He exaggerates, I assure you.

SATAN. And you mean to tell me they have nothing
To look up to, nothing to worship?

DON JUAN. A minority among them
Look up to these.
　　　*He indicates the poets.*
And show reverence to culture.
And what is unfashionable is their only heresy.

SHAW. Don't be distressed. Take no notice of him.
What can he know of contemporary life on earth
Who's been up there only for a day?

BISHOP. And then only in the company of women.

SATAN. What else would you expect of Don Juan?
And that is why I sent him. For when women
Cease to make men suffer,
What chance has God or Satan?
I do not understand. Tell me, do you mean to say
They suffer less because they sin less?

DON JUAN. They do not sin at all.

SATAN. What!

DON JUAN. For nothing is accounted sin. They experience no
remorse,
Only the irritation of opportunities lost
To express their personalities. . . .

SATAN. This is my fault! I am to blame!

WILDE. No, no.

BYRON. Do come and lie down again.

SHAW. And relax.

SATAN. Leave me alone. I wish to hear the worst.
It seems I did my work too well and tempted man
Too much. Now it is I who must confess:
My purpose was to make man suffer
As I have suffered. For generations I have sought
To undermine man's conscience, tempt him to sin,
Then torture him with sorrow. In a way, I was doing God's
work.
Though I got small credit for it—for the soul
Only grows through sorrow. The pity is, it seems
I've succeeded beyond my purpose. For by destroying
Man's conscience I have taken away the only thing
Which could make him suffer, as I have suffered.
—And you say they know only comfort?

DON JUAN. And loneliness. They've wired up the world;
Everybody is in touch with anybody and
Nobody has anything to say. They can go anywhere
But everywhere is so alike, they have nowhere to go.
They've freed themselves of the belief in God or you
And are all imprisoned in themselves.
The strata of geological time weighs
On each man's shoulder. Expanding space
Echoes his despair. It is a world crowded
With loneliness. The wind blows through the wires.

SATAN. May God be merciful to man! Not in all my Satanic spite
Could I devise a hell more horrible than this:
To leave man conscious, but bereft of purpose!
The little flame which was his faith
Was all the hope he had; but with that,

The callous universe could hurl its futile meteorites
Yet not put out his light. Without it,
Hemispheres of darkness must tread on his eyelids
And he must be alone. . . .

BYRON. Rhetoric.

WILDE. I often wondered where Milton
Got his style from.

SATAN. . . . Glaciers of loneliness to confine him;
Canyons of futility to yawn about him;
Deserts of despair searing his tiny heart.
No, I never envisaged this; I'm not as cruel as that.
This is not what I intended. This leaves me lonely too.
How can that have happened? Tell me,
Has man lost all his faith?

BISHOP. Not all.

SHAW. He has refined it.

DON JUAN. He believes in nothing but himself,
And doubts everything but his own reason.

WILDE (Whispering). Ssh . . . Can't you see you're killing him?

SATAN. What perverse paradox is this? Can't the fools realize
That they could not doubt if they could not reason,
And that to believe in their reason
Is the same thing as to believe in God.
For without Him, Man would have no reason:
Mind is a miracle, matter is a fact?
Can't the dolts realize that
The very ability to doubt the existence of God
Is proof that man was created by God?—That was His wish.
The more they can doubt, the more reason for their faith . . .
And you, my son, tell me you still believe in Him,
For unless you do, you cannot believe in me.
Answer me: for I feel lonely too, and am sick
And I must die. . .

DON JUAN (Turning away). I know that I am insufficient in my-
self.
Sometimes I feel grateful
But I do not know whom to thank.
Sometimes I feel sorry

But I do not know from whom to ask forgiveness.
I believe yet I do not believe.
I know that I am insufficient in myself,
And that being is a burden I would put down,
But where I do not know.

SATAN. What is that you hold in your hand?
Come closer. I can scarcely see.

DON JUAN. It is a cross which Dona Ana wore round her neck.
To test her love for me, I made her deny her love for Him.
But the sacrifice was meaningless,
This thing meant nothing to her. She thought it pretty.

SATAN. What does it mean to you?

DON JUAN. Something yet nothing.
Perhaps it takes someone who was known as a great lover
To recognize one who was a greater lover?

SATAN. That's true; and recognition must precede
Betrayal. So why don't you wear it yourself
And put it round your own neck, as Judas did?
Put it on, I say. Well? Your hesitation
Wounds both Christ and Satan. What are you waiting for?
For one of these to help you to some compromise.
There is no compromise. There is no middle way
Or Satan himself might have taken it.
So wear that Cross and bear its weight, as He did;
Or spit on it and deny Him, as they did,
And, for a different reason do what I did.
Can't you see there are only two alternatives:
Either believing or denying; either for Him
Or against Him. It's no use looking at them
Even poets can't evade this issue:
That Jesus is the Son of God as He claimed to be,
Or, that He was the greatest mountebank and charlatan
That ever led humanity astray. Which? Still you can't decide?
Then give that thing to me.

SHAW (*Beneath his breath*). Of course there is a third possibility . .

SATAN. And what is that?
*The poets close on* SATAN, *who appears cornered.*

SHAW. That He was the more deceived.

SATAN. God! how they wriggled from your hand!

BYRON. It is also possible that though He resisted
The three temptations, He fell for your fourth.

SATAN. It takes a poet to improve upon the devil!
Tell me what that fourth temptation was.

WILDE. To project upon the beloved
The reality of His love. The temptation to create God
Out of His need for God.

SATAN. Made in Man's likeness. Never was insult
More precisely fashioned! Is there nothing
You believe in?
*Now it is as though the poets were assassinating* SATAN,
*stabbing him with words. He cowers, turning from one to
another.*

WILDE. In time.

SATAN. Yet you have so little time.

BYRON. In facts.

SATAN. You have so few facts.

SHAW. In reason.

SATAN. You have such little reason.
*He breaks away to* DON JUAN.
And Don Juan?

DON JUAN (*As though drawing a knife*). In death.

SATAN (*Broken*). Even you, my son? Have you no pity?

DON JUAN. In death. The death she died!

SATAN. Their disbelief wounds me, yours destroys me.
And for that: Death shall be a mercy
You shall be denied. It is finished.
Now faith has withered on earth, I must perish here in Hell.
Man has undone himself. It leaves me nothing to do.
There can be no suffering where there is no hope,
Nor can there be evil where there is no virtue.
This is the death of Satan, now Christ has died in you,
It is finished. Won't you even lift me?

Come, carry me back, and let me lie
In sabled indolence again.
Bring me my robes and with my last breath
I'll curse you if I can.
    *They lift him up.*

WILDE. Lift him gently.

BYRON. Bear him solemnly.
    SATAN *now lies in state upon the sofa.*

SATAN. Bring another pillow, prop my head
And let a muffled funeral bell toll and tell
Those on earth that Satan dies in Hell.
Now may the rivers drain their source
And the oceans turn with their last tide.
Listen to that thunder, echoing Golgotha.
May the malicious lightning nail the limbs of light
And universal darkness bleed
Over all creation as it withdraws into the womb of night,
Leaving nothing but the loneliness of God
Borne on a wind which mourns through space
With nothing to blow upon. So shall it be.
And so it is; yet I perceive
His Lordship still plays patience. . . .
    *He sits up to curse.*
Donnerblitzen! Mater Dolorosa!
Yet the anaemic episcopal eunuch doesn't hear
Even when I curse him in Church Latin.
    *He sinks back.*
This is the end. Adoremus in aeternum.
Sanctissimum Sacramentum! . . .

WILDE (*Whispering*). Shouldn't someone get a priest?

DON JUAN. It's too late.

BYRON. Fold his hands.

SHAW. Bring clean linen.

SATAN. Stop whispering like relatives guessing about the will!
You have no need. Come close, you shall hear it.
This is my last Will and Testament.
To those agnostics on the earth, worshippers of man and mediocrity,

I, Satan, hereby bequeath: equality, democracy and boredom,
Together with all my chattels and effects.
May they who've sought security, find it;
And, knowing that world without saint or sinner, good or evil,
Without excess for sin or art,
Without vitality for love or hate,
May they be without passion or piety, without poverty or charity.
To the men, I give opportunity without desire;
To the women, desire without fulfillment.
And may they breed and reproduce themselves,
Knowing birth without joy, and death without grief,
Till maggot eats maggot on the bare bone of the eroded earth
And the last expires with vomit.
But to you three who never believed in Heaven
Sufficiently to suffer any discomfort here in Hell, I bequeath:
Complete release from fear of retribution
Or hope of your redemption.
I absolve you from all spiritual doubt
And leave you this material certainty: death.
Do not smile, you will not find that it's a quick escape to
nothingness.
But a slow running down of your consciousness.

WILDE. How?

SATAN. You do well to ask.
You, the sensualist, who believed in nothing but your sensibility
Shall experience the senses slowly become insensitive.
You will smell the wreath and not see the rose.
You will knock on your coffin and bruise your knuckles.
Touch is the last sense to go.
And you, the rationalist, who refused to trace the origin of
reason,
Shall suffer thought without revelation.
May you be, and cogitate, without the power
Of making a logical deduction,
Or the ability of reaching even the wrong conclusion.
Non sequitur nonsense is the last thought to fade.
And to you, who lived for experience,
May you suffer sentimental emotions without their object
And recall memories without their emotions.
Self pity is the last feeling to go.

Thus will you three lie after I am gone,
Entombed in your personality,
While the roots reach for your brain
And the nettles leech your heart.
> *The poets join the* BISHOP *and the four begin to play poker.*
> JUAN *moistens* SATAN's *lips.*
But you, who moisten my lips with wine,
To you, I leave the gift of sorrow.
Kneel and receive from him who was Christ's brightest angel
That symbol of faith which will make you suffer for ever for
Him. Amen.
> SATAN *puts* DONA's *cross round* JUAN's *neck.*
For you the light, which comes from despair.
For them, the darkness of indifference.
> SATAN *expires;* JUAN *remains kneeling; the poets playing
> poker. It grows darker, till only their faces and hands can
> be seen and these are bones. The italicized refrain is de-
> livered naturalistically, the verses should be spoken in a
> more stylized manner. The game is never interrupted.*

WILDE. *It's you to cut, the cards are shuffled.*

SHAW. It seems a little colder, distinctly colder.
Draughty too. I'd swear somebody hadn't shut the window,
But there is no window.

BISHOP. *Two, Three, Two. Dealer takes four.*

BYRON. How dark it is. When it's as dark as this
It's impossible to discover
Whether there is no light, or whether one is blind.

SHAW. *You're seen. Two pairs. Three kings.*

BISHOP. What is this falling through the air?
I have the impression something is falling through the air
But there is no air. It is dust which is falling.

BYRON. *It's you to cut, the cards are shuffled.*

WILDE. How quiet it is. This silence weighs. My own cry cannot
lift it.
Does it mean I am deaf or does it mean I am dumb?
For me it would be mercy enough to hear the sound of that
word.

BISHOP. *Three, Two, Three. Dealer takes four.*

SHAW. Like being in a telephone kiosk
Having dialled the number, heard the voice and pressed the
button,
But the voice which answers is my own. Exasperating conversation . . .

WILDE. *Two pairs, three queens to a flush.*

BYRON. With unseeing eyes I see crimson of cyclamen
White wet jasmine, the aubretia's violet waterfall,
While sheep crop my eyelids, the ox treads my tongue.

SHAW. *It's you to cut, the cards are shuffled.*

BISHOP. Rest in peace. There is no rest. There is no peace
For us who lie folded in the slate of Time. Yet we are free
Fleeing from ourself, the self we still pursue . . .

BYRON. *Two. Three. Two. Dealer takes four.*

WILDE. To laugh without lips, weep without tears
While regret gnaws at my memory
And I can remember nothing but the feeling of regret. . . .

BISHOP. *Two aces? Five, six, seven, joker, nine.*

SHAW. . . . Exasperating conversation, especially since his replies
Beg the question and prove him incapable of logical deduction.
This is the delirium of the inconsequential.

WILDE. *It's you to cut, the cards are shuffled.*

BYRON. There is no sleep. There is no dream for us who lie
In this embrace. Faithful to a mistress one doesn't love;
Intimate without desire.

SHAW. *Two. Three. Two. Dealer takes four.*

BISHOP. I spent my life worshipping God. Now that I've passed
over
I've found the God I worshipped: but it's disappointing
He should be like that portrait in my shaving mirror.
Most disappointing.

BYRON. *The cards are slow. Let's have the black twos as jokers.*

WILDE. Regret for time wasted. Now that I've nothing but time
to waste.

Nausea for the remembered excess, the appetite forgotten.
Nausea for the remembered embrace when the desire cannot be
imagined.

BISHOP. *It's you to cut, the cards are shuffled.*

SHAW. . . . Inconsequential as an encyclopaedia compiled by a
jackdaw.
A jigsaw where no two pieces fit. But for all that—
Cogito ergo sum: twice two are four, twice four are six.

WILDE. *Two. Three. Two. Dealer takes five.*

BYRON. This is a fine and private place
But what is this bone I hold in my right hand?
It is my left hand. There is no bracelet of bright hair about it.

SHAW. *It's you to cut, the cards are shuffled.*

BISHOP. Nothing can wake us for we do not sleep.
Listening to the rough surgery of the wind
Watching the blind butchery of the sea.

BYRON. *It's you to cut, the cards are shuffled.*

WILDE. And no release from the tedium of the mind.
Believe me, the shock after death at finding life's eternal
Is almost enough to kill a man outright.

BISHOP. *This is a jackpot, can nobody open?*

WILDE. *This is a queen pot, can nobody open?*

SHAW. *This is a king pot, can nobody open?*

BYRON. *This is an ace pot, can nobody open?*

### CURTAIN

# THE SOCIALITES

*by*

KENNETH JUPP

# CHARACTERS

SNOWBALL, a Negro

FLON, a scarred little man who wears a beret throughout

RIKKI, a handsome man with a stammer

SHEBA, a blonde (who is Snowball's girl)

MAXINE, a dark girl (officially with Rikki)

(*All the above are employed by* Cato.)

SIMON ASHER

EVA, Cato's daughter

CATO

DAX, Cato's servant

TESSA ASHER, Simon's mother

LUCIAN, Tessa's friend

*Scene: A house near an estuary*

*Time: Evening*

# SCENE ONE

*As the curtain rises, we see past a dark frontroom into a harshly lit backroom of* CATO's *house. A gauze wall, solid for the frontroom scenes, transparent for the backroom, divides the two.*

SNOWBALL, RIKKI *and* FLON *sit around a table with an arc light above it, playing cards.* SHEBA *and* MAXINE *sit near the table, watching. A colourful crowd of very dubious-looking types.*

*A television set and a radio-gram are prominent, and under the entire scene to come, jazz beats loudly.*

*At first, the noise in there reaches us muted, for the door between the front and back rooms is closed. Then a sudden argument springs up, ending with the Negro leaving the table, opening the door, and almost falling into the frontroom for air. He is followed by the blonde, the only one to show concern.*

*As the door opens, the noise hits us full blast. The Negro and the blonde are lightly spotlit in the frontroom, which still remains dark.*

SHEBA. Peter's gone, hasn't he? (*She catches his sleeve*) **Let's** forget him!

SNOWBALL. I know he's gone—I know that, you don't have to tell me—(*Pulls himself away*)

SHEBA. So let's forget him. There's nothing else to do.

SNOWBALL. It's alright for you! You're just like the others—it doesn't matter to you, does it?
(*Turns back toward the group*) Nothing matters to you, does it?

RIKKI. Calm down.

FLON. He's gone, that's the end of it.

RIKKI. You're interrupting the g-game.
*The Negro stands, wavering.*

113

SHEBA (*Reasonably*). He was a nice boy. We're all very sorry.

MAXINE. We'll miss him.

FLON. The place won't be the same.

RIKKI. Pass that bottle over. (MAXINE *does so*)

SNOWBALL. You talk as though . . . "a nice boy!" Anyone'd think—

FLON. As far as I'm concerned, that's what he was.

RIKKI. You're making too m-much of it.

SNOWBALL. How can you? A person like that . . . how can you make too much of it?
> *He re-enters the back room.*

SHEBA (*Coaxingly*). Sit down, Snowball . . . sit down with the boys again. (*He does so*)

FLON. Alright? That's it then.
> *He starts to deal, stops when he sees the Negro still isn't concentrating.*
Are you okay now? Are we playing?

RIKKI. Come on—we've got a lot to do tomorrow.
> FLON *resumes dealing.*

MAXINE (*Thoughtfully*). It's always the way . . . when you get to like someone. They sail away—out to sea . . .

SNOWBALL (*Vaguely*). Yes.

RIKKI. That's what happened.

FLON. Cato said so.

SNOWBALL (*Even more vaguely*). Yes.

RIKKI (*Suddenly leans forward*). D'you know where you'd be today if it wasn't for Cato? Well, d-do you?
> *The Negro looks down.*
Where any of us'd be, if he hadn't let us work here?

SNOWBALL (*Mumbling*). No one else'd *do* the work.

RIKKI. That's not the point. Where would *we* be?

SNOWBALL (*Grudgingly*). In the ash can.

FLON (*Coldly*). Then don't be so stupid.
> *Pause.*

SNOWBALL. I don't see . . . how Peter could just GO! . . . without even saying goodbye—

MAXINE. People do.

SNOWBALL. To me at least! He should've said good-bye to me—

SHEBA. Why to you—?

MAXINE. What's special about you— } (*Loudly and indignantly*)

SHEBA. You great black ape—!

SNOWBALL. Alright then—to any of us—

FLON. How could he? We were all in bed when he left.

SNOWBALL. Couldn't he've seen us the night before? Why couldn't he—?

FLON. He was out all evening the night before. We were all in bed when he got back.

SHEBA. We spend too much time in bed.

RIKKI (*Grins at her*). There are w-worse places.

SHEBA. Not with you, there aren't.
*Pause.*

FLON. He got fed up with us, and I don't blame him. You didn't expect him to stay forever, did you? (*Bitterly*) There wasn't much to stay for. It's a lot of fuss about nothing. Let's play cards.
*They pick up their cards.*

SNOWBALL. Maybe you're right.

FLON. Thanks.

SNOWBALL. But I still think Cato should've found out more details.

RIKKI. What're you talking about n-now?

SNOWBALL. Where he went—if he was coming back—his family'll want to know—

MAXINE. Peter has no family.

SHEBA. Of course he has. He's got a mother and a brother, you know that.

SNOWBALL. Real socialites, they are.

SHEBA. Always in the papers—

MAXINE. He was alone, just the same.

SHEBA. He always spoke well of them—

MAXINE. He spoke well of *everyone!* Can you imagine him not speaking well of anyone? (*Pause*) Simon Asher and his mother won't be worrying about Peter. They're both too far gone.

RIKKI (*Triumphantly*). L-look at that! Full house!
    FLON *looks at it, throws down his own hand in disgust.*

FLON (*To* MAXINE). Who the hell *cares,* anyway?

*Jazz* . . .

## THE SCENE DIMS OUT

## SCENE TWO

*An hour later.*
*The lights come up on* SIMON ASHER, *waiting in the front-room.* (*The gauze wall is now solid.*)
*Although the cash value of all the objects in this room would be* (*unlike the backroom*) *extremely high, the total effect is cluttered and un-chic. This is the effect created by a man with money to spend, but no sense of conventional style or taste. The furniture, painting, etc. have been collected at random, each thing for its own sake, in a manner which reveals the owner* (*to anyone who has studied these things*) *as either a peasant, or an eccentric, or possibly both.*
SIMON, *a good-looking, fashionable young man in the twenties, surveys all this with a condescending curiosity. He is expensively dressed in a fur and leather travelling coat, and, although he has been drinking heavily, he is perfectly in control of himself.*
*After a moment,* EVA *enters. She is young, simply dressed, and attractive—and somehow fits very well into the room described above. She and* SIMON *are worlds apart.*

EVA (*With warmth*). I'm Cato's daughter. I've heard so much about you . .
> *She comes towards him smiling, hand outstretched.*

SIMON. I'm sure you have.
> *He takes her hand and looks coolly at her.*

You're exactly as he described you.

EVA. Am I? Well. . . .
> *She removes her hand.*

He was good at descriptions. (*Slight pause*) We can't seem to find my father at the moment—he doesn't even know you're here—

SIMON. Never mind.

EVA. Of course, if we'd known you were coming—

SIMON. It doesn't matter. I prefer dropping-in. You learn more about people that way.
> *He continues to regard her—insolently.*

I would have recognized you anywhere.

EVA. From Peter's letters, you mean?

SIMON. From Peter's letters, that's right.
> *Abruptly, he seems to lose all interest in her, turns away— examining things in the room.*

EVA (*Slightly unsure of herself*). Did you have any trouble finding u

SIMON. Not much. (*Absently*)

EVA. We're a little remote out here—miles from anywhere. People often get lost, especially at night—

SIMON. You're not surprised to see me, are you?

EVA. Why should I be? You're his brother, after all. (*Pause*) How was St. Moritz this year?
> SIMON *looks round in surprise.*

I was reading about you the other day. In the social column.

SIMON. The snow was excellent.

EVA. I'm so glad.

SIMON. I suppose Peter talked a lot about me?

EVA. Quite a bit—about you and your mother. It was fascinating. We don't have much excitement . . . Would you like something to eat, or have you—

SIMON. No thank you. I stopped on the way.

EVA. A drink then?

SIMON (*Deciding to climb down a little*). Thank you very much.

EVA. Whisky?

SIMON. Thank you.

> *She goes to the inset bar and pours drinks.*

EVA (*Conversationally*). You know . . . you're amazingly like Peter to look at.

SIMON. So they say.

EVA. You could almost be his twin. If I hadn't been told who you were . .

> *She hands him a drink. They toast each other briefly and drink.*

How long would you like to stay?

SIMON. I'm not staying—I'm just driving through. Why should I want to stay here? (*Sharply*)

EVA. I don't know . . . (*She smiles*) I just assumed . . .

SIMON. Oh, did you? Did you really?

> *He is oddly annoyed by this, whereas EVA becomes correspondingly calmer.*

EVA. Anyhow, you're in for a late night if you don't. It's a two hours' drive to town, and the hotels are packed this week for the exhibition. But please yourself . . . (*Pause*) I'm sorry if I've annoyed you, Simon. . .

SIMON. You haven't.

EVA. I think you expected a different kind of welcome.

SIMON. I didn't expect anything.

EVA. Would you be happier if I was rude to you? I can be, you know—

SIMON. I don't doubt it.

EVA. Look . . . we're hospitable in this part of the world—why not? We're nice to everybody, even perfect strangers. And as for Peter's family. . .

SIMON. I'm glad to hear it. (*Pause*) You were fond of him then?

EVA. Of course we were.

SIMON. Especially you?

EVA. We all were . . . (*She withdraws a little*) Very fond of him.
*Silence. She finishes her drink.*
Well, if you don't mind, I'll—

SIMON. No, don't go—(*The social act is cracking a little at the seams*) Tell me what he said about me.

EVA. I'm surprised you care.

SIMON. I suppose you got a brilliant analysis—the full works—a list of my failings a mile long, with built-in motives—

EVA (*Coldly*). He spoke very well of you.

SIMON. Did he? (*Pause*) Poor Peter.

EVA. He thought a great deal of you, don't you know that?

SIMON. Yes, I know. (*Suddenly tired, he turns away*)

EVA. He did say you were spoiled and hard to get on with.
*She turns and moves toward the door.*
I see what he meant.

SIMON. True . . . (*Following her*) No one's denying it . . . What else?

EVA. He thought it was worth the effort.
*She turns back to him, all her directness coming out.*
He said you were disappointed and bitter, Simon—your own worst enemy—

SIMON. Did he say why?

EVA. Something about your mother . . .

SIMON. Was that all?

EVA. No . . .
*Pause.*

SIMON. He did talk, didn't he?

EVA. I've told you—he thought a lot of you. He thought you had great possibilities.

*This appears to destroy* SIMON's *last vestige of poise.*

SIMON. Possibilities! How typical. How bloody typical! We're all potentially something or other, aren't we? It's such a comfort to know you have possibilities! (*Pause*) Why d'you think I've come here?

EVA. Because of Peter, I suppose.

SIMON. Because of my brother, that's right. My brother who lived in this house for six weeks and then disappeared.

EVA. Went abroad—

SIMON. Went abroad . . . oh yes, of course. (*Sarcastically*) He'd never been abroad in his life. He'd never done an unexpected thing since the day he was born. But he's gone abroad, just like that! He's gone away without *seeing* us or *telling* us—!

EVA. He wrote to you, didn't he?

SIMON. We received a note . . . not a letter, mind you, but a note! . . . Two lines saying nothing at all. . . .

EVA. P'raps he'd nothing to say.

SIMON. He *always* had things to say—he *always* explained himself and everyone else as well!—how he felt, how I felt, even how our mother felt! (*Pause*) He was forever trying to explain what made the world go round—he had that sort of mind. I can't believe he wrote that note—I can't believe he'd do that.

EVA. P'raps he changed. People do, you know?

SIMON. They can't—who can change? People can't change basically like that, don't be so ridiculous—!

*He stops, conscious of going too far.*

Do you expect me to believe he just *went*?

EVA. I'm sure you'll believe whatever you want to.

*She turns to go again.*

SIMON. There's no need to go . . . I mean . . . you can understand me being curious, can't you? It's not unreasonable, is it? . . . Is it? (*With great urgency*)

*She seems to hesitate.*

You see . . . if something happened while he was here, then I must know about it, you can understand that?
*She turns and looks at him; their first moment of contact. JAZZ ROARS SUDDENLY . . . as the door to the back-room flies open, and* SNOWBALL, *now very drunk, totters over to the door up right.*

SNOWBALL (*Formally to* EVA). Pardon me, I'm sure.
*He practically falls out of the door up right.* EVA *closes the backroom door, cutting off the jazz.*

SIMON (*Tiredly*). Is there a party on?

EVA. No, they're always like that. They drink too much, that's all.

SIMON. Who are they?

EVA. They work for my father. He lets them live here as well.

SIMON. What does your father do?

EVA. He's in the export business.
*They look at each other.* EVA *somehow defiant.*

SIMON (*Softly*). I need your help, Eva. It isn't easy for me to say that. I just want to talk to you, that's all.
*A strange, underplayed appeal, which very nearly dislodges* EVA *from the position she has taken up. For a moment, she seems on the point of saying something important. Then . .*

CATO'S VOICE (*Off*). Eva . . . ! (*A deep voice, demanding instant attention*)

EVA. That's my father. Excuse me.
*The moment is broken. She goes to the door.*

CATO'S VOICE (*Off, impatient*). EVA!!! Come here a minute—
*She opens the door and goes out.*
This idiot's passed out in the hall again and I can't find Dax. Whenever there's work to do he hides in the lavatory—p'raps you could . .

EVA'S VOICE (*Interrupts quietly*). We have a visitor.

CATO'S VOICE. What?

EVA'S VOICE. We have a visitor—come and meet him.
    CATO *enters slowly. He is a grey-haired powerful-looking*

*man in the sixties, permanently confined to a high wheel chair. A scarlet rug across his legs.* EVA *enters behind him. As he sees* SIMON, *he sits quite still.*

EVA (*Speaking softly*). This is Simon Asher. He's just driving through.

### THE SCENE DIMS OUT

## SCENE THREE

*Immediately afterward.*
SIMON, CATO *and* DAX, *who is* CATO's *servant. He is a huge man, incoherent and illiterate—he could be a brokendown boxer or wrestler.*

CATO. Simon Asher! . . . Well, well . . . Peter's brother. You could be his twin! (*He laughs*). Shook me for a moment, I must say—I thought he'd come back.

SIMON. Changed his mind, you mean?

CATO. That's right . . . changed his mind and come back.
*To* DAX, *who is fixing drinks.*
Make mine strong, Dax.

DAX (*Nodding*). Strong.

CATO. Well—it's nice to see you! (*He exudes hospitality*)

SIMON (*Briefly*). Thanks.

CATO. Smart car you have outside—German, isn't it?

SIMON. Mercedes . . . (*A touch of arrogance*)

CATO. I should've known! (*He smiles*) We've heard all about you of course . . . you and your mother—she's quite a girl, isn't she?
*The coarse directness makes* SIMON *stiffen slightly.*
(*Remembering*) Have you had anything to eat, or—

SIMON. Thank you—I stopped on the way.

CATO. Any trouble finding us?

SIMON. Not much.

CATO. This place is a bit out of the way. People—

SIMON. I know. (*He nods*) Often get lost, especially at night.

CATO. That's right . . . of course—you've been talking to Eva
. . . what did you think of her? (*A touch of pride*)

SIMON. I think she's pretty. (*He drinks*)

CATO. You'd never believe she was my daughter, would you? I
mean—she doesn't look a bit like me, and she's so 'refined'
. . . (*He laughs*) Of course, she's educated, that makes a difference—me, I'm entirely self-made. Self-*created*, you might
say . . . no one else had anything to do with it.

SIMON. That's a big responsibility you're taking. (*Finishes his
drink*)

CATO (*Looks at him for a moment, then smiles*). Have another!
We shall get on fine! . . . Dax!
     DAX *takes* SIMON's *glass.*
She's a good girl though, Eva. She's had a mixed-up time lately,
but she's coming through it alright.

SIMON. Mixed up? (*Without interest*)

CATO. Through being married, you see—she wasn't his type. He
was one of these city intellectuals. Went around thinking all
the time. Tried for months to get her at it too, and as soon
as she did she left him. (*He laughs*) Poor chap. . . .
     *He drinks.*
But it upset her, just the same.

SIMON. I can imagine.

CATO (*After a slight pause*). You seem to know what I'm talking
about, which is a change. Eva always says I don't express myself clearly . . . (*He sighs heavily*) I'm tired out and my back
aches like hell! (*He stretches in his chair*) We're building a
new wing to this dump round the other side, and if you can
imagine the trouble—

SIMON. That must be expensive.

CATO. What must? (*Not having understood*)

SIMON. Building a new wing.

CATO (*Briefly*). I'm not short of money.
> *He glances at* DAX, *who stands silent at the bar, then back*
> *to* SIMON.

I don't quite get the point of that.

SIMON. I just said it must be expensive.

CATO. I heard you—it was the point I didn't get.

SIMON. Where does your money come from, Cato?

CATO. I'm in shipping. Why?

SIMON. Your daughter said the export business.

CATO. They're very much the same . . . Why don't you sit down?
> *Pause.*

How many of these things have you had?

SIMON. Three, so far.

CATO. Then take it easy. It's special stuff, and if you're not used
to it—

SIMON. I'm alright—

CATO (*With authority*). Sit down anyway . . .
> SIMON *does so.*

That's better. . .
> *Pause.*

You seem worried, Simon—you don't mind if I call you Simon?
. . . You seem to have something on your mind. Want to tell
me about it?
> SIMON *looks at him in silence—trying to judge this man,*
> *and failing.*

Well, (*He shrugs*) whenever you're ready. I like to get things
straightened out. Problems bore the ass off me.

DAX (*Who has been staring at* SIMON). How long you here for?

SIMON (*In mild surprise*). It talks!

CATO. Of course it talks! (*He laughs*) He's human, what d'you
think?

SIMON. I don't know the answer.

CATO. As far as I'm concerned, you can stay as long as you like,
but you'd better check with Eva—she'll have to make the
arrangements. (*Complete unconcern*)

*He suddenly winces—puts his hand to his chest—leans forward in pain.*

DAX (*Anxiously*). What?

CATO. The same thing.
*He shakes his head and straightens, recovering immediately.*
(*Smiling at* SIMON) Sorry about that—I get shocking indigestion . . . (*He takes a pill*) Belch all day long. Dax talks quite a lot, as a matter of fact. He not only talks, he does tricks, too—here! (*Clicks his fingers*)
DAX *lumbers over*—CATO *takes something out of his pocket.*
(*To* SIMON) See that? Six-inch building nail—we're using them round the other side, in case you wondered . . . here, feel it.
SIMON *feels it.*
Now watch this—(*To* DAX) Bend it!
DAX *puts the nail between his teeth and bends the two ends down. Returns it to* CATO *in the shape of an E.*
Fantastic, isn't it? Bloody incredible! He can bust a three-inch-thick iron bar round his shoulders, but we've run out of three-inch-thick iron bars . . . Good boy!!
*He smiles at* DAX, *who beams happily and vacantly.*

DAX (*Eagerly*). Bust poker?

CATO. Leave the poker alone! It's the last one in the place. (*To* SIMON) That's the trouble with him—never knows when to stop. Impetuous, that's what he is.
DAX *returns to his position by the bar.*
He's nice though, don't you think? I found him in a circus a couple of years back—he was the strong man, but they had to let him go.
DAX *makes a deep growling noise.*
Shut up! (*Silence*) He overdid it, you see—he always overdoes it.
*Pause.*

SIMON (*A trifle weakly*). I think I'll have another.
*He holds out his glass to* DAX, *who looks at* CATO *for approval.* CATO *nods.*

CATO (*To* SIMON). OK . . . We'll see what you're like drunk.

SIMON. I'm much better. I become very frank, for one thing—

CATO (*To* DAX). Make it a big one.
　　DAX *doubles the dose.*

SIMON. Like the night I left my wife. (*Laughs briefly*) I was frank with her alright.

CATO. You're divorced, aren't you?

SIMON. Did you read about it?

CATO. Peter told me . . . I can't stand newspapers.
　　SIMON *takes his drink from* DAX.

SIMON. Did he say he was in love with her himself?

CATO. No.

SIMON. Probably didn't even mention he knew her first?

CATO. No.

SIMON. That's right, he wouldn't. How would he put it? Let me think . . . (*Regards the ceiling drunkenly*) I know . . . ! (*Exaggerating his voice*) We fell in love, through no fault of our own—married—then fell out of love, through no fault of our own . . . Right?

CATO. Something like that.

SIMON. That was Peter . . . (*A trace of contempt*) He never could see it.
　　*He waits for* CATO's *question, which doesn't come.*
　　(*Volunteering*) What really happened was that I wanted her, took her away from him, and when I was fed up I cleared out. It cost me a packet.
　　*Waits for* CATO's *reaction.*

CATO (*Completely unmoved*). Is that so?

SIMON. I suppose it's all in the point of view.
　　*He drinks.*

CATO. P'raps he thought you couldn't help it.

SIMON. But I could! I did it on purpose. I told him so.

CATO. P'raps he thought you couldn't help it—just the same.

SIMON. I don't know . . . he was a fool.

CATO. Yes . . . (*Thoughtfully*) And still you've come all this way—

SIMON. I'm passing, that's why. I'm just driving through.
*Pause.*
Anyway, he's my brother.

CATO. Your brother, that's right . . . your perfect brother.
(*Laughs abruptly*) The black sheep of the family.
SIMON's *head droops slightly as he begins to feel the full
effect of the whiskey.*
It's strange, when you think about it—Tessa having two sons
so different—

SIMON. We had different fathers, that's all. There's nothing
strange about that.

CATO. She was attractive, so they say.

SIMON. She still is. *Very* attractive . . .
*He sinks lower in his chair—drowsily.*
I don't even know who mine was.

CATO. I thought Paul Asher—

SIMON. He was Peter's father, not mine! (*A flash of emotion*)
He was nothing to do with me. He died before I was born.
(*Closing his eyes*) Peter should've mentioned it.
*He fights his sleepiness.*
Now p'raps you'll be so kind as to tell *me* something—
*He tries to sit up.*

CATO. Whatever you like.

SIMON. It's very simple, what I want to know . . . (*Trying to
concentrate*) I just want to know if he really went abroad.

CATO. Of course he did.

SIMON. Then why isn't his name on any of the passenger lists?
I checked them all.

CATO. You poor boy—what a lot of trouble you've been to—

SIMON. I want an answer—

CATO. He left in a private launch—that's the answer, Simon—

SIMON. I don't—

CATO. He left in a private launch, and he went to Spain—so his
name wouldn't *be* on any passenger list, would it? (*Reasonably*)
*Pause.*

SIMON. Spain? . . . he went to Spain?

CATO. That's right.

SIMON. At this time of year?

CATO (*Smiles slightly*). That was his first port of call.

SIMON. And after that?

CATO. Africa—somewhere in Africa, wasn't it, Dax?

DAX (*Starts*). Huh? (*Thinks, painfully*) Yuh—Africa.

SIMON. That's a big place.

CATO. He didn't tell us any more.
    *Pause.*

SIMON. Who's launch was it?

CATO. His own—he bought one.

SIMON. He didn't have the money.

CATO. He'd thirty thousand in trust from his father—

SIMON (*Violently*). How do YOU know that—?

CATO (*As to a child*). I know because he told me. You're for-
    getting—he was here a long time. We were friends. I
    wouldn't've let him stay otherwise, he was no use to me.

SIMON. He wrote he found this place by accident.

CATO. That's right. He was heading north and lost his way. We
    put him up for the night—

SIMON. Is that a habit of yours?

CATO. Not exactly . . . I'd never have done it if he hadn't been
    in such a state.
    *He looks straight at* SIMON, *who looks away.*
    Anyway, we talked, got to like each other, and I invited him to
    stay on . . . (*Shrugs*) God knows why.

SIMON (*Muttering*). Who'd he buy this launch from?

CATO. Some dealer, I think . . . down in the estuary.

SIMON. Do you know the name?

CATO. I can't remember. Can you remember, Dax?

SIMON. Don't bother, you'll wear him out. (*Tiredly*) There are
    hundreds of boat-dealers in the estuary.
    *His head droops again, down to his chest.*

CATO. Don't you think you're making a fuss over nothing? You're building a mystery out of something that happens every day. Look . . . your brother, along with thousands of others last year—got tired of his own country and went abroad . . . Is there anything extraordinary about that?

SIMON (*Sleepily, drunkenly*). To somewhere in Africa . . .

CATO. Why not? P'raps he had a reason—

SIMON. In a launch . . .

CATO. P'raps he wanted to be left alone for a bit—is that impossible?

> SIMON *is almost asleep.* CATO *speaks softly, soothingly.*

Anyone can see you're taking it to heart—too much to heart— Your best move'd be to forget him. That'd be the best thing you could do . . .

> *Pause.*

You know . . . you'll end up with a nervous breakdown, the way you're going on. I've seen it happen . . . Breakdowns aren't nice, and they come from worrying about things you can't help. You don't want that, do you?

> SIMON *doesn't move.*

Anyway—he'll be in touch when he's ready—so what's the point of worrying?

SIMON (*Mumbling*). That's right. What's the point?

CATO. You ought to be pleased, in a way . . .

SIMON. Pleased?

CATO (*In a very friendly manner*). Well . . . he always bothered you, didn't he? Let's be honest—it can't be much fun having a brother like that around the place . . . showing you up . . . making you seem more of a bastard than you are . . . (*Pause*) Now he's gone you won't have to feel so inferior.

SIMON. You're right. You're quite right. I should be pleased . . .

CATO. Of course, you should! (*He sits back, smiling genially*) It'll make all the difference—

SIMON. Maybe I would be, if I didn't have these doubts—

CATO. Doubts? Listen . . . anything you don't understand, just ask me—there's no need for you to be worried. Let's have these doubts out in the open *now* . . . then we can all relax . . .

SIMON *regards him through half-closed eyes.*

SIMON. Where does your money come from, Cato?

CATO. We've already—!

SIMON. I know we have! It just bothers me, that's all. Especially as Peter drew all his *out* the day before we got that note.

CATO. For the launch, and his expenses—

SIMON. And he was the third person to do that . . . living in this house of yours!

CATO *sits a little straighter.* DAX *moves slightly.*
(*A sudden fear*) Why does Dax sway around like that?

CATO. He's not moving—it's your imagination.

*He makes a sign to* DAX.

(*Quietly*) Is that all?

SIMON. No . . . (*He sits up a bit, gathering power*) No it isn't —the other two sent notes to their families just before they closed their accounts. He moved again! (*Looking at* DAX)

CATO (*A trifle grimly*). Never mind him—what else?

SIMON. What else? You need more, do you? Alright . . . they both disappeared *immediately after!*

*With a huge effort, he raises himself halfway out of his chair.*

Those are my doubts!

DAX *moves, unchecked behind* SIMON, *looms over him. The door up right opens and* EVA *stands, framed in the doorway.*
*Pause.*
*Jazz beats loudly.* . . .

## THE SCENE DIMS OUT

# SCENE FOUR

*Ten a.m. next morning.*
*The stage is now brilliantly lit by 'sunlight,' which pours in through the open window up left.*
*Standing by the window, looking out, is* TESSA ASHER, *a woman of about 45, beautifully dressed.*
*On the other side of the room,* LUCIAN, *a handsome youth of about 20, stands impatiently, glancing at his watch.*
*They both appear to be waiting for something.*

TESSA (*Without looking round*). Give me another cigarette, please.

> LUCIAN *gives her one of her own, from her bag on the table. As he lights it, her hand shakes so he has to flick the lighter several times.*

LUCIAN. What are you so shaky about?

TESSA. Nothing. I'm a bit cold, that's all.
*Pause.*

LUCIAN. How long are we going to hang around here anyway?

TESSA. Until I've talked to Simon.

LUCIAN. I can't understand it. You don't bother to see him for weeks when he's living in town and now—when he comes to a Godforsaken hole like this—

TESSA. I know.
*Pause.*

LUCIAN. If we don't hurry we'll have to eat on the plane.

TESSA (*Briefly*). I'm sorry.

LUCIAN. You know perfectly well I hate eating on planes . . .
(*Pause*) We've driven a hundred miles out of our way, and for what—

TESSA. I know it's a bore for you, but it matters to me! (*With force*) Can you understand *that*?

LUCIAN. Alright . . . (*He shrugs*) I just think it's a waste of time, that's all. (*Pause*) It's not as if you had anything in common with him.

TESSA. He's my son, you know?
 LUCIAN *sighs deeply, turns to go.*

LUCIAN. I'll wait in the car.

TESSA (*Quickly*). No, don't go. I . . . Wait until Simon comes.

LUCIAN (*In surprise*). Do you want him to meet me?

TESSA. It doesn't matter anymore.

LUCIAN. No—I expect he's used to it by now—

TESSA. Oh, for God's sake don't snap at me—I've enough on my mind. . .
 *Pause.*
They're taking their time alright. . . .

LUCIAN. The ape-man looked half-witted to me. Probably didn't understand who you wanted.

TESSA. He knew who I wanted.

LUCIAN. Perhaps they don't like visitors then. Maybe this isn't the sort of place where you just drop in . . .
 *He surveys the room with distaste.*
Though why anyone'd *want* to, I can't imagine.

TESSA. I hope he's alright . . . (*Sudden anxiety*) He does such stupid things—

LUCIAN. Yes, doesn't he? (*Sarcastically*) When did you last bail him out?

TESSA. I haven't seen him lately.

LUCIAN. You don't have to see him, to bail him out of prison.

TESSA. Who told you about it?

LUCIAN. A friend of mine. She read about it.

TESSA. Was I mentioned?

LUCIAN. Of course—with your news value? There was a picture of you.
 TESSA *goes to the window.*
Don't worry—it was a good one. Left profile, that's the best,

isn't it? (*He laughs*) "The Beautiful Tessa Asher, widow of our Country's Greatest Writer—"

TESSA. Shut up, will you?

LUCIAN. Why are you so touchy? Everyone knows about Simon. He's an international celebrity.

TESSA. No one knows about him. That's the trouble.

LUCIAN. Well! . . . Motherly love from you of all people! (*Suddenly spiteful*) Can't you face the fact that you've produced a drunken hooligan?

> TESSA *flinches, but doesn't move.* LUCIAN *wanders around the room.*

My friend gave me a full report. As far as I can see, he's a public menace.

TESSA. Your "friend" exaggerated. He . . . gets drunk, that's all.

LUCIAN. That's all! He smashed up a night club and half-killed two policemen last time . . . (*Regards a vase*) Look at that ghastly object!

TESSA. He gets into arguments—people pick on him because he's well-known, and he flies off the handle. He can't help it.

LUCIAN. All I can say is, it's a good thing you've got money.

TESSA. Yes, isn't it?

> *She looks at him, he becomes silent.*

Anyway, he can't help it. He's not vicious, or criminal, or anything like that. He's just—

LUCIAN. Don't tell me . . . misunderstood? How contemporary! A pure soul, warped by Society!

TESSA. Purity isn't your line. Let's drop it.

LUCIAN. And as for the things he did to Peter—

TESSA. *Alright!* . . . I said let's drop it.

> *Pause.*

There's more to this than you'll ever know. And you wouldn't understand it if you did.

LUCIAN. I'm only repeating what—

TESSA. Don't judge everything by appearances! Don't be more of an idiot than you can help!

LUCIAN. Thank you, Mrs. Asher. I see where Simon gets his manners from.
*Pause.*
You're always insulting me when you're in a temper, aren't you? But of course, you'll be sorry later . . . about midnight, as usual, you'll want to make friends again—
*SIMON enters quietly, unobserved by either of them for a moment.*
One of these days I may get tired of making friends again, just remember that! I may begin to wonder if it's worth it after all—and you'd be worried then, wouldn't you?

TESSA (*Seeing him*). Simon!
*LUCIAN stops, and turns.*

SIMON (*Quietly to* TESSA). I had a feeling you'd come.
*He moves across the stage, not looking at her.*

TESSA (*In a rush*). We were just driving through, you see . . . I'm flying to Rome, and I thought . . . it seemed . . . a good opportunity. . . .
*She trails off, glances at* LUCIAN.

LUCIAN (*Nastily*). Is this my cue?

TESSA. I shan't be long.

SIMON (*Looking out of the window*). George can stay, as far as I'm concerned.

LUCIAN. My name is not George.

SIMON. George, Jeremy, Charley . . . what's the difference?

LUCIAN (*Tensely*). It makes a difference to me.

TESSA (*To* LUCIAN). Please . . . wait in the car.

LUCIAN. Alright, I'll go. You can have your family chat in peace. I'll give you ten minutes.
*He goes, slamming the door violently.*

SIMON. What a charming young man.
*A long pause—*TESSA *seems very nervous.*

TESSA. There's a party on in Rome, did you know? For the Wilders. It starts tomorrow. It should be fun, everyone's going to be there . . . you remember the Wilders? You met

them in New York last August—the daughter found you attractive—remember?
> *Pause.*

They're always asking about you.
> *Pause.*

Why not come down as well? I know they'd be pleased, and if you're not really busy . . .
> *Pause.*

(*Softly*) Are you alright, Simon?

SIMON. Quite alright.

TESSA. I've been so worried . . .

SIMON. There's nothing to worry about.

TESSA. But I was thinking—

SIMON. I'm *alright!* (*Pause*) How did you know I'd be here?

TESSA. I guessed—it wasn't difficult—and we happened to be passing, you see—

SIMON. Yes, I see.
> *Pause.*

TESSA. Where has he gone?

SIMON. I don't know. Somewhere in Africa, they say.

TESSA. Do you believe them?

SIMON. I don't know.

TESSA. Is there any reason *not* to believe them?

SIMON. The whole thing's peculiar. People've disappeared from here before. Then there's this ape . . . roaming around . . . (*Meaning* DAX)

TESSA (*Nods*). I've met him.
> *Pause.*

But there's still nothing definite, is there? I mean . . . we're no further forward. We're still only guessing, aren't we?

SIMON. What else can we do?

TESSA. Nothing, I suppose . . . unless . . .

SIMON. What? (*Softly*) Unless what, Mother?

TESSA. Unless we just accept the fact that he's gone away.

SIMON. He couldn't do that to us! You know perfectly well he wouldn't just *go!* There must be more to it—there has to be a reason—

TESSA. Of course . . .
*She turns away.*

SIMON. Anyway, he drew all his cash out, before he wrote that stupid note—did you know that?
TESSA *shakes her head.*
All his money—every bit—and now no one knows where he is! If you don't think that's suspicious—

TESSA. If he went abroad—

SIMON. But would he go without even *seeing* us? Without giving us a chance . . . ? (*Pause.*) There's something behind it all—there's some motive—some mystery or other and I'm going to find out what it is. I'll never believe he just went! I'll never believe he could do that to us!

TESSA. Perhaps we'd better see the police.

SIMON. I already have. (*Pause*) I saw the local ones yesterday. They were polite, but not interested. They said people often go abroad without giving details—especially people like Peter.

TESSA. How do they know what he was like?

SIMON. They don't—that's the hell of it! They were just fobbing me off. They didn't want to be bothered—no one wants to be bothered with it. (*Almost hysterically*) That's the trouble with this bloody place—(*Kicks a sedate chair violently*) nobody *cares* about anything!
*He stands, trembling and overwrought.*

TESSA (*Taking him by the shoulders*). Sit down darling . . . (*He sits, with his head in his hands*) Don't . . . don't be silly . . .
*She strokes his forehead, nervously at first, then confidently as he accepts it.*
You know that isn't true . . . you're just upset—like you used to be . . .

SIMON (*Allowing himself to be comforted*). That's right . . .

TESSA. Did you see that doctor in Switzerland?

SIMON. No.

TESSA. You should've done—you know how he helped you last time—

SIMON. He didn't help me one bit. You don't know anything about it.

TESSA (*Kneeling beside him*). Yes, I do . . . I know how it is . . . I've been through it. But you mustn't blame other people all the time—after all, it doesn't mean anything to them. You get upset too easily . . .
*She kisses him gently.*

SIMON. I know I do . . . I'm sorry . . .
*He is barely audible, his arms around her shoulders.*

TESSA. Just relax, darling . . . don't think anymore. . . .
*She holds his face tenderly between her hands.*
It's a long time, isn't it? Since we sat together . . . like this. . . .

SIMON. Yes, it is.
*Pause—he slowly disengages himself and stands up.*
(*A dull voice*) It's a very long time.
*They look at each other for a moment.*

TESSA (*Trying to speak in a normal tone*). Why not just tell this man Cato what you think? Come right out with it and see how he reacts?

SIMON. I've done that, too. Last night.

TESSA. What happened?

SIMON. Nothing. Nothing at all. I think he knew I was bluffing anyway. He treated me like a child. . . .

TESSA. You are sometimes. . . .

SIMON. I passed out in the middle of it. They must've carried me up to bed. This morning Dax . . . gave me some stuff for my headache. It worked.

TESSA. Did you have to be drunk?

SIMON (*Briefly*). It was special stuff—pure alcohol.
*Pause.*
I don't know what to think.

TESSA. What are you going to do?

SIMON. Stay here for a bit—what else can I do? Perhaps if I get to know them better, I'll—

TESSA. There were only two that Peter wrote about—

SIMON. That's right. The old man and his daughter.

TESSA. Have you met her?

SIMON. Yes . . . she's attractive.

TESSA. Is she? (*Coolly*) How nice for you. What about him?

SIMON. I don't know. I can't make him out. He's an old peasant with a lot of money. He says he's in shipping. . . . I get the feeling nothing could surprise that man. I threw the lot at him last night and it had no effect at all.

TESSA. What did he say?

SIMON. Oh, he told me exactly what I ought to do. He advised me properly . . . he was very wise and logical. He even said I should feel relieved that Peter's gone . . . (*With venom*) because of us being so different, you see.
    TESSA *turns away.*
He said I was making a lot of fuss about nothing. It was an everyday occurrence. He'd get in touch when he was ready. (*Pause*). In the end he said I should just forget him. That it would be better for my health if I just forgot him.

TESSA. P'raps he was right.

SIMON. You think so too? You're worried about my health as well? My *health*—!

TESSA. Simon! You must get a grip on yourself! What's the use of—

SIMON. Are you going wise and logical on me, too? That would be wonderful—just what I need—and considering you're in it as deep as I am—

TESSA. Don't you think I know that? Don't you think I feel everything you do? I may not see you for months or years on end, but I feel *all* the same things as you! You must believe that!
    *Pause*

SIMON (*Turning away*). It's a pity you didn't for Peter.
*Silence.*

TESSA (*Dully*). I'd better go. Will you phone if you hear anything?

SIMON (*Not looking at her*). You are concerned, aren't you?

TESSA. You know the hotel.

SIMON. I know it.
    *Pause.*
Remember me to the Wilders.

TESSA. We're both to blame. Whatever's happened, it's our fault.

SIMON. OUR fault . . . ! That's good!

TESSA. Oh, it was *me* then, was it? All by myself, is that right? I sent him driving off into the night—!

SIMON. You know you—

TESSA. I was all alone with him, I suppose? (*With vicious sarcasm*) You weren't *there!*
    *Pause*—SIMON *doesn't answer.*
(*Quietly now*) We did it between us, Simon. For years . . . we did it between us—until finally he couldn't take any more, and he got into that ridiculous car of his and drove . . . and drove . . . and ended up here. And now he's gone and we're sorry and we're here too. You know I'm right. How could I've done all that alone? Just *me*, doing nothing?

SIMON. Because that's what you were for him—nothing. A bloody great void.

TESSA. Alright . . . if it helps to blame me, then you'd better do it.

SIMON. You don't agree? You think you've been a model mother, perhaps, with your strange parties and your unusual friends and your little boys . . . getting younger every year? (*Pause*) They'll be in school caps before long!

TESSA. So what? What of it?
    *Pause.*
What do you care anyway? If I sat at home with a book and an apple, would you ever come to see me?
    *Pause.*
There's no point in this.

SIMON. You had responsibilities . . . that's all.

TESSA. And you! Didn't you have any? Were you a model son?

SIMON. We're not talking about me. We're talking about Peter, not me. (*Pause*) That's a very different thing. (*Pause*) Can't you see? I'd've *understood* you not caring for me—after all, why should you? I was a mistake right from the start—

TESSA. Simon—!

SIMON. It's true . . . I was a lapse at a party and you know it alright! I was a bit of bad timing on someone's part, and that's about all—

TESSA. How can you—

SIMON. But we're not talking about me. We're talking about Peter and that's different because he was *intended!* He's the son of your husband, he's the son of Paul—the Great Writer —the Great Philosopher—he's the son of the man you're supposed to have loved and I should've thought he deserved *better* of you!
*Pause.*

TESSA. We've been through all this before.

SIMON. I know—
*Takes her by the shoulders and roughly turns her round.*
I know we have but let's . . . let's go through it again because I still don't understand it!

TESSA. Alright! He deserved better of me—you've made your point—I know—

SIMON. You admit it—!

TESSA. I know! But I couldn't help it—I couldn't stand it—

SIMON (*Almost shaking her*). Couldn't stand *what?* He was Paul's son, wasn't he? Why couldn't you—?

TESSA (*Violently*). It was *because* he was Paul's son that I couldn't stand the sight of him!
*Silence.* SIMON *releases her and steps away, suddenly exhausted. She goes to him.*
Will I ever make you understand? Couldn't you try? Couldn't you put yourself in my place, just for a minute? (*She holds his arm*) Couldn't you at least *try?*
*He turns and they look at each other.*

(*Quietly—with an effort*) You know very well what Paul meant
to me—everything he was to the millions who read his books,
and twice as much besides—he was my *world*, you understand? I was his deepest convert—a sort of high priestess—
everything that was right and true on earth could be summed
up in two words—Paul Asher.

    *Pause.*

I never began to know why he married me—a flighty little chit
of seventeen, I was a complete nobody. I only know there was
nothing I wouldn't have done for him . . . and not a day
went by but I didn't try to be a little more worthy of him.
I'd've gone on, too, Simon! I'd've gone on, and I'd've been
happy, and I'd never have stopped—

SIMON. But he died.

TESSA. Yes, he died. Stupidly, senselessly—

SIMON. He had the sense to leave you a fortune—and that
must've helped a bit—

TESSA. You don't understand even now, do you? You think of
Paul Asher as some kind of monument—representing all the
virtues—all the best things—

SIMON. That's what you *told* me—!

TESSA. I know I did! (*Pause*) But he was a man—a man as *well*,
my husband . . . That's what made him real to me—that's
what made it all so easy. While he was alive everything was
possible—I could reach the stars when he was there—but it
was a *man* I worshipped, not a monument . . . (*Pause*) At
nineteen I was already a widow—I'd tried so hard to live up
to him, and then suddenly . . . he wasn't there anymore.

SIMON. His books were there—everything he stood for—

TESSA. Books! Are you mad? What use were his books to me,
or his ideals, or his teachings? Can't you understand? Everything collapsed!—fell around my ears—all that stuff meant
nothing if he wasn't there himself to love me. I had to know
he was with me. I had to be able to see him and hear him.
I couldn't be alone with it!

    *Pause.*

He'd given me a code . . . a way of life all worked out in
books . . . and left me alone to live it. It was as though he'd

said—"There you are—you know what I expect of you—now get on with it!" (*Pause*) I just couldn't do it alone, that's all.

SIMON. You had Peter. You could've lived for him.

TESSA. I wanted to. That's what I always meant to do, but somehow . . . the more he grew like Paul, the more I went the other way.

SIMON. You did—

TESSA. I couldn't help it—I didn't want it, but when your whole life revolves around someone—when it's just built on one *thing* and *that's* taken from you . . . you slide, Simon . . . you go right down. . . .

SIMON. On his cash, which is very funny. (*Pause*) What's all this to do with Peter?

TESSA. Everything—because he was Paul all over again . . . As he grew up—every day—it was like a knife in me—how could I be with him? Knowing I was too far gone . . . to ever get back . . . I couldn't even look at him in the end—without remembering . . . feeling. . . .

SIMON (*Prompts ironically*). Ashamed?
　　TESSA *turns away.*
—and feeling *bored!* Go on, admit that too! Admit you found Peter a great big pious BORE! (*Pause*) Just the same as I did.
　　*Silence.*

TESSA (*Softly*). Then why are you so worried?

SIMON. You know . . . you know why.

TESSA (*Going to him*). You're so much like me, aren't you? Like the worst of me . . .

SIMON. How do you know what I'm like? You've spent more time with your *hairdresser!* (*Spitefully, to hurt her*) P'raps I bore you as well?

TESSA. You know that's not the reason! (*With passionate sincerity*) You know it's the *reverse* of that! I've always felt close to you, Simon—if I've stayed away it's because I thought it better.

SIMON. Better?

TESSA. Because . . . I feel *so* close that . . . Simon—
*Pause.*

SIMON. If you'd been around when I was growing up there'd *be*
no reason now!

TESSA. I know—it was a mistake—

SIMON. To me you were just a beautiful woman I saw once a
year if that—we were *strangers* until I was twenty and *then*—

TESSA. I know. I'm sorry.

SIMON. You used to drop in, I remember. When I was a child
you dropped in now and then—just back from Greece or Italy
or somewhere—all brown and gold with presents under your
arm—presents for the little boys, the dear little boys, so sweet,
so good . . .
*He pauses, slightly choked-up.*
It's no wonder I'm like you.

TESSA. Yes it is—it *is* a wonder . . . With me there was a reason
for it—I lost Paul—

SIMON. That's an *excuse*, not a reason!

TESSA. I lost all that strength and wisdom—

SIMON. You'd've been like this anyway—

TESSA. I lost the only thing—

SIMON. You were BORN LIKE THIS!!
*Pause.*

TESSA (*Closing her eyes*). I lost the only thing that held me together. But you are twenty-five. What can you possibly have
lost?

SIMON. Nothing. Nothing at all. You never gave me anything
to lose. There's been no one doling out strength and wisdom
in my lifetime—he died before I was born, remember? You
said so yourself— Everything's collapsed. So nice of you to pass
the ruins on to me.

TESSA. You must build your own life—

SIMON. Oh that's fine! That's really profound—"You must build
your own life!!" (*Into her face*) And what d'you suggest I
build it on? A heap of rubble? Be a little constructive, if you—

TESSA. But you must try! What's going to happen if you don't even try? It's too late for me now, but you have every advantage—

*A car horn hoots loudly. Then silence. . . .*

SIMON (*Echoing her tiredly*). . . . every advantage. . . .

TESSA. I must go.
SIMON *nods. It's as though she's already gone.*

SIMON. Enjoy the party.

TESSA. Will you phone, if you hear anything?
SIMON *nods.*
Try to understand . . .
*Going to him abruptly.*
I love you, Simon—more than anyone, you know that. I'm your mother, and I love you.

SIMON. I know. . . .
*She embraces him.*

TESSA (*In a last attempt*). But I don't *want* to leave you here! Where will it get you? What can you do?
SIMON *breaks away.*
Listen—come with me—I'll get rid of Lucian—I shan't need him if you're there—

SIMON. I can't.

TESSA. You're all I want, you know that, Simon. I was wrong to leave you, and I want you back.
*The horn toots—loud and impatient.*

SIMON. You'd better go.

TESSA. Come to Rome—you've got your own car—you know everyone there—

SIMON. No.

TESSA. All the usual set—they'll help you relax—you *must* relax—

SIMON. No.

TESSA. Look—Peter's gone—everyone says so—why can't you—

SIMON. I—DON'T—BELIEVE—IT!
*Silence. Realising the futility of saying any more, she goes slowly to the door.*

(*Following her*) I *can't* believe it, that's all.
*She reaches the door.*

TESSA (*Quietly, without looking round*). Goodbye . . .

SIMON. I just don't believe he could do *that!*
*She goes. He stands, looking after her for a moment.*
Not Peter . . .
*He bangs his hands down on the table in futile rage, then half falls on to it, his head in his arms.*
Anyone but Peter. . . .
*There is the sound of a car door slamming, the roar of a powerful exhaust.*
Anyone else, but not Peter. . . .
*He mumbles, shoulders shaking.*
*A final, ironic toot on the horn.*

THE CURTAIN FALLS

END OF FIRST HALF

SCENE FIVE

*Evening, two weeks later.*
*The backroom of* CATO's *house—exactly as at the beginning.*
*The men playing cards, the women watching.*

FLON (*After a moment*). It seems to me he's in a bad way.
*Plays a card.*

RIKKI. I don't know w-what he h-hangs around for. It's not as if he liked the company.
*Picks up a card, examines it, throws.*

FLON. He never talks to us, does he? Has he spoken to anyone here?

MAXINE. You wouldn't talk either, when you first came.

FLON. That was different. I'd lost the habit.
*Pause.*

SHEBA. It's all to do with his mother—you can see it a mile off.

RIKKI. I had a l-look at her—through the window—

SNOWBALL. She was alright, wasn't she? (*Sighs*)

SHEBA (*Ironically*). Don't I satisfy you anymore?

RIKKI. She had a l-l-lov-l- (*He gets hopelessly embroiled*)

SHEBA. Spit it out then!

MAXINE. He made a packet out of that stammer. People're sorry for a man with a stammer, and once they're sorry for him, they've had it.

SHEBA. Pity the cops weren't. (*To* RIKKI) What were you stuttering?

RIKKI (*To* SNOWBALL, *ignoring the women*). Beautiful car, wasn't it?

SNOWBALL (*Dreamily*). Alfa-Romeo . . .

FLON (*Correcting*). Mercedes. Just like Simon's, only bigger.

SNOWBALL. They've got wonderful taste, those two.
> *Pause.*
(*To* RIKKI) You know, I don't see it either! He's been here two weeks—they must've told him what happened—

FLON. P'raps he doesn't believe them.

SNOWBALL. That's stupid! Why shouldn't he?

MAXINE. Hark at that!

SNOWBALL. Well, there's no mystery, is there? It's all simple enough—

MAXINE. I seem to remember, two weeks ago—

SNOWBALL. That was different. I hadn't talked to Cato then. Cato explained it all to me—there's no mystery at all.

FLON. Simon should do that.

MAXINE. He hasn't had a chance yet.

FLON (*Briefly*). Well, he'll get it tonight. Cato'll be free tonight, after he's seen the doctor.

SNOWBALL. P'raps he'll go away then. I hope so.
> *Throws a card.*
You know, he still makes me nervous—stalking around—

FLON (*Tiredly*). Don't start—

SNOWBALL. I can't help it! He reminds me of Peter! He looks like him! I see him walk by, and I suddenly . . . all of a sudden I—

RIKKI. There you go again! Why d'you have to keep *talking* about it? It's always the same—just when we get settled down you have to open your b-bloody great mouth—

SNOWBALL. I can't help it! I can't help it while he's here. If he went away I'd be alright—I'd forget it then. He bothers me, I tell you—looking like him—sounding like him—

SHEBA. And that's all!

SNOWBALL. Maybe that's all but it's enough! What does he want here? He's not like us—he's got nothing in common with *us*, has he? He's in a different class—I mean . . . there's no *reason*—!

SHEBA (*Harshly*). He's staying because of Eva. Can't you see that? Now shut up about it! You give me a pain.

THE SCENE DIMS OUT

*Followed by an immediate lighting switch to* SIMON *and* EVA *who are downstage left in the frontroom.*
*As before, the gauze wall becomes solid.*

SCENE SIX

*Immediately after.*

EVA. Don't start again. I couldn't stand it!

SIMON. Don't you think I'm sick of it, too?

EVA. I had enough yesterday.

SIMON. So did I.
　　*He moves around restlessly.*
D'you imagine I enjoy thinking of you with someone else?

EVA. There's no *need!* I explained—

SIMON. I don't enjoy it but I must! I must know all about it—

EVA. You already do—I explained the whole thing—

SIMON. I know what you told me.

EVA. I told you *everything* last night!

SIMON. We stopped talking after a while, remember?

EVA. You didn't seem to mind. You didn't object at the time. . . .
*Pause.*

SIMON. You admired Peter—we got that far. You thought he had wonderful qualities—we established that, too—

EVA. That's all—

SIMON. You were in love with him, weren't you?

EVA. No! . . . I wasn't . . .
*She hesitates—he looks at her.*
He was the kindest person I'd ever known. I met him at a time when I needed kindness . . . that's all. It was nothing like this.

SIMON (*Bitterly*). No, I'm sure. (*Pause*) Look—you were sorry for me last night—let's admit it—I'm turning into a pretty sad spectacle, I know that—it wouldn't have happened if you hadn't felt sorry for me.

EVA. Since when have you been so modest?

SIMON. It's true—

EVA. It doesn't suit you, Simon—it's out of character.

SIMON. It's true. Why not—?

EVA. There are other ways of showing pity! (*Pause*) You're in a bad way if you think THAT was pity! I don't show it like that—!

SIMON. Then how did you show it to Peter?

EVA. Oh, God! Must we talk about him *all* the time? Can't we forget him for five minutes? Why does everything have to—
*Jazz roars out as the door to the backroom is flung open, and* SNOWBALL *totters through to the door up right exactly as he did in Scene Two.*

SNOWBALL (*To* EVA). Pardon me.
> *He practically falls out of the door up right, The backroom door is shut from inside, cutting off the jazz.*
> *Pause.*

EVA (*Softly, almost pleadingly*). You can't go on like this—it isn't possible—

SIMON (*Wearily*). I want the truth, that's all. That's why I came here . . . is it so unreasonable?

EVA. You can't . . . (*She is suddenly very disturbed*) You won't get it by firing questions—things are never that simple. . . .
> *She is almost on the point of tears—for her this is the climax of days of "questioning."*

SIMON (*Relenting*). Alright . . . okay. . . .
> *He goes to her.*
We'll say no more about it.
> *He puts an arm around her shoulders.*
We'll give it a rest.
> *He smiles at her, and she turns swiftly, into his arms.*

EVA. Simon . . . I know we could be good for each other. . . .

SIMON (*Absently stroking her hair*). Do you?

EVA. We're both pretty useless but perhaps . . . together. . . .

SIMON. I suppose it's possible . . . just possible. . . .

EVA. You don't really think that was pity, do you?

SIMON. No. (*He smiles*) Certainly not all of it. . . .

EVA. All of it! (*She giggles suddenly*) If I could act like that I'd be . . . Well, not here anyway . . .
> *Pause.*

SIMON. Why are you here, Eva?

EVA. It's my father's house—
> *She gently disengages herself.*
Where else should I be?
> *They both pause, as though sensing how delicately this scene is poised between dark and light.* EVA *comes in quickly, taking the initiative.*
Let's behave like other people, shall we? Let's say all the things that lovers say . . . shall we try that for a bit?

SIMON (*Smiling*). I'm out of practice—

EVA. You'll soon pick it up again . . . look . . . we'll rehearse a
little—
  *She stands in front of him and looks into his eyes with
  comic intensity.*
What are you thinking about?
Why are your eyes so blue?
I wonder if you really love me?
  *She kisses him lightly, though there is an air of sheer
  desperation about the whole thing.*
Simon, it's so easy . . . it's such fun . . . won't you help me,
just a little?
  *A pathetic, almost childish plea.*

SIMON. I will . . . I'll help you if you'll answer one more question.
  *Smiling still, he takes her arms from around his neck.*

EVA. Questions . . . questions . . .
  *Slightly lost, she seems very young.*

SIMON (*Gently, as to a child*). Just one more, that's all—
You slept with Peter, too, didn't you?

EVA (*Starting violently from him*). For God's sake—!

SIMON (*Turning her round*). Didn't you?

EVA. You're hurting me!

SIMON. Didn't you? You wrapped yourself all round him just
the same—

EVA (*Struggling*). What *right* have you—!

SIMON. —all the same—used your little tricks—

EVA. You're crazy—

SIMON. ANSWER ME!!

EVA. Alright—!
  *Pause.*
Alright, I did!
  *He releases her and moves away.*
I did, now are you satisfied?
  *She rubs her shoulder.*
(*Quietly*) I did . . . but it wasn't the way you think.

SIMON. There are fifty-nine of them, I hear.

EVA. You *want* to know about it then? You really want the whole story?
>Pause.
I didn't tell you, because it would hurt you, and it isn't important—

SIMON. Not important—!

EVA. No! It has nothing to do with this. (*Pause*) I'll never make you understand.

SIMON (*Viciously*). Never mind, you go ahead and try—everyone else does! People always want to make me understand things— I must be thick-headed or something—but I *try*—I really put myself out. So you go ahead, darling—I'm half-sold already.
>Pause.

EVA. Then try to imagine—

SIMON. Yes—

EVA. Oh, how can I—?

SIMON. Go on—get on with it—I'm listening!

EVA. I'd just come home after a long time.

SIMON (*Brutally*). You'd just walked out on your husband, let's have it exact.

EVA (*Quietly*). Alright . . . I had . . . But I'm not going through it. I'm not going through all that because it doesn't matter— only *believe* me! When I first came here it mattered—it mattered then alright . . .
>Pause.
I must have reached about the lowest point of sheer *misery* a person like me *can* reach. I was more in pieces than . . . even than you are now. I came to Cato because . . . this place is quiet, and I thought I'd be able to rest.

SIMON. Rest . . . ?

EVA. He couldn't help me like he does the others—he tried, but we couldn't talk somehow—because I'm his daughter, I suppose —that made it harder . . . Anyway, I found myself getting worse instead of better. Worse and worse until—(*She pauses*) Until Peter came.
>*She hesitates.*

SIMON. Go on. You're doing fine.

EVA. It was a week before he even spoke to me—

SIMON. He always was a slow starter.

EVA. He didn't feel much like it either—can't you imagine?
    SIMON *looks away. Pause.*
But later . . . (*She almost glows at the memory*) If you could've
seen him later, the way he was with me . . . I'd never met
anyone like him. All he wanted was to *be* with me and *talk*
to me . . . If you knew what a relief it was to be with a man
without motives! One who wasn't the whole time scheming-up
and leading-up to things . . . He took one look at me and
just . . . *understood* . . . the whole thing. I didn't even have
to tell him.
    *She pauses, still amazed by it.*
I never understood him though . . . not for moment. The
only thing I understood was that I could never repay him—
never in a lifetime. We became *friends,* you see—all of a
sudden. In a way I'd never imagined . . . He made me realize
what friendship can mean—

SIMON. Friendship! Christ!!

EVA. Let me finish! I know what you—!

SIMON (*Savagely*). He taught you what friendship can mean . . . !

EVA. THAT'S RIGHT!
    *This with such force that even* SIMON *stops. For the first
    time, we can believe she's* CATO's *daughter.*
I daresay it's news to you, but such things still exist.
    SIMON *is silent.*
They exist, Simon . . . I'd nearly forgotten myself, but they
do. Such things as kindness, unselfishness, gentleness . . .
haven't entirely disappeared from the face of the earth. They do
actually still exist! (*Pause*) Peter reminded me, that was
all . . . he made me want to live again. Oh, not *for* him—I
wouldn't be capable anyway—but just because of him . . . Because, if there were still people like that in the world it couldn't
be such a bad place . . . (*She pauses*) Is this all too difficult
for you?
    SIMON *looks at her, waiting. She hesitates, like someone
    who knows they will not be believed.*

I wanted . . . I wanted to show my gratitude somehow . . . for all he'd done. I knew he thought I was attractive . . .
> *She pauses.*

(*Defiantly*) It seemed inadequate at the time, and it still does.
> SIMON *still looks at her.*

That's all.

SIMON. Surely that can't be all?

EVA. D'you want the details? Haven't you—!

SIMON. What was he like in bed, this perfect brother of mine?

EVA (*Wildly*). Why not get a whip and beat yourself? Or p'raps a hair-shirt would—!

SIMON. What was he like? I really want to know—I mean . . . he was so bright at everything else it must've been something *marvellous*—

EVA. How can—!

SIMON (*Suddenly shouting*). What was he l—?

EVA (*Frenzied*). Like he was in everything . . . sweet, affectionate and . . . uncomplicated . . . d'you know what I mean? He was charming. Is that enough?

SIMON (*Wearily*). That's enough.

EVA. So you see—it was nothing like this.

SIMON. Nothing at all. (*Pause*) Nothing at all like this.
> *He stands, his back to her. She goes to him, rubs her face tiredly against his shoulder.*

EVA (*In a dull voice*). What is it with us, Simon? Why can't we be simple and straightforward and . . . ?

SIMON. I don't know.
> *He turns and they look at each other—balked somehow, and frustrated.*

I don't know. It just never works out. We go around loaded with experience—we know all about it—oh, we're good alright . . . But we mess it up . . . in the end we mess it up— every time.

EVA. Maybe we think too much. P'raps if we could stop thinking and let things just . . . (*Pause*) (*She rallies*) Anyhow—there

are two of us. After all, that should make it easier . . .
(*Quickly*) I didn't love him, you see—he was the most wonderful person I'd ever met, but I didn't love him. He didn't *need*
me anyway—I couldn't do him any good . . . (*She pauses*)
We're animals, Simon—we can only love our own kind.

> *Jazz roars again . . . as* SHEBA, *now happily plastered,
> totters off in* SNOWBALL's *footsteps. The door is shut, the
> jazz stops.*

SIMON. Our own kind . . .

> *His eyes have followed* SHEBA *through the room.*

Maybe you're right. (*He moves about*) I suppose it's possible . . . you and me . . . ?

EVA. We could try anyway—what harm could it do?
It's not as if we had anything to lose.

> *They look at each other.*

SIMON. Isn't it time we had a drink? I'm tired of thinking! I'm
tired of it . . . !

EVA. We're young, too, aren't we? It's not as if—

SIMON. Of course we are! (*Laughs*) We have Youth On Our Side.

EVA. We have everything on our side.

SIMON (*To himself*). . . . every advantage. . . .

> *Pause.*

Tessa was right—I've been a fool—

EVA. Cato was right, too.

SIMON. Everyone was right! (*Determined now*) There's no point
in this—it gets me nowhere! He went away, that's all there is,
he sailed away—

EVA. In a launch—

SIMON. Which he bought up the estuary! He bought a launch
and went away in it, there's no more than that? It happens all
the time.
Anyway, I'm sick of it—I'm just going to relax—I'm going to
calm down, and if you'll help me—

EVA. You know I will.

> *She goes happily to the bar. The determined gaiety grows,
> until not a trace of self-deception remains.*

SIMON. I'm going to relax. I'm going to stop thinking and asking questions. I don't even want to know! I'm going to relax and stop thinking and forget him!
    *Pause.*
We'll be happy, you and I . . .
We'll behave just like lovers do, that's what you want, isn't it? We'll say stupid things in baby voices and spend three weeks in bed—

EVA (*Smiling*). People might talk.

SIMON. P'raps you're right. I'll take you away then— Anywhere you like—you just name it—London, Paris, Rome . . .
    *On "Rome" he stops abruptly. Pause.*

EVA (*From the bar, softly*). Whiskey?

SIMON (*Smiling ruefully*). Isn't there anything else?

EVA (*Looking at the bottles*). We have a nice line in gin, some very old brandy for special occasions, some vodka, some . . .
    SIMON *comes behind her.*

SIMON. Did I ever tell you you have a beautiful neck? (*Kisses it*)

EVA. It's too long—like an ostrich—

SIMON. I like ostriches—big furry things with their heads in the sand—

EVA (*Turning to him*). We'll never do that—

SIMON. Never! We'll look everything straight in the eye—

EVA. And to hell with the lot of them!

SIMON. To blazes with them!
    *They embrace—feverishly . . .*
    *Jazz blares again, in the darkness . . .*

## THE SCENE DIMS OUT

# SCENE SEVEN

*One hour later.*
*In the darkness, the voice of* CATO—*booming above the jazz—*

VOICE OF CATO. Dax! . . . (*Rising inflection*) DAX!
    *A sense of threat.*
    . . . that bloody Snowball's passed out in the hall again—!
    *The jazz fades a little.*
Come and shift him! Take him away! People who can't hold
it shouldn't have it—
    *As the frontroom is slowly lit,* EVA *rises from the couch
    down left. She doesn't leap up, but rises slowly, almost
    lazily.*
    *There is a bottle of brandy beside the couch.*
    SIMON *moves into a sitting position, a half-smoked cigarette
    in his mouth, his collar open, an air of happy befuddlement.*
    CATO *enters alone, up right.*
I don't understand it . . . Six months here and that fool *still*
gets drunk! Anyone'd think— . . . uh . . .
    *Seeing* EVA *and* SIMON, *he trails off. He looks closely at*
    SIMON, *who beams at him amiably.*
I'm sorry.
    *With some surprise, but no resentment,* CATO *turns his chair
    and starts off.*

EVA (*Indulgently*). Where're you going?

CATO (*Briskly*). I'm going out again—where does it look as if I'm
going?

EVA. There's no need.

CATO. Oh, I hate to interrupt—

SIMON. But you're not. (*Positively*) Really you're not.

CATO. No?
*He looks at* EVA, *who smiles at him.*
Oh . . .
*Pause. He regards* SIMON *with considerable interest.*
You look alright . . . (*A slight smile*)

SIMON. I *am* alright—didn't you know?
*He rises and stretches—unsteadily.*
I'm a hell of a nice chap really—you've only seen one side of me so far—

EVA. The worst one.

SIMON. Right.

CATO. I see . . . (*The smile deepens as he begins to understand*)

SIMON. That's it. Like most people, I have a many faceted personality—

CATO. A many—?

SIMON. Which means my nature is many sided, or, if you prefer it, double-bottomed. (*Giggles slightly*)

EVA (*To* CATO). He means he's feeling better.

CATO. Does he? Thank God for that.
*He wheels himself downstage.*

SIMON. Much better—a hundred percent—I can't tell you . . .
*Pause.*
In fact, I'm almost embarrassed.

CATO. Embarrassed?

SIMON. For the way . . . for the things I said to you . . .

CATO (*Briefly*). Nuts.

SIMON. . . . on the night I arrived. I was very rude. I was offensive—

CATO. Think nothing of it.

SIMON. I *do* think something of it—

CATO. Forget it.

SIMON. I will not forget it! I'm not often able . . . I'm not able often to do this, so let me get on with it—

EVA *smiles at* CATO.
You're the first person I've apologized to since—I don't know—

CATO (*Protesting*). But it doesn't—

SIMON. It does! . . . I've come to realize—that is—it's been pointed out that I've got too much imagination.

EVA. Far too much.

SIMON. I've got too much imagination and I think too much—in fact, I do too much of everything—it's a sort of disease, which I'm told can be fatal—

EVA (*Smiling*). Unless taken in time.

SIMON (*He nods deeply*). Right.

CATO (*Calmly*). You were worried about your brother. What's peculiar about that?

SIMON. I know but—

CATO. I understood perfectly—what's all the fuss about?
SIMON *tries not to be nonplussed. As always, in the presence of* CATO, *he feels like a child of five.*

SIMON. *You* may have understood, but I didn't. It hadn't been explained to me—that's the whole point. Now, if I could just tell you—

CATO (*Protesting*). I don't—

SIMON (*Ignoring this*). You see . . . I've never been able to accept the obvious—especially if I don't like the look of it. I mean . . . I can't take anything on its face value, I never have been able to, you see? And that's why—

CATO. I don't want—

SIMON (*As though it's impossible for him to stop talking*). That's why I couldn't *accept* that Peter's gone away. I always have to complicate things. Nothing's ever simple for me. If I don't want to believe a thing *nothing*'ll make me—

CATO. I don't want to know! Can you understand that?
*Pause.*

SIMON (*In wonder*). You don't?
*Another pause.*
But *why*? I mean . . .

CATO. Look . . . when you first arrived, God knows why, I liked you. I told you so. You've been here two weeks and I still like you. I'm telling you again.

SIMON (*Almost humbly*). Thank you.

CATO. Forget it. When you came here you weren't feeling good, so you behaved like you did. Now you're feeling better and behaving different and I'm glad. That's all. It's as simple as that. I'm not interested in your motives.

SIMON. Not interested?

CATO. Why should I be? I hate explanations—they give me a pain. You can spend your life digging out motives, and where does it get you? It all goes round and round. People are too complicated. I've given it up.
    SIMON *suddenly looks down.*
(*Softly*) So don't spew your soul all over me . . .
    *There is a burst of raucous singing, as* DAX *enters upper right carrying* SNOWBALL *in his arms, as easily as if he were a baby.*

SNOWBALL. Why was I born so bee-oooooo-ti-fooooool-
Why was I born at all?
    *A comic commotion of almost vaudeville standard is now called for.* SNOWBALL, *in passing, sees* EVA *whom he admires. He struggles in* DAX's *arms, almost bringing them both down in a heap on the floor. Eventually, they exit, upper left.*

EVA (*Calming down after her laughter*). Why don't we throw a party?

CATO. What for?

EVA. For Simon. I mean . . . now that he's better, don't you think he should meet the others?

CATO. Maybe. (*Shrugs*) I don't know.

SIMON. Not yet. I don't feel—

EVA. They're a nice crowd—they'll amuse you—

SIMON. I'm sure—

EVA. They're very good company—they've been asking about you—
    *Already there is a sense of possessiveness—a touch of ownership.*

SIMON. I'm sure they have—

EVA. They've all been wondering about you for weeks—

SIMON (*With a flash of earlier tension*). I just don't *feel* like a party! At least, not yet . . . d'you mind?

EVA. I only wanted to cheer the place up a bit—that's all.
     DAX *enters, without* SNOWBALL.

CATO (*Telegraphically*). Fix him?

DAX. Yuh. (*He beams*) In the bath.

CATO. All his clothes on?

DAX. Yuh.

CATO. Good. Cool him off . . . (*To* SIMON) I don't want you to think I'm anti-liquor, or anything else—but some people abuse it. I have to watch them like hawks.

SIMON. Well . . . (*He looks from one to the other*) Why don't *you* have a drink, Cato? I feel as if . . . I'd like to pour you a drink.
     *His manner is eager. He is bending over backwards to be pleasant.*

CATO. Dax'll do it. He knows what I have.
     *Pause.*

SIMON. I just think we should get to know each other better. I mean . . . I've hardly seen you since I arrived—

CATO. I didn't think you wanted to.

SIMON. I . . .

CATO. Anyway, I've been busy.

SIMON (*Insistently*). I know you have but you're not any more. You've finished the . . . whatever it is. . . .

CATO. The new wine.

SIMON. And so you should be *around* more from now on!
     *He pauses.*
     (*To* EVA) Am I overdoing it?

EVA. Yes.
     CATO *suddenly explodes with laughter.*

CATO. No you're not—we *should* get to know each other—

EVA (*Relieved*). It's time we had some fun—everything's been so gloomy—

SIMON. It was my fault—(*Eagerly again*) It's been my fault right from the start. I've got a suspicious mind—

CATO (*Holding up his hand*). Don't start!
*They all laugh.* SIMON *ruefully.*
CATO *takes his drink from* DAX, *who also hands one each to* SIMON *and* EVA.

EVA (*Lightly to* CATO). What did the doctor say?

CATO. The same old thing.

EVA. You eat too much.

CATO. That's right. . . .
*A slight pause.*
Well, let's drink to it then . . . to whatever, or whoever, has managed to calm you down!

SIMON. Then it's to Eva—

CATO (*Drinking*). Quite an achievement.
*He looks at* EVA *coolly, over the rim of his glass.*

SIMON (*Drinking*). To Eva—with love.
*He looks at her.*
To Eva—for making me stop thinking—so clever—
*He kisses her cheek lightly.*

CATO. She's had that effect, ah? (*Chuckles*)

EVA. Now don't you spoil it! It's taken a lot of time—

SIMON. And trouble—

EVA. And—(*She can't think what else it has taken*)
*They both laugh, in a kind of bewilderment and lean together, arms about each other. A huge atmosphere of relief.*

CATO (*Expansively*). Well . . . all this is very nice. There's nothing like an air of . . . what's that word?

EVA. Bonhomie. (*Some private joke*)

CATO. Bonhomie. An air of bonhomie is very pleasant—very restful—very *unusual*.
*Pause.*

(*Suddenly to* SIMON) D'you know . . . you remind me of a fellow . . . the more I think . . . you remind me of the man who went to the psychiatrist . . . d'you know that story?

SIMON (*Laughing*). I know dozens of—

CATO. So do I, but this one's different. It sort of fits the situation. I expect you've actually *been* to a psychiatrist, haven't you?

SIMON (*Quietly*). Yes.

CATO. Exactly—so it's appropriate—you'll get the point. Especially now you're better and you've stopped worrying and everything—

EVA (*Smiling*). Well, tell it!

CATO. Well . . . this man, y'see . . . was always wetting himself.
    EVA, *already mildly hysterical, sputters.*
Always wetting himself. I'm using the refined term because my daughter's here. And he was telling his friend about it—he says, "It's terrible! I'm so worried! I sit down to breakfast in the morning, I wet myself. I go to the station, someone says good-morning, I wet myself. I . . . everything that happens to me on my journey through life, I wet myself."
    EVA *and* SIMON *giggle helplessly.*
So his friend says—"Is your bladder alright?" and he says, "Of course it is, I've had it checked." (*He pauses, wipes his eyes*) So his friend says, "Well, it must be psychological. You should see a good psychiatrist, and I know just the man . . ." Have you heard it?

SIMON. No. . .
    *He produces a cigarette, and fumbles for matches, shaking with laughter. The reception being given to this anecdote is pointedly out of all proportion to its actual worth as a story.*

CATO. Good . . . anyway . . . a week later he meets this friend again, and he says, "I can't thank you enough for sending me to that psychiatrist—what a wonderful man he is—he's absolutely cured me." And his friend says, "What did I tell you? Psychiatry is a wonderful thing—you've stopped wetting yourself, have you?" "Oh no," he says, . . . "but I don't *worry* about it anymore!"
    CATO *is convulsed with laughter.*
    DAX *tries to light* SIMON's *cigarette with an oddly shaped lighter which doesn't work.*

Don't you think that's—
> SIMON *notices the lighter, and freezes suddenly. He grabs*
> DAX's *hand to see it better.*
. . . appropriate. . . .
> *The laughter dies away. Silence.*

SIMON (*Almost whispering*). Where did you get that? (*To* DAX)
> DAX *tries to pull his hand away.*
Where did you get it? WHERE—!
> *He jerks* DAX *forward, tearing the lighter out of his hand.*
(*To* CATO) You know whose lighter this is! You know, don't
you? (*To* EVA—*savagely*) And so do you—!

EVA (*Moving toward him*). Simon—!

SIMON. Get away from me! Don't come near me! How could
you—(*He is semi-articulate as his rage grows*)
(*To* CATO) What's this ape doing with Peter's lighter? Why
has he got it? This was his mascot—his *lucky charm*—!

EVA (*Desperately*). SIMON!

SIMON. He'd never have parted with this—he'd never leave it
behind—he was superstitious, you know? (*To* CATO) Of course
you do—you know *everything*, don't you?
> *In a futile attempt to stop this tirade in time,* EVA *rushes*
> *forward toward him as* CATO *backs himself toward the fire-*
> *place.*

EVA. Can't you—

SIMON (*Catching her wrist and gripping it*). As for you—so sweet
—so clever—
> *He hits her violently across the mouth.*
—lying, twisting, whoring bitch!!
> *She reels and falls across the couch on which they were*
> *before.*
You knew too!—you ALL knew—you've been lying, lying, the
whole murdering lot of you—!
> *In a hysterical frenzy of passion he turns on* CATO.
I'll make you tell the truth!
> CATO *grabs the poker to defend himself with. Then, with*
> *incredible speed,* DAX *gets* SIMON *from behind, and hits him*
> *scientifically on the back of the neck with the edge of his*
> *hand;*

SIMON *drops like a stone.*
EVA *lies, twisted and shaking, over the couch.*
CATO *drops the poker and tiredly rubs his face with his hands.*
DAX *bends over* SIMON *and examines him.*

DAX (*After a moment*). I think I hit him too hard.
*Jazz*

## THE SCENE DIMS OUT


# SCENE EIGHT


*Three hours later.*
*The stage is in complete darkness except for one brilliant vertical column of light which shines down upon the prone figure of* SIMON ASHER.
*He lies, spreadeagled across the couch in the frontroom, head back, arms thrown wide.*
*From the pitch darkness of the back room we hear the now familiar voices of the gang.*

SNOWBALL'S VOICE. You know what I think his trouble is?

FLON'S VOICE (*Without interest*). No.

SNOWBALL'S VOICE. He's got a guilt complex. I've worked it out.

SHEBA'S VOICE. You're a genius.

SNOWBALL'S VOICE. The boy is riddled with guilt.
*Pause.*

RIKKI'S VOICE. He's got no self-control, that's the trouble with him —he doesn't s-stop to think.

SNOWBALL'S VOICE. That's what I'm saying, isn't it? No self-control, charges up and down, can't relax—people suffering from guilt always carry on like that.

FLON'S VOICE (*Bored*). So do people with wind.
*Sound of* SHEBA *giggling.*

*The spotlight figure of* SIMON ASHER *moves slightly. Lifts one arm, which falls weakly back again. The head moves a fraction.*

SNOWBALL'S VOICE. You're very funny. You're a real scream.

FLON'S VOICE. It's your play.
    *Pause.*

RIKKI'S VOICE. This business of chasing Eva all over the place, f'rinstance—I mean, now that's typical—

SNOWBALL'S VOICE (*Wistfully*). The only clever thing he's done.

RIKKI'S VOICE. Will you shut up? D'you mind? When I want to p-play you get serious—when I want to talk you ass around—now what are you? D-d-different, or something?
    *Pause.*
    SIMON *repeats his previous movements, a little stronger than before, but still falling back again.*
As I was saying—he's like a bull in a tea shop—doesn't stop to think—

FLON'S VOICE. It's your play again.

RIKKI'S VOICE. Me? Uh . . . Uh . . . But that's it, see? He doesn't think—he just charges up and down. . . .

MAXINE'S VOICE. You're all wrong—it's the other way round . . . he thinks *too* much . . . a child could see. . . .

FLON'S VOICE (*Interrupting*). All right . . . OK . . . You're interrupting the game. Do we have to talk about him all the time?

MAXINE'S VOICE. It makes a change from talking about you!
    SIMON *gets his hands up to his face, puts them over his eyes.*

SNOWBALL'S VOICE (*Slurring the words*). You can't blame Cato for staying out of the way . . . What can you *do* with a man like that? What can you say to him?

FLON'S VOICE. Nothing.

SNOWBALL'S VOICE. How can you *help* a man like that?

FLON'S VOICE. You can't.

MAXINE'S VOICE. No one'll help him, poor kid . . . because the whole thing's in his head. It's all in his mind, so no one'll be *able* to help him.

FLON'S VOICE. He needs a psychiatrist, that's what he needs.

SNOWBALL'S VOICE (*Blankly*). A what?
> SIMON *emits a low-pitched moan, full of pain. One hand against each temple, he turns his head from one side to the other.*

SNOWBALL'S VOICE (*Softly*). But he must have a *load* on his mind, that one . . . eh? (*Awed*) A *real* load . . . I don't know what he did to that brother of his but . . . *whew!* . . . It must've been *something!*

SHEBA'S VOICE. It's all to do with his mother—just like I said.

SNOWBALL'S VOICE (*Mimicking her*). "Just like she said!"

SHEBA'S VOICE. Whatever he did's to do with her—she's the root of it, can't you tell? You ignorant ape?

SNOWBALL'S VOICE. Don't you call me ignorant—I've been to school—

SHEBA'S VOICE. Reform school?

SNOWBALL'S VOICE. You never been to any at all, stupid whore.
> *Sound of a hard slap.*
> *Followed instantly by a moan from* SIMON. *He makes a spasmodic effort to sit up, fails, falls back again. A second attempt is more successful, and he swings his legs from the couch and sits, head down, painfully massaging the back of his neck.*

RIKKI'S VOICE. There's only one thing I'd l-like to know. I'd l-like to know why it all *matters* so much to him.

SNOWBALL'S VOICE. You know all right.

MAXINE'S VOICE. He's just been telling you, hasn't he? (*Pityingly*) Haven't you got any imagination?

SNOWBALL'S VOICE. A guilt complex is a nasty thing to have. My old man had one . . . that's how I know about it.
> SIMON *rises shakily to his feet and, during the following dialogue, he crosses to the bar, pours himself a brandy, drinks it, pours another.*

*The overhead spot follows him throughout—at no point in this scene have we had anything to look at apart from* SIMON.

MAXINE'S VOICE. He and his mother carried on so it broke Peter's heart. He wants a chance to make it up, that's all.

SNOWBALL'S VOICE. He wants to be able to sleep nights—haven't you ever felt that way?

MAXINE'S VOICE. He won't be told that Peter just went—*voluntary*—of his own free will—because then it'd be HIS fault—HIS responsibility—

SNOWBALL'S VOICE. With never a chance—no chance to tell him —like when someone dies and you know you'll *never* get the chance to *tell* them—

FLON'S VOICE. Tell them *what?*

SNOWBALL'S VOICE. That you're sorry . . .

MAXINE'S VOICE. You just have to live with it, for the rest of your life. I've seen it.

SNOWBALL'S VOICE. Like my old man.

SHEBA'S VOICE. What happened to him?

SNOWBALL'S VOICE. He died.
*At the bar,* SIMON *drinks another brandy in one abrupt swallow, shakes his head violently as though to clear it. Then he looks towards the back room as if becoming aware, for the first time, of voices through the half open door.*

MAXINE'S VOICE. That's why he blames everyone else, isn't it? Tessa, Eva, even Cato—

SNOWBALL'S VOICE. Especially Cato!

SHEBA'S VOICE. P'raps he thinks Cato did Peter in?

SNOWBALL'S VOICE. Probably hope he did?
SIMON *starts, coming fully to his senses. He turns to face the still dark backroom.*

SHEBA'S VOICE. For his money, d'you suppose?

SNOWBALL'S VOICE. That's the only reason he'd understand.

SHEBA'S VOICE. He's off his rocker! As if Cato hadn't got money.

FLON'S VOICE. As if Cato'd *bother* to do anyone in.
> *As* SIMON *moves nearer, actively listening for the first time,
> the backroom is slowly lit.*
> *We now see the gang sitting around, exactly as before.*
> SIMON *remains spotlit in the frontroom.*

SNOWBALL (*An air of discovery*). And even *that* isn't the whole story!

FLON (*Wearily*). Oh for God's sake . . . !

SNOWBALL. How can it be? When you work it out—

FLON. Stop *working* it out! No one's interested!

SNOWBALL. The more you think about it, the more you see—

FLON. We don't *want* to think about it!

SNOWBALL. But you *must!* How can you ignore a thing like that—

FLON. Easy! You talk to your friends, have a drink, play *cards*—!

SNOWBALL. Will you *listen* to me?
> *Pause.* FLON *resigns himself.*
I didn't have a guilty conscience, and I'm sane enough. I'd never laid eyes on Peter before he came here—neither had any of you but you ALL cared—when he disappeared—

FLON (*Correcting*). Went away—

SNOWBALL. You *cared!* You may've pretended not to but you did! So why'd it matter to you? You didn't ALL have guilt complexes—

FLON. All right! You've made your point! Don't go on about it!

RIKKI. P-Peter made an impression. P-people like us are easily impressed.

MAXINE (*Wistfully*). D'you remember what he said? D'you remember what he told us? . . . (*She hesitates slightly*) . . . there was hope for us? . . . Jesus! . . . hope! He knew all about us—what we'd done—he knew we were the most hopeless bunch that ever . .

SNOWBALL. He was a saint, that boy.

FLON. He was a *boy*, that's all.

SHEBA. I wonder why he stayed?

SNOWBALL. I can guess—after seeing Simon and his mother I think I can guess.

SHEBA. We must've been a change.

MAXINE. Yes . . . compared with *that* lot we must've been almost refreshing!

RIKKI. Just simple, honest p-peasants.
*A cackle of laughter from Sheba.*

SNOWBALL. I think he'd had everything else anyway. He tried the lot and we were the end.

SHEBA. That makes sense.

MAXINE. And yet, somehow . . . he made life seem *possible* . . . all of a sudden, you know what I mean? He knew what we were—why we were here, and yet . . . he said there was hope— in spite of it all, I believed him . . . HOPE!!

FLON (*In total weariness*). It's a great consolation, isn't it?
*Now only* SIMON's *face is spotlit. We see it in profile, motionless, like the head on a coin.*
I didn't listen to him.

SNOWBALL (*Flaring at him*). Oh yes you did! You don't get away with that. You listened all right—your great ears flapped every time he came into the room! Don't tell *me* you didn't listen!
*FLON looks away.*
And if he meant all that to us—we hardly knew him—what must he mean to that poor, twisted bastard out there?
*He hiccups sadly.*
You think it over.

SHEBA. But . . . if he . . . if it's like that why didn't they *treat* him better? Look after him? Why'd they have to treat him like dirt—?

FLON (*Muttering*). Why-why-why-why—

SHEBA. Why do people *do* these things to each other?

FLON. If you must know, it's human nature! No one can stand goodness . . . no one can *live* with it—I've noticed it before, here and there . .

SHEBA (*Sarcastic*). You've noticed everything.

MAXINE. He was in politics, remember?

*We see* SIMON *with his eyes averted, his head lowered.*

SNOWBALL. I don't know about all that . . . I only know what he meant to me. (*Pause*) You'll never believe this, but he meant so much I stole from him! Yes . . . look at me! I stole from Peter!

MAXINE (*Astonished*). What did you take?

SNOWBALL. I took his lighter.

MAXINE. But you've got a lighter!

SNOWBALL. I know—and it wasn't even force of habit. I wanted to have something of his. Seems silly, doesn't it? I just wanted to have something that belonged to him.

SHEBA (*Turning away*). You disgust me.

SIMON's *face registers no emotion whatsoever.*

SNOWBALL. After I talked to Cato, I saw how stupid it was . . . then I didn't want it anymore.

MAXINE (*Eagerly*). Why not let's send it back to him?

SNOWBALL. We don't know the address.

MAXINE. No . . .

SNOWBALL. Anyway . . . (*He shrugs*) I've given it to Dax now, and—

FLON (*Interrupting harshly*). There's no point in going on about it, is there?

SIMON *moves slowly away from the door.*

*He takes a few tired paces downstage, facing the audience.*

FLON. I mean . . . we don't know much about it anyway—just bits and pieces—which we pick up . . . (*Bitterly*) These damned lunatics come here! . . . Carry *on* all over the place! Giving and taking and *caring so much* about everything . . . Dashing out . . . rushing off . . . Lying—dying—*where does it get us?* It just upsets us, doesn't it? I mean . . . it doesn't actually do us any *good,* does it?

*He looks around at their faces, all averted.*

(*Scornfully*) Look at you! This bloody Asher family's helped you a *lot,* hasn't it? Done you a world of good, anyone can

see . . . You look as miserable as bloody sin! (*He sits down*)
The only one to be with is Cato. I've always said so. He's the
only one who knows how to live—the only one with a system
which *works*—he's got common sense. He doesn't waste time
worrying about the past.

*He picks up the cards.*

Neurotic young men are a pain in the neck. You've got to be
calm . . . calm, the way Cato is. You've got to learn to accept
everything in a calm, logical manner—that's the only way . . .
Otherwise you just get morbid. You get morbid and miserable,
all for nothing . . . It doesn't get you anywhere. Things that
are over and done with are best left alone.

> SIMON *closes his eyes, his moment of giving-up has arrived.*
> *The spotlight gleams on his face.*

(*Shuffling the cards*) It's no good digging away into people's
souls. It's no good *concerning* yourself with these things. Psychiatry's out of date. This Asher family should've lived in the
19th century—Freud would've had a *time* with them!

RIKKI. What is it Cato says? "Explanations give me a pain."
That's about right. C-Cato's a great man.

> *They are all, somehow, unable to look at each other.*

FLON. I'll put my money on him. He'll still be here when all the
saints and lunatics have gone . . .

> *He finishes dealing.*

All right? (*To the others*) Are we playing?

> *No one looks at him. No one moves.*

Come on . . . (*A kind of plea*) Shall we start?

> *Utter silence. All eyes averted. He puts down the cards.*
> SIMON *turns, slowly, toward the door up right.*

Look . . . (*In sudden desperation*) We have to try, don't
we? We've got to go on, that's what I've been trying to tell
you.

> *Pause.*

We have to GO ON . . . There's nothing else . . .

> *The backroom fades out slowly.*
> SIMON *moves, still spotlit, toward the door up right. He*
> *resembles a man who has run a long race, and lost it. Just*
> *before he reaches the door, it is thrown open and the front-*
> *room is lit.*
> CATO *enters, in his chair.*

SIMON *stops, visibly pulling himself together.*
*The two men face each other.*

### THE SCENE DIMS OUT

# SCENE NINE

CATO (*Cheerfully*). Well . . . feeling better?
> *He wheels himself downstage, past* SIMON, *his manner calm, matter-of-fact.*

You've been out three hours, I suppose you know that? (*Chuckles*) Poor old Dax! He was scared to death. He always overdoes it, I told you that didn't I? He was scared he'd killed you.
> SIMON *gives no sign of having heard.* CATO *looks from him to the half open door of the backroom, through which jazz softly pours.*

Oh, I see . . . you've been listening to them.

SIMON. Who are they, Cato?

CATO. Does it matter?

SIMON. What is this gang of yours, in the backroom?

CATO. Well, that's just about it—a gang in the backroom.

SIMON. Look—I don't want to know anything else—

CATO. They *work* for me! I *employ* them—they knew me in the old days.

SIMON. It's my last question—d'you understand?

CATO. They live here—what does it matter?

SIMON (*Automatically—as though his mind has ceased to function*). The time for mystery's over, isn't it? Surely we've reached that point—

CATO. They're just a crowd of nuts, Simon—special cases, every one—nothing to do with you. (*Pause*) Society can be ruthless, you know? It throws out the rejects . . . Sometimes I pick 'em up, that's all. (*Pause*) What've they been talking about?

SIMON. Peter.

CATO. I might've known it! He was bad for them, can't you imagine? How could they cope with that—faith, hope, starting again and all that business? It wasn't their fault—they've never been educated for it.

SIMON. And what about you? Have you been educated for it? Could you cope?

CATO. I said we were friends, didn't I? In a peculiar way . . . I could cope better than anyone. (*Pause*) By the way, about that cigarette lighter . .

SIMON. Never mind. (*He turns away*)

CATO. Well, your doubts then—those "doubts" you had the day you arrived—

SIMON (*Muttering*). It doesn't matter.

CATO. Of course it matters—you see, those other two men you mentioned—they were both in trouble.

SIMON. Good for them.

CATO. They were in big trouble, and they had to get abroad— *quick*, you know?

SIMON (*Vaguely*). I know.

CATO. It's not exactly legal, but then that's how I am. I just like helping people.

SIMON. For a large fee, naturally.

CATO. Naturally. (*He laughs*) But you're not really interested, are you, Simon?

SIMON. Not a bit. Could I have a drink?

CATO. Of course . . . (*He pauses*) What're you on?

SIMON. Whatever . . . I don't know . . . whatever's in that bottle there. (*Points to the one he's been at*)

CATO. Oh, yes . . . (*Regards the level*) Naturally. Wonderful taste in everything, you and your mother.

SIMON. Where's Eva?

*The clipped social manner of the beginning has returned.*

CATO (*Briefly*). Upstairs.

SIMON (*Drinking*). Is she all right?

CATO. Now what do you think?

SIMON. This is good . . . (*Drinks again*)

CATO. You were rough with her, weren't you? That's called re-
verting to type. If Dax hadn't half-killed you I'd've done it
myself. (*Gently*) You were kidding anyway—you were both
kidding yourselves—you know that. (*Pause*) She knows it
anyhow. That's what hurt her, not the sock in the mouth.
That's why she's upstairs. (*They drink silently*) I suppose
you'll be leaving us now?

SIMON. That's right.

CATO. Where'll you go—Rome?

SIMON. I expect the party's still on.

CATO. Or if not, there'll be another.

SIMON. Of course. I know everyone down there.
*The social mask is almost exactly back in place.*

CATO. I used to know a few people too . . . different ones I'm
sure. I was there in the war, as a matter of fact. That's how
I got in this thing. (*Pats the chair*)

SIMON. I don't know anything about you, do I, Cato?

CATO. No . . . (*Thoughtfully*) But I shouldn't worry. It
wouldn't do you much good.
*A roar of sudden laughter from the backroom.*

SIMON. Could I meet them, before I go?

CATO (*Pleased*). Of course you can! I'd like you to—let's do it
right away . .
*They both start toward the backroom.*
. . . they'll be so pleased—they've all been asking about you
. . . They're curious, it's only natural . . .
*SIMON stops abruptly, his head down.*
What's the matter?

SIMON (*Slightly choked*). Nothing . . . it's nothing . . .

CATO (*A touch of compassion*). Take your time.

SIMON. So he just went—after all . . . he just *went*, like you said. He didn't even give us a chance—

CATO (*Gently*). What d'you think you could've done? . . . made amends? Come on—come and meet them . . .
*He moves again toward the backroom.*
They'll amuse you, I'm sure—you'll be a big hit with them . . .
*The noise from the backroom increases.*
Good company too—listen to that! (*He laughs*)
*Sounds of laughter, talk, music.*
They enjoy themselves, why not? You can hear for yourself—they really work at it. Sometimes, for short periods, they're even gay . .
*He looks at* SIMON.
Go in and introduce yourself—that'll please them more than anything.
*They exchange a final glance.*
I'll tell Dax to bring your bags down.
SIMON *walks into the backroom, and as the noise swells again with greetings, Hello's, etc.,* CATO *wheels himself downstage, looking for the first time old and tired and beaten.*
*He winces violently with pain, then recovers.*
EVA *enters.*

EVA. Where is he?

CATO. In there.

EVA. I've decided. I'm going to tell him the truth.

CATO. I wouldn't do that.

EVA. But I *must*—

CATO. What's the point? He's given it up already.

EVA. What'll happen if I don't?

CATO (*Quietly*). He's off to Rome in a minute.

EVA. Rome? (*She turns away*)
*Pause.*

CATO. He'll forget Peter, that's what'll happen. He'll forget the way Tessa's forgetting, the way everyone forgets . . . (*Gently*)
It's just a question of time.

EVA (*Muttering*). That suits *you* all right, doesn't it?

CATO. It's the best way. You know it is.

EVA. I'm going to tell him, just the same.
　　*Pause.*

CATO (*Abruptly harsh*). Please yourself. He probably deserves it anyway.

EVA. What're you talking about? As if *that* was ever the reason—

CATO (*Tiredly*). I know.

EVA. That was never the reason for keeping quiet, was it? When you asked me to keep quiet it wasn't to spare anyone's feelings—

CATO (*Quietly*). Then why did you?

EVA. You KNOW why!! I kept quiet for *you*—for *your* sake—! Don't look at me like that! I didn't feel guilty! I don't feel a thing about Peter—it was nothing to do with me!

CATO. He loved you, didn't he?

EVA. It was nothing to do with me! I kept quiet because of you— because *you* were afraid—!

CATO. All right—

EVA. Afraid no one'd believe us! Afraid it'd go beyond your tame local cops and start real enquiries! You were afraid they'd find out about your rotten set-up!
　　*Pause.*

CATO. I don't care anymore.

EVA. Scared they'd find out about your gang of jailbirds—your crooked affairs—you'd let everyone believe a lie to protect your filthy racket—!

CATO. I tell you I don't care anymore! Can't you understand plain English?
　　EVA *is silenced.*
Look . . . (*With difficulty*) I found out something today for the first time . . . that doctor. . . .
　　EVA *stands very still, watching him.*
If the whole works blow up in my face, I don't really mind.
　　*She doesn't move.*
So you have my full permission. If that's all that held you

back, then just feel free . . . OK? Walk right in there and
explain to Simon how his brother hanged himself from a high
beam in the new wing. (*Pause*) And tell him why—in case
he's forgotten.
*Silence.*
Mention that he gave all his cash to charity, and that it took
him an hour and a half to die. Tell the gang, while you're
about it. They're all in there. . . . What're you waiting for?
    EVA *doesn't move.*
After that, you could phone Tessa in Rome—I'm sure she'd
be happy to know . . . In fact you could tell everyone who
ever knew him. You could make a life's work of it. Tell them
all what they did to him. Tell them what they're responsible
for. Tell them the boy . . . died. . . .
    *He rests his head back on the chair.*

EVA. It was our fault too—I know it was—we didn't care—

CATO. Don't flatter yourself. He was half-dead before he even
got here. (*Pause*) Anyway, peasants like us aren't capable of
that kind of damage. We're not complicated enough . . . But
these others—the Tessa's and the Simon's of this world—that's
another story. That's the real set-up, didn't you know? In these
rich bourgeois—with their middle-class perversions and their
good taste. Their psychiatrists—their Mercedes—and their international comic circus! Nothing worth having ever survives
them—they'd strangle anything between them. Not just boys
like Peter . . . anything! And the joke is, they hardly know
they're doing it.
    *Pause.*
I'm the weak one, Eva, can't you see? I only break the law. But
these others . . . they can break the world in half.
    *He closes his eyes.*
But you go in there and tell him all about it. It should be
interesting.
    *He sinks a little, in his chair.*
I'll just sit here and listen.
    *The noise from the backroom swells to a crescendo of talk
and music.*
    EVA *doesn't move.*
## THE CURTAIN FALLS

# ENTER SOLLY GOLD

A *Comedy*

*by*

BERNARD KOPS

# CAST

A Prostitute, 35 years old

Solly Gold, 35 to 40 years old

A Policeman

Tailor's Wife, 45 years old

Tailor, 45 years old

An Old Woman

Morry Swartz, 60 to 65 years old

Millie Swartz, 55 to 60 years old

Romaine, 28 years old

Sarah, 23 years old

Melvin, 26 years old

Herbert Fink, 50 to 55 years old

Sadie Fink, 50 years old

Alan Fink, 25 years old

# PROLOGUE

*Street scene. Dark stage and simple setting. A row of small houses near Aldgate in London's East End. The set is in a stylised manner and the interior can be seen as well as the exterior. When action takes place in a particular house or area that place is simply lit up. It is one o'clock in the morning; late summer. A* PROSTITUTE *stands outside her streetdoor and* SOLLY *enters. As she sings he sizes her up from afar.*

PROSTITUTE (*Sings*).
>Yours for a short time, how about it honey?
>I'll give you five minutes, if you've got the money.
>You can have me once or have me all night.
>I'm very very versatile if the price is right.
>I can be naughty if you pay me cash,
>Now don't be so bashful, come and have a bash.
>If you want what I've got you can have it honey
>I'll give you five minutes if you've got the money.
>*She beckons* SOLLY.
Hello darling, do you want a good time with a bad girl?

SOLLY. Do you mean me?

PROSTITUTE. Why not? I'm not particular. I'll take anyone, as long as they're not jockeys or fishmongers, or Negroes.

SOLLY. What's wrong with jockeys? Some of my best friends.

PROSTITUTE. Whores are not horses, they tend to dig their heels in and treat the bed post like a winning post and fishmongers stink.

SOLLY. What's wrong with Negroes?

PROSTITUTE. You've got to draw the line somewhere. Come on, don't let's waste time.

SOLLY. Changed my mind, I thought you were fatter.

PROSTITUTE. You don't know what you want—eff off, go on.

SOLLY. But maybe I could stretch a point just this once.

PROSTITUTE. Make up your mind or it'll soon be closing time. Now come on, I want cash on delivery.

SOLLY. How much will you charge me to have a chat?

PROSTITUTE. Cut it out. What do you take me for? None of that kinky stuff for me, at least not unless you make it worth my while.

SOLLY. You mean you charge more for talking? Why?

PROSTITUTE. Cos I've heard it all before. How much do you think psychiatrists charge for listening? Five quid for five minutes, that's the fixed rate.

SOLLY. I could become Catholic for less and they'd listen for nothing.

PROSTITUTE. Take it or leave it, that's the standard charge.

SOLLY. How much do you charge ordinary rate for the ordinary thing?

PROSTITUTE. Two quid and no beating about the bush.

SOLLY. Two quid? You're a profiteer! It was only thirty bob before I left.

PROSTITUTE. You're living in the past, grand-dad, prices are rising all the time.

SOLLY. Sorry I wasted your time, fact is I've been daydreaming in the middle of the night. I'm flat broke—stoney—skint—haven't even got a bed for the night—take a look at the soles of my shoes.

PROSTITUTE. You're breaking my heart.

SOLLY. I'm hungry too, haven't eaten for days.

PROSTITUTE. Don't come the old acid with me. You might have heard of sentimental tarts with soppy hearts but yours truly is not like that—times are hard, can't even walk the streets these days. The likes of you should be shot—you've got no morals, no principles, that's your trouble.

SOLLY. Well, this is as far as I can go tonight.

*He sits on his case.*

PROSTITUTE. Your mother should see you now.

SOLLY. My mother! Mum! I can just see her now. I was bad to her but she forgave me—she knew in her heart of hearts that I wanted to help her—she was a famous debutante—Martha Goldberg—I dragged her down and she died in the workhouse —I was just too late—I arrived in my Rolls to take her to the south of England.

PROSTITUTE. Poor boy—(*She shakes herself*) What! You've got the spiel all right. You never had a mother. Bet you could melt the heart of a judge. Well, I'm off, I hear the Swedish Navy are pulling in tonight. I hope you don't catch cold and die of pneumonia. So long.

    *She goes.*

SOLLY. What time is it?

    *A clock strikes one.*

Thank you!

    *A* POLICEMAN *enters and watches* SOLLY.

My watch is stopped; wonder if I can pawn it for a few bob?

    *He doesn't see the* POLICEMAN.

What can I do about kip tonight? Coo, I could kip right here and now I'm so tired—so here we are back in the old country— It's so old it's got one foot in the grave and the other foot's got ingrowing toenails.

    *He takes his shoes off, and his socks, and starts cutting his toenails. The* POLICEMAN *who was just about to pounce has temporarily held off.*

What am I gonna do for cash? For the old lolly? Must think of something. But there's one thing I'm sure of—I'm not gonna work—never! Never!—never!

    *He stands on the case—mocking the Hyde Park orators.*

Comrades, if you want work you can have it, as for me, work's too much like an occupation—I've committed no crimes, work is all right for workers, just the job for the working class, but for Solly Gold? There's only one thing he wants, money! And there's only one way he wants to get it—by doing nothing.

POLICEMAN. What do you think you're doing?

SOLLY (*Jumping off case and quickly putting on his shoes*). Hello, Officer—I remember you from way back. I've just returned from a world trip and do you know the world's nothing to write

home about. They wouldn't let me stay in the States so I
returned here—to little old England, the greatest littlest country this side of the universe.

POLICEMAN. What are you doing?

SOLLY. Isn't it obvious? I'm out here studying the stars—contemplating the infinite.

POLICEMAN. I'll contemplate your what-you-may-call-it if you
don't move sharpish. What have you got in that case?

SOLLY. My worldly goods, Officer.

POLICEMAN. You're a saucy bastard, aren't you? Open up.

SOLLY (*Opens it*). One toothbrush—you know—for cleaning
the teeth. (*Goes through the motions*) One shoe brush—for
brushing the shoes and one clothes brush for—

POLICEMAN. Alright, alright—what else?

SOLLY. That's the lot—I've flogged the rest. Three brushes and
a brain, that's all I've got.

POLICEMAN. Where have you come from?

SOLLY. I've just landed—from Australia. Started on the boat as
a dishwasher. By the time I got to Gib I was head steward,
but by the time we got to Tilbury I'd lost my position, my
clothes and my money all in a card game. That's the way it
goes—up and down—everything's up and down. Ever been to
Australia?

POLICEMAN. No.

SOLLY. Do yourself a favour—never go.

POLICEMAN. You said they threw you out of America, why?

SOLLY. Because I was a member of the blue and white shirts
when I was five.

POLICEMAN. What were the blue and white shirts?

SOLLY. How should I know? But I'm going to get into the
States, you see. It's my spiritual home. It's dog eat dog there,
that's the way I like it.

POLICEMAN. Got any family here?

SOLLY. No—no family—no one (*Sings*) My mother got struck
by lightning, my father crashed in a plane, my sister drowned in

the Serpentine, my brother got shot down in Spain. My cousin died in a madhouse, my aunt from the sting of a bee, my uncle jumped off a skyscraper— Oh what's gonna happen to me?

POLICEMAN. I don't believe you.

SOLLY. I don't blame you. No, chum, the things I do remember I try to forget and the things I try to forget, I try to forget that I'm forgetting.

POLICEMAN. You'd better hop it out of here or I'll run you in.

SOLLY. A nice feller like you wouldn't do that to me. Where shall I go?

POLICEMAN. Go up to the West End—another crook there, more or less, won't matter—so beat it. I'm on my rounds now and if you're here when I come back I'll lock you up.

SOLLY. You've got me wrong.
> POLICEMAN *starts to go.*

Oh what's the use. Thank you! Thank you! You're a very nice man—I think the English police are wonderful—

POLICEMAN. None of that moody. I'll be back in five minutes— so watch it. (*He goes off muttering*) Spiv! Lazy good-for- nothings—

SOLLY. I resemble that remark, I may be good for nothing but I'm not lazy. He should try living on his wits. Conning people is a full-time job—you've got to use your loaf to get through this bloody world without work and believe me it's a damn sight harder than your union would let you work—and I'm always on duty—twenty-eight hours a day.
> *He shouts after the* POLICEMAN, *then picks up case and moves, but after a few feet he notices light in a window of a tailor's shop: he knocks on the door and falls on his face—on the doorstep.*

(*Groans*). Oh help me—help me—oh God—
> *The tailor's wife comes to the door, opens it.*

RITA (*Calls*). Joe! Joe! Come here, someone's in trouble.

JOE. Who isn't?
> *He is busy sewing in the interior.*

RITA. But he's on our doorstep.

JOE. So? We won't charge him any rent.

SOLLY (*Desperate*). Help me—oh lady—I'm in terrible trouble. *He pulls on her skirt and at the same time tries to look up her legs; she doesn't see this.*

RITA. We've got enough of our own, son.

SOLLY. If you only knew—I can't face it.

JOE. Tell him to go somewhere else—I've got this armhole to finish.

SOLLY (*Loud*). I'm so choked—I can't talk—you're a Jewish woman, aren't you? *Sholem Alecheim.*

RITA. I don't care what your name is—what do you want?

SOLLY. I'm gonna die—I'm spitting blood. Oh God, that it should happen to me. I'm gonna die.

JOE. Tell him please not on our doorstep—bring him in.

SOLLY (*As he is helped inside*). No tongue can tell the things I've suffered.

RITA. Just take it easy, son—try and relax. Oh the poor boy— he's as white as a sheet.

JOE. What's he doing out this time of night?

SOLLY. Oh I'm all water, my legs are just like water—I can't go on. Take me too—kill me also. *He collapses on the floor.* JOE *won't leave the machine so* RITA *pulls him into a chair.* I'm just like water—water.

JOE. Rita, fetch him some water.

SOLLY. Haven't you got something a bit stronger?

JOE. Rita, bring him some of that Palestinian wine.

SOLLY. I prefer brandy if you've got it. RITA *brings him wine.*

JOE. I'm only a poor tailor.

SOLLY. Alright, I'll settle for this, I'm not so particular— Oh no, I don't believe it—Becky—where have you gone?

RITA. He's delirious.

SOLLY. Nice wine—thank God I found you up.

RITA. You'll always find us up—he says he can't afford to sleep.

JOE. Alright. (*To* SOLLY) So, what's your story?

SOLLY. I can't talk, not yet. Just let me sit here. I'll be alright in a minute. Could I have another glass of wine?

JOE. Alright. Now listen, you don't feel so well, have a little rest, put your feet up and in two minutes you'll be as right as rain and be able to leave.

RITA. He drives me mad. Joe, can't you see he looks like death, what's the matter, 'fraid you'll lose a few stitches? Work is all he knows. Never marry a tailor (*She tells* SOLLY) That's what my Aunt Sophie said. He borrows a few hours from the next day, then a day from the next week and a few weeks from the next year and then he dies owing all that time.
*She goes to* JOE.
What's the matter with him, Joe?

JOE. I don't like the look of him.

RITA. He's a Jewish boy, he can't be bad.

JOE. Yeah? What about Schnorrer Morry?

RITA. Can't you stop working? Can't you ever get away from that machine?

JOE. You can grumble; did you ever go without?

RITA. Yes, without you, all my life. I'm married to a sewing machine.
*Returns to* SOLLY.
You feeling better, son?

SOLLY. Oh Becky! Becky! What's the matter with you? Why don't you jump—save the children—the children!

JOE. I don't want him having delusions on my sofa.

RITA. Oh shut up!

SOLLY. Becky, my poor wife—all burned (*Bursts into tears*)

RITA. What happened to her? It's good to tell someone.

SOLLY. I'm a traveller, I only heard before. I live in Glasgow—and my wife—oh—God rest her soul—died this morning with the children.

RITA. Died? Oh, you poor feller.

JOE (*Leaves machine*). How?

SOLLY. Oh it was such a big fire, there were twenty engines, masks they had on. They all got burned to death, my Becky, my little Renee, the twins, Michael and Angela—they were so beautiful. Becky had long black hair—she was a picture.

RITA. Oh, I'm so sorry.

JOE. I wish we could help you.

SOLLY. I wish I could help myself. I've been wandering in a daze, I haven't eaten.

RITA. The good die young. Don't talk no more, rest.

SOLLY. No, no, it eases me, I've cried enough. Becky tried to save them—she stood on the parapet with all the children in her arms—little Renee, she was such a lovely dancer—tap and ballet. What can I do?

RITA. Let me make you something to eat.

SOLLY. No, I couldn't, I'm all choked. Alright, if you insist, a chicken sandwich with some mustard pickle or some smoked salmon—nothing much—something light.
> RITA *goes off to prepare it.*
I must go to Glasgow—now! I must give them a decent burial.

JOE. Stay here tonight, go tomorrow morning.

SOLLY. I must fly tonight—I'll have to charter a plane—

JOE. Of course, I understand.

SOLLY. I wonder if you could help me? God is good, in times of stress He sends good friends. You know your friends when you're in trouble. Listen—I need a few quid for the plane fare—the banks are closed and I must fly tonight.

JOE. How much?

SOLLY. At least twenty-five—yes, that will cover me. Oh, Becky, Becky, by my mother in the grave I'm sorry—forgive me, I tried to be a good husband.

JOE. I'm afraid I can only afford five.

SOLLY. That's no use, make it twenty then.

JOE. What about ten?

SOLLY. I'll tell you what, I'll settle with fifteen and try and manage with that.

JOE. Alright, fifteen it is!
*He gives* SOLLY *the money.*

SOLLY. It's a deal.

JOE. Done!
*They shake hands on it.*

SOLLY. It's only a loan, mind. I'll send it back tomorrow morning.

JOE. There's no hurry, wait till the afternoon. I'll get it.
SOLLY *lies back, smokes and pours himself another drink.*
JOE *meets* RITA *coming in with sandwiches.*
I must be crazy, I'm lending him money.

RITA. It's good to know you've got a heart, we must all help each other. I'm pleased with you; he's the first person you've lent money to in the past twenty years.

JOE. Ah well, he's different—you can see it, it's obvious, he's a decent boy in trouble. I'm a good judge of character.
JOE *goes off and* RITA *brings the sandwiches to* SOLLY.

SOLLY. You're so kind—how can I repay you? (*Stuffs the sandwich into his mouth*) You're too good. I bet no one appreciates you.

RITA. You can say that again. My husband takes me for granted.

SOLLY. When you're dead, then he'll appreciate you, just like me and Becky.

RITA. Try and look forward now, we have to get over things, life goes on.

SOLLY. You're very nice, you're an angel. Has anyone ever told you that? You've got a light in your eyes; does he ever say a kind word to you?

RITA. He hasn't got time. He's not a bad boy exactly, just got no time.

SOLLY. I'd have time for someone like you, I would—you're so nice— Oh comfort me—my Becky is dead.
*She pats him on the shoulder and puts her arms around him.*
I'm so lonely, let me cuddle you.

*He pretends to cry and soon he is completely embracing her and touching her hair.*

Oh, you're lovely, so lovely, just like my Becky.

RITA. No—no—I shouldn't—
*She tries to break away as she realises he is getting amorous.*

SOLLY. You're lovely, you're a good woman—so big and kind. I'm in trouble, don't leave me—I need you—you're strong and fat—and oh—

RITA. Please, you'd better stop.

SOLLY. You're just my size—don't go—come closer. Can you blame me—you're so lovely, you're a friend, a real friend. You're just the right size—I'm mad about you.
*He tries to kiss her but she breaks free and still they speak quietly, urgently.*

RITA. How could you? With your wife just dead? How could you get fresh with me—no-one's ever done that to me. How could you?

SOLLY. How should I know what I'm doing—I'm so sad and emotional. It was a sudden urge, blood is thicker than water.

RITA. With your wife just dead how could you do it?

SOLLY. Don't tell your husband, he wouldn't understand. I'll come back some other time—I'm mad for you and so unhappy.

RITA. Men! Men make me sick.

SOLLY. Me too. I was being affectionate; you're too good for your husband. I'll make it up to you somehow. Please forgive me, I'm only human and you're a beautiful woman; kiss me and tell me you forgive—for poor Becky's sake.

RITA (*Wanders off and looks in a mirror*). How could you do that to me?
        JOE *returns.*

JOE. Here you are, fifteen quid.

SOLLY. You're a pal, how can I repay you?

JOE. With money.

SOLLY. I'll be on my way now, God bless you all, my Becky will be so pleased, I mean as she looks down on all this. Goodbye!

May you live long and die happy—may you live to be a hundred and three.

JOE. Don't do me no favours.

SOLLY. You're one in a million, both of you. I must fly now.
*He leaves the house and lingers outside, but the light goes off him for a moment.*

JOE. Nice feller, ain't it funny how the good always suffer?

RITA. How could he do it to me?
*She rejoins her husband.*
I knew there was something fishy all along.

JOE. Well darling, I gave him the money.

RITA. Money? You bloody fool! You stupid silly sod! Didn't you see how he mauled me—he tried to rape me and you gave him money? Couldn't you see that he was just a lying thief? You gave him money? Why didn't you give me away while you were about it?

JOE. I wish I did.

RITA. Go on, back to your sewing, you silly so and so.

JOE. Why don't you go to bed? I've got a busy night ahead.

RITA. Why don't you drop dead? It's all your fault. Yes, I'm going to bed and don't wake me up whatever you do—cos the answer's no. You've had it from now on; you don't know how to treat a lady—you don't appreciate me. It's alright, I'm not so bad looking; people still think I'm attractive. I'm not finished yet. Good night.
*She goes to bed, the tailor continues sewing and the light in the room darkens.* SOLLY *is now seen again, counting the money. The* PROSTITUTE *comes up to him.*

SOLLY. What happened to the Swedish Navy?

PROSTITUTE. They've got an attack of German measles on board. Bang goes another night's business. I'll have to sleep.

SOLLY. Don't go, I've changed my mind, I need a room and I fancy something so I may as well kill two birds with one stone.

PROSTITUTE. No one's gonna kill this bird— My my, you've got a wad there. I'm in the wrong racket.

SOLLY. How much you charge for all night?

PROSTITUTE. Special rates for night work—time and a half.

SOLLY. Do me a favour, I want it cut price. How much?

PROSTITUTE. A fiver.

SOLLY. Come off it, I'm only a poor working man.

PROSTITUTE. Oh alright, four.

SOLLY. Make it two.

PROSTITUTE. You out of your mind? Don't you know about the cost of living index? Three pounds ten and that's my final word.

SOLLY. Two pounds fifteen, on the nose.

PROSTITUTE. You'd auction your own mother—alright, three quid and not a penny less.

SOLLY. Right, it's a deal.
*They shake on it.*

PROSTITUTE. That's done. Let's go.

SOLLY. You're not as fat as I would like but you can't pick and choose all your life.
*They exit into her door and the stage darkens completely— now there is a passage of time and the stage lightens again and it is dawn—a cock is heard crowing and SOLLY comes out of the PROSTITUTE's door, yawns and does some exercises.*

A cock crowing? In Whitechapel? Impossible.
*It crows again. He looks over a fence beside a third house.* Chickens—that's handy. Come on you pretty little darlings— come and get stuffed. Oh boy, that takes me back . . . chicken soup, stuffed neck, chopped liver, giblet pie. There's one, two, three, five, eight, eleven birds in all, and one lovely rooster— beautiful bird. Looks as if you've had a heavy night like me. Never mind—I'll cut your throat and then you can have a long sleep and then I'll flog you and your girl friends down the lane.
*He is about to climb over the fence when an old lady comes out of the house with some food for the chickens.*

WOMAN. What do you want?
*He jumps back quickly but soon relaxes.*

SOLLY. I want you. Good morning, my good woman, I'm the bird inspector.

WOMAN. Bird inspector? What do you want? Where are you from?

SOLLY (*More to himself*). As a matter of fact I've been inspecting a bird all night. I'm from the Ministry of Agriculture and Poultry; I've been inspecting your birds.

WOMAN. What's wrong with my birds?

SOLLY. What's right with them? They're suffering from foot and mouth disease and they're all having a nervous breakdown. This won't do. This is a serious business.

WOMAN. Please sir, I can't help it; since my husband died I've been struggling to carry on alone.

SOLLY. Your husband dead?

WOMAN. Yes, a week ago, did you know him?

SOLLY. Of course I did, who didn't?

WOMAN. Who didn't know my Hymie? Who didn't know him and love him? He was such a wonder, he knew everyone.

SOLLY. Wonderful Hymie, with the heart of gold. As a matter of fact he owes me some money.

WOMAN. Money? He never owed anyone.

SOLLY. I mean the government. He never paid his last instalment of the Chicken Registration fee—didn't you know he owed us ten pounds?

WOMAN. Chicken Registration? No, I didn't know—he took care of everything, I'm so lost without him. I'll pay you.

SOLLY. Poor Hymie, the world won't be the same without him.

WOMAN. It's good to talk to you—I haven't spoke to a soul since he died.
    *She gives him the money.*
You make me feel better—I'm glad you liked my husband so much.

SOLLY (*Looking over the fence*). The birds will have to go of course.

WOMAN. Why?

SOLLY. Neurotic birds are a menace to society—they're totally maladjusted and what's more I'll have to kill them here and now, I'm afraid. And that will be of course another six pounds disposal fee—

WOMAN. Take them, kill them. Who can be bothered feeding them anyway? Who eats eggs since Hymie died? Here, six pounds.

SOLLY. I'm letting you off light—because I like you and Hymie was a friend of mine. Actually I could report you because you didn't register the disease and then it would mean a heavy fine and even imprisonment, but Hymie was a wonderful guy, and also there will be just one further charge, two pounds ten shillings for the death entry certificate which we will send you in a matter of a few days.

WOMAN (*Gives him more money*). Take it, take it, who cares anyway.

SOLLY. I'm letting you off light.

WOMAN. Thank you, thank you—I know, you're very kind. Death is an expensive business—all I've done since my husband died is lay out, lay out.

SOLLY. I hope I'm not leaving you too short.

WOMAN. As my husband always said, you can always find money for bread and coffins.

SOLLY (*Puts away money*). Now please, I will need a sharp razor to cut their throats.
> *She goes inside and he jumps over fence and inspects the birds. She returns and hands him a cut-throat razor. He sets to work though we cannot see his hands or the birds but very soon amidst a flury of sound and feather, he emerges with a cluster of dead birds.*

We'll send you receipts.

WOMAN. One minute, do you know anyone who could use some clothes? I've got some, my husband's things, they're in marvellous condition. I can't bear to see them anymore.

SOLLY. I might be able to help you out, let's have a look.

WOMAN. Do me a favour, pull out that trunk.
*He puts the chickens down and pulls out a large suitcase.*
Only the best, as you can see—take it all.

SOLLY. A rabbi's clothes?
*He holds up some jackets and trousers and soon lifts out some rabbi's clothes.*

WOMAN. But you knew my husband was a rabbi, didn't you?

SOLLY. Who didn't know? From Tel Aviv to Tell me the Tale he was famous—the best rabbi in the racket. It's just that I didn't think you'd part with such personal items.

WOMAN. You're right I wouldn't. Don't touch the Rabbi's clothes and his Bible. Take everything else—I can't bear to see them anymore. I must go now and sweep up. Thank you.
*She goes inside.*

SOLLY. These clothes are not worth a light—she must be blind, they're all moth eaten; but this Rabbi's gear might come in handy—and I hear there are some very hot tales in this black book. Well, Solly boy, you're not doing too bad—last night you had sweet Fanny Adams and this morning you're worth twenty odd nicker, a dozen chickens and this odd clobber. You're in business somehow. The world owes you a living, my boy, and you've come to collect.
*He kneels down and prays.*
Oh, Rabbi Hymie—forgive me but I mean well—I'm a bad boy, but I've got my part to play, and I promise to spread love and happiness everywhere I go—cos money don't bring happiness so I'm gonna take it away from them.
*He suddenly gets an idea.*
Solly boy, you're a genius and you're in business.
*He quickly puts the Rabbi's clothes on and puts the chickens in his case.*
First I'll go from door to door, flogging these kosher chickens for charity, my charity. Thank you, Rabbi Hymie, you're a pal— I'll walk in your shoes. (*As he changes shoes*) And take the word of God—promises of redemption, love, kisses—anything they want—as long as they're happy. Watch out, world, I'm coming! Hendon! Golders Green! Hampstead Garden Suburb! —I'm knocking on your door!
*He does a little dance and some mock prayers.*

I'm Rabbi Solomon Goldstone, I'm knocking on your
    door
With a new kind of religion and a brand new kind of law
If you can't get in heaven, he'll fix it in a flash
I've got the right connections, if you have got the cash.
*He exits hurriedly.*

THE CURTAIN FALLS

## SCENE TWO

*The next day. Interior. Living room of the house of*
MORRY SWARTZ. *Known as The Castle for obvious reasons.*
*First because they've named it that and secondly because*
*they've tried to furnish it and make it appear very grand.*
*The furniture is in a mishmash of styles—good taste and*
*the appalling are side by side. A garish glassy cocktail bar,*
*for instance, stands next to a great Gothic-looking bookcase,*
*without books. A suit of armour, and animals' heads all*
*around. A television screen set in an antique case. Peach*
*mirrors all around the room. The huge ugly table is set*
*for a wedding although it appears the wedding feast has*
*almost been finished. This castle is in Golders Green.*
*Around the table the people are eating furiously.* SARAH
SWARTZ *is dressed as a bride. She is attractive in a slightly*
*overblown way. Beside her is the groom* ALAN FINK, *a*
*nervous slight boy, dressed in a dinner jacket. Next to him*
*his parents sit—*HERBERT FINK, *in a flashy American get-up,*
*and his intense wife. Next to them sit* ROMAINE SWARTZ—
*a buxom girl in late twenties—she seems very hungry, as*
*usual. And there is her brother* MELVIN—*who wears a sports*
*blazer and flannels—he is always slightly aloof and seems*
*to despise the surrounding people. Next to him* MILLIE
SWARTZ, *a rather attractive woman who tries to look younger*
*than her years, heavily made-up and wearing a lot of ex-*
*pensive jewellery.* MORRY SWARTZ *is not at the table but*

*is feeding a bird in a cage—he too is dressed in a dinner jacket but he has his slippers on. There are streamers and balloons about. When the curtain goes up there is a silence for a while as we just see the spectacle of people stuffing themselves.*

MILLIE. Morry, come back to the table, we're supposed to be celebrating.

MORRY *takes no notice but is swaying with a champagne glass in his hand.*

FINK. Come on, Alan, make a speech.

ALAN. I've already made four.

FINK. Make another one.

*All except* MELVIN *and* MORRY *bang on the table with their forks.*

ALL. Speech! Speech!

ALAN (*He pulls* SARAH *to her feet and they cuddle*). Mum and Dad! My dear Mother- and Father-in-law, Melvin, Romaine, my darling wife—I promise to be a loving husband, to bring you breakfast in bed for the first three months, to look after the shop and make lots of money.

*They all clap.*

SARAH. I'm so happy, I could cry.

MILLIE. Don't do that, your eyeblack will run.

SARAH. I could eat him, he's so handsome.

SADIE. What a handsome couple, don't they look lovely together?

MILLIE. Yes, it's a good arrangement.

HERBERT. Your turn next, Romaine.

ROMAINE. Don't do me no favours. I don't trust men.

HERBERT. Alan, you've got a lovely girl there, cherish her. She's a lovely well-made girl and you're a lucky well-off boy. Look, he's blushing, you naughty boy. Bet you can't wait for tonight, eh? It's lovely to see young people coming together. Wish I had my time over again—that's the way I used to like them— well covered.

SADIE. Herbert!

MORRY (*Sings*).
Here comes the bride, short, fat and wide,
See how she wobbles from side to side.
Here comes the groom, skinny as a broom,
If it wasn't for the bride he would have more room.
*All laugh nervously.*

SADIE. Aren't we having a lovely time? I love a party. This is the happiest day of my life, by my life. Don't they look lovely standing together? I could cry.

MILLIE. Why you?

SADIE. I don't know, brides always make me cry.

HERBERT (*He is also very tipsy and holds a drink up*). Please God by me—I'll sing a song now.
*The others take it up.*

ALL. For they are jolly good fellows, for they are jolly good fellows, for they are jolly good felel—ows
*At this moment* SOLLY *walks in and holds up a solitary chicken.*

SOLLY. And so say all of us.
*They are all astonished.*
I rang the bell, but I heard singing so I came in.

MORRY. Please excuse us, we're all upside down.

SOLLY. That's alright, my son, it's good to see people happy. What a lovely house.

HERBERT. Isn't it marvellous? What do you think of it? Do you know it cost twenty thousand to build.

SADIE. It's just like a palace, you could eat off the floor.

MORRY. Excuse us, but we're right in the middle of a wedding.

SOLLY. Carry on, it's so nice to see such a nice happy family gathering.

HERBERT. This is a nice stroke of luck, a rabbi calling on our children's wedding day. Heaven's happy with this match.

SADIE. Who wouldn't be? Look at them, they're so lovely.

MILLIE. Well, Rabbi, what can we do for you? How much money do you want?

MELVIN. Mother! You do go on—money, money, that's all you talk about.

SOLLY. Business can wait.

MORRY. Have a drink with us, please.

SADIE. Drink the health of our children.

SOLLY. Some of that Three Star brandy please. No soda.

MILLIE. What charity do you represent?

SOLLY (*Holds up his glass*). *Lechaim.*

MELVIN. Can I go now? I have a game of squash booked.

HERBERT (*Points to couple*). So have they.

MILLIE. No, you can't go. What's the matter with you? (*She pinches his cheek, he squirms*) He's so highly strung and sensitive. Are you feeling alright, darling? Let's feel your forehead. Spit out three times and go and eat some fruit. Well, Rabbi, it's nice to see you in this house.

SADIE. Perhaps he'd like to bless the house—believe me, it's worth it.

MILLIE. Alright, why not? We've got everything but it can't do no harm.

MORRY. We've got nothing, we kid ourselves.

ROMAINE. Oh, Daddy's getting all philosophical again.

MELVIN. Dad's right and we're a load of hypocrites.

HERBERT. It's a lovely party, isn't it? And soon our dear children will be pushing off on their honeymoon.

MORRY. Thank God.

MILLIE. I agree, it's good at last they'll almost stand on their own feet. After all, you push them out of you—into the world—and then it seems you have to push them right through life. And now at last they're gonna push off. It's not fair—they leave you so suddenly—look at her, she's only a baby.

HERBERT. Some baby.

     SOLLY *takes another drink, walks around the couple, digs* ALAN *in the ribs and kisses* SARAH.

SOLLY. Have a nice time, don't be greedy—in life. Love thy neighbour as—

*He starts kissing all the women on the forehead, lingers over* ROMAINE.

Be fruitful and drink lots of malt and may you have peach mirrors in your house and apricots on your table.

MILLIE. They're not moving out yet, we've still got them for a little while—until the architects have finished their house. Then they'll move away; they grow up and leave you.

MORRY. What do you mean? Look, Rabbi, see that building next door? (*Shows* SOLLY *through the window*) That's how far they're moving.

MILLIE. They've got the best of everything—I've seen to that. It cost a fortune, but who's complaining?

MELVIN. There she goes again. Must you always mention money?

MILLIE. I'd like to see you manage without it.

MORRY. For once I agree with your mother. I wouldn't care if you worked—you're supposed to look after the shop but what do you do all day? You're out playing golf and in the Turkish baths, trying to be like an English gentleman—Gandhi was more of an Englishman. Something for nothing, that's all you want. I had to work for it.

MILLIE. He's not that bad.

MELVIN. He's almost right, but can I help it if I don't belong?

ROMAINE. There he goes again, don't belong. Go out and don't belong—just fifty years or so.

MELVIN. Shut up you, you silly fat cow.

SOLLY. Children, children, remember the Sabbath day and keep it holy.

SARAH. But this isn't the Sabbath.

SOLLY. I never said it was. You must learn to respect your parents.

MILLIE. That's what I keep on telling him, he's killing me—killing me.

MELVIN. You're a long time dying.

SOLLY. Peace, peace, my children. We must forgive and love each other.

MILLIE. Alright, Mel darling, I'll buy you your glider.

ROMAINE. I want a car.

MORRY. Two years ago she bought him a sports car and last year
she bought him a yacht, and now, a glider. We've had the
ground and the water and now we'll have the air. What happens when we run out of elements? I suppose next year it'll be
a spaceship. Alright, let's change the subject. Rabbi, it's a
great honour to have you here; tell us the purpose for your visit
to our humble—big house.

SOLLY. I'm Rabbi Solly Gold, at your service. I bring the word
of God, I spread love and happiness. I'm on my usual pilgrimage through Golders Green and I pass this way but once—
for today of all days is the day of days.

ALAN. You said it, today's my wedding day.

HERBERT. And tonight's the night.

SARAH (*Pinching* ALAN's *cheek*). Isn't he lovely? I could eat him.

SOLLY. Apart from that, it's still a very special day.

SADIE. It's a holiday or festival or something, isn't it?

HERBERT. No, I know them all.

MELVIN. It's the Amateur Gliding championship today.

ROMAINE. It's just another Sunday.

MORRY. And I've got heartburn as usual and a splitting headache.

MILLIE. And I've got heartache, and backache and stomach-
ache—

SOLLY. I'm ashamed of you all. All of you. Look at you! Call
yourself good Jews? And you didn't even know it was rabbinical
chicken Sunday? I'm disgusted.

MILLIE. Rabbinical chicken what?

MORRY. Forgive me, Rabbi, but I don't follow religion—too many
hypocrites.

SOLLY. You've all heard of Mother's Day? And Father's Day?
And Doomsday? Well then, you surely must know that seven
years ago the American Reform Orthodox Proxy Rabbi's As-
sociation proclaimed this Chicken Sunday. In the old days
it used to be a great Hasidic feast. Don't you remember?
*He dances around wildly and mumbles gibberish.*

We revived it. Five times a year it falls. Surely someone must
know the famous song?
> *Sings and dances again.*
>> On the second Sunday of December,
>> Don't forget to remember,
>> Give, give and give some more,
>> To the Rabbi at your door.
>> The third Sunday that comes in May,
>> That most auspicious Rabbinical Day,
>> Give, give, and give your all,
>> To the Rabbi who comes to call.
>> On the fourth Sunday in July,
>> If a Rabbi passes by,
>> Give! give! Don't ask why
>> It's Rabbinical Chicken Sunday.

HERBERT. Of course, now I remember, I was only reading about
it the other day.

SOLLY. Then as you know, the idea is for an esteemed rabbi, like
yours truly, to go humbly from door to door, giving a chicken
as a symbol of life and collecting a small amount for charity.

HERBERT. Ah, charity—what a lovely word that is. I'm a Mason,
Rabbi, and that's the basis of our creed. Ever thought of going
on the square? I'll propose you.

MILLIE (*Takes out purse*). We always give to charity. That
should be my middle name—Millie Charity Swartz. What
charity this time?

SOLLY. The Rabbinical Chicken Sunday fund for the prevention
of cruelty.

MILLIE. Cruelty to who? Chickens?

SOLLY. Cruelty to anyone.

HERBERT. You're a man after my own heart. Here, let me give
you something. (*Hands* SOLLY *a note*) Honestly, I give, give
and never think about it. (*Turns to the others*) Just gave him
a fiver. Why not?

MILLIE. But we don't want a chicken, we've just eaten half a
dozen. I'm beginning to look like a chicken.

MORRY. You always did.

SADIE. I never get tired of chicken.

SARAH. Neither do I—I love them casseroled.

ROMAINE. I prefer them fricassee with breadcrumbs.

MORRY. Take no notice of any of them. Put the bird on the table. Go on, Millie, give the Rabbi some money. As a goy named Bacon once said—

MILLIE. Please don't mention that word, this is a kosher house. What will the Rabbi think? You give him the money, you want the bird.

MORRY. Who should I make it out to?
*Takes out cheque book.*

SOLLY. Please, please. I'm surprised with you—you must surely know that truly spiritual organisations don't believe in banks. It's unholy—it's usury, it cuts across the holy act of giving from one to the other.

MORRY. How much?

SOLLY. Shall we say ten pounds?

MILLIE. Expensive chicken!

SOLLY (*Taking money from* MORRY). Fine—wonderful. Now, let's forget all about money and get down to business, the business of blessing. (*To* SARAH *and* ALAN) What kind do you want? The special super de luxe deep significant kind, or the simple blessing of the bedchamber?

SARAH. How much do they cost?

SOLLY. Let me see—
*Takes out little book; consults it.*
The significant, cabalistic eternal marriage blessing costs enough —mind you, it's worth it—two hundred and fifty pounds.

MORRY. The man who thinks up them charges should be in charge of my business.

SOLLY. It all goes to charity mind you.

HERBERT. Our children deserve special prayers. After all, God can't be expected to be tuned in everywhere—we must have a strong transmitter. And the money goes to charity after all, don't let's stint ourselves. Mr. Swartz, you can afford it—if it was my house I'd give willingly.

SOLLY. Good, I'm glad you take that attitude. According to the law you must pay—

HERBERT. Me? Oh—

SADIE. But we—

HERBERT. How much does the cheaper blessing cost? You know, the bedchamber kind?

SOLLY. Only twenty-five pounds, and it's a pretty good blessing. For as the good book says: When the bedroom is happy every room is happy.

HERBERT. We'll have to have that one then—I haven't got the loose change here and I've left my cheque book at home—I'll owe it to you, don't forget to remind me.     .

SOLLY (*Points to* MORRY). He'll lend it to you, won't you, Mr. Swartz? Of course he will.

    MORRY *nods slowly and gives* SOLLY *more money.*

That's twenty-five pounds this gentleman owes you. Now on with the blessing. Oh, what a wonderful couple they are—they take my breath away. All I can say is they deserve each other. How I envy them—wish I could get married.

MORRY. Why can't you? Rabbis can.

SOLLY. I was married once. She was beautiful. Miriam! She died in childbirth.

MILLIE. I'm so sorry.

SOLLY. That's alright—we have to get over these things. But no other girl will take her place; besides, now I've taken my vow of chastity. . . . Right, now the—let me see—the bedroom all-purpose blessing. . . .

    *He takes up wine and starts to mumble gibberish and sways backward and forward.*

Mayyoulivelonganddiehappy. Pleasegodbyyouyoushouldliveso longmayyougetwhatIwishyoufrompurimtoshobosnochmaohgod unitetheminmorewaysthanonewhatsdonecanneverbeundone mazelmazelmazeltovmazelmazelmazeltov.

    *He now repeats this over and over again and claps his hands until he virtually hypnotises himself and starts dancing suggestively around the couple. He does this so completely and with such conviction that he has the others following him—going round and round in a circle, copying him. Seeing his power he dances around the room in conga-fashion and the others still follow him in and out of the rooms. The couple still stand where they were, completely oblivious to all this. When* SOLLY *stops dancing he shrugs, all the others seem rather stunned and dazed.*

HERBERT. Your Hebrew was the funniest I ever heard.

SOLLY. That's the new semantic Semitic based on the emetic antics of the yigdal incorporating the Aztectoltec Ashkenazim. We're branching out.

HERBERT. Of course, I was only reading about it the other day in the Jewish *Chronicle*.

SOLLY *sits down at the table and eats a chicken leg with great relish.*

SOLLY. This is a lovely house.

SADIE. It's a palace. You could eat off the floor.

HERBERT. It's a castle. Believe me, a king could live here. And Rabbi, come here, look at these peach mirrors—all embossed— what do you think of them? I tell everyone about them. They cost the earth.

MORRY. I hate them, they're designed to make you look better than you are. Every day I feel lousy but the mirrors make me look in the pink of health.

MELVIN. Mirror mirror on the wall—who is the peachiest of us all?

HERBERT. Do you know how much this house cost?

SOLLY. You told me. But tell me, Mr. Swartz, who are you that you can afford such opulence?

HERBERT. You mean to say you never heard of him? Didn't you see that full page ad in the Jewish *Chronicle* last week? This is Morry Swartz—*the* Morry Swartz—the shoe king. He's rich, he's famous—haven't you heard the jingle on Tele? Swartz's Shoes—Swartz's Shoes are the shoes for You. Get some, get some, for your wife, and your children too. My son married his daughter. His shoes are the best.

MORRY. Don't you believe it, I never wear them—they cripple me. Don't talk about business, it's a millstone round my neck. Let's change the subject. What synagogue are you from?

SOLLY. Synagogue? Oh no, I'm a peripatetic rabbi—I travel. Of course I have many synagogues under me, for between you and me—I don't want to boast, but I'm a fully fledged Synog. Regalia and all. You should all be ashamed of yourselves— don't you know your own religion? (*They all look ashamed*) I have now renounced ceremony, severed myself from paraphernalia and am having a Sabbatical year, for the whole world is a place of worship. Every house is a synagogue.

MR. FINK. I think I read about you in the *Daily Express* and the good work you are doing.

SOLLY. Of course you did, though I shun personal publicity. I've just returned from the provinces where I've been making fifty conversions daily.

ROMAINE. But Jews don't go in for conversion.

SOLLY. Don't be ridiculous, I've been converting the Jews back to their own faith.

MORRY. You've got your work cut out.

SOLLY. I'm so ashamed, of all of you, everywhere I go the same story—everyone only interested in money, no thought for the spiritual.

MILLIE. What's the name of your organisation?

SOLLY. The Liberal Orthodox Hasidic Reform United Union of Peripatetics.

SARAH. Well, Mummy, it's time we started on our honeymoon.

MILLIE. Oh darling, I'll miss you.

SOLLY. Going somewhere nice? Bournemouth? Cliftonville?

ALAN. No, we're going to the Mount Royal Hotel at Marble Arch.

SOLLY. Eh?

SARAH. What's wrong with that? All sorts of interesting foreigners come and go and it's opposite the park and it's not too far away.

ROMAINE. And the food's smashing.

MILLIE. Five miles away is far enough—she's never been that far from me. Don't forget to phone me tonight, darling. If there's anything you want or want to know, I'm here at the other end of the phone. And remember I'm always here and you've always got a home here.

MORRY. Alan, look after my baby and we'll look after you.

ALAN. Don't worry, Dad, she's in safe hands.

SARAH. You ready, Alan?

ALAN. What do you think?

MELVIN. Thank God for that. Now I can get to that game—I'll drop you off in my car.

SARAH. No thanks, we're taking Daddy's Rolls.

*There is now a lot of kissing and pinching and crying by the women and back slapping by the men, then all the people talk in a group near the door as* ROMAINE *and* SARAH *exchange a few words.*

Don't worry, Romaine, it'll soon be your turn.

ROMAINE. Who's worried? Make sure you have their barbecued trout—it's out of this world.

SARAH. I wish it was you who got married today, really I do.

ROMAINE. I've got no time for men. But be careful of their horse-radish sauce.

SARAH. I know it's going to be lonely for you without me around but maybe I'll find a nice boy there for you.

ROMAINE. Men are horrible, they only want one thing. Of course, the speciality of the house is smoked salmon rolled up with capers and stuffed into cold Scotch salmon.

SARAH. Oh I do wish you could get married—you've got such lovely eyes.

ROMAINE. I told you I don't trust men. You going to cook for Alan or employ a cook?

SARAH. I want to cook myself—I can make omelettes. Oh look at him, he seems half-starved.

ROMAINE. What he needs is plenty of lockshen soup, gefilte fish, apple strudel, cheesecake.

SARAH. You're so clever, you must teach me.

ROMAINE. And steaks—lots of steaks, for breakfast. It's the latest rage—and salt beef always goes down well.

SARAH. You're so good, so good, you deserve a man.

ROMAINE. Don't do me no favours.

ALAN. Coming, darling?

MR. FINK. Well, Kinderler, be happy, tonight we'll really be related, eh Morry? You know you haven't lost a daughter you've gained a son.

MORRY. Looks like I've gained a family.

MRS. FINK. My boy is a good boy and she's a good girl, don't they look lovely together?

MORRY. Alright, alright, go then—and if you need any more money, I know that you know where to come.

MILLIE. I'm so happy, so happy for both of you.

SOLLY (*Blessing them*). Eat plenty of fruitcake and may all your troubles be little ones.

MELVIN. Well, Sis, Alan, lots of splendid luck and all that sort of rot and play the game and all that kind of thing.
*He hurries out and he is followed by* SARAH *and* ALAN.

MILLIE (*Shouts after them*). Wrap up warm—don't forget, phone me.

MRS. FINK. Alan! Don't forget your tablets—well, they've gone now. Suppose we'll go also.

MR. FINK. Can't we stay a little longer? Play cards or watch Tele or something, after all our families are now united? Come on, Romaine, put some records on, let's be lively.

MILLIE. Alright, let's all go to the other room and play canasta— I feel funny tonight.

MRS. FINK. Believe me, Millie, I've also got the shivers—I know how you feel. My baby got married—
*They all start for the other room but* SOLLY *and* MORRY *don't move.*

MILLIE. Coming, Morry?

MORRY. No, I don't feel well.

MILLIE (*To the others*). You all go, I'll be in in a moment.
*They all go in.* SOLLY *goes to the bar and drinks.*

You drive me mad you do. If you don't act a bit more sociable I'll brain you.

MORRY. I can't stand them.

MILLIE. You're ruining everything.

MORRY. Everything ruined anyway. I wanted Alan for Romaine, you married off the wrong one.

MILLIE. Well, at least we got one of them off our hands. Alan's a good boy, he's a plodder.

MORRY. Can't stand his father!

MILLIE. Well at least he's not badly off—even if he is stupid.

MORRY. He's nothing, just nothing in trousers.

MILLIE. He's a turf accountant, rolling in it.

MORRY. Turf accountant? In my day they called it bookmaker. He hasn't got two pennies to rub together. Street corner spiv.

MILLIE. He's got an office with a typewriter and two girls working for him.

MORRY. I bet!

MILLIE. Besides, he must be respectable, he's a Mason.

MORRY. That explains everything.

MILLIE. He's got marvellous connections.

MORRY. I need unconnections. I've got too many. We'll never get poor Romaine married now.

MILLIE. Why not? She's got nice eyes.

MORRY. Let's face it—she's fat and ugly and she's not a chicken. I told you to tell that marriage broker that I wanted a husband for her and not Sarah. Sarah could always find a husband.

MILLIE. She'd have got swept off her feet for a lowlife who only wanted her for her money.

MORRY. What about Alan? You think he's marrying her for love? Every time he looks at me, cash registers ring in his eyes.

MILLIE. I know, but this is different; we chose him, it's respectable this way. Anyway, who wants Romaine married? She's such a good girl around the house—no romantic-shmantic nonsense about her.

MORRY. We sold the wrong one—the wrong one. Poor Romaine, running to seed, well—hardly running—hobbling. It's all your fault.

MILLIE. Do me a favour, go to sleep—you're uncouth. A rich man with nothing. Look at him. At least I know how to treat guests, even if I don't like them.

*She goes into the other room and we can just see them in there playing cards.* ROMAINE *is dancing rather sadly around the card table.*

SOLLY (*Giving* MORRY *a drink*). One thing I don't understand, if you're so rich, why so few guests?

MORRY. Who do I need to impress? Anyway, I don't like anyone, not even myself. I'm surrounded by enemies, all after my money.

SOLLY. You're right, and listen, your enemies praise you but your friends tell you the truth, and I'm telling you that there's something missing in your life.

MORRY. I don't trust no one. I love my children but what's the use, they're spoilt and take no notice of me. I love my wife but we're miles apart—getting further away every minute. I'm finished.

SOLLY. They're sucking the life out of you. Bloodsuckers, that's what they all are.

MORRY. Riches? You can keep them. All my life I slaved. For what?

SOLLY. It's obvious to me you're a highly spiritually developed man. Ah well, it's time to be gone.

MORRY (*Breaking away from his own thoughts*). No, no, Rabbi! Please don't go. You give me a certain peace, when you sit beside me.

SOLLY. I've work to do, my son.

MORRY. Please spare me a little longer, I want to talk to you. I feel I could pour it all out, you have such a beautiful face. Please, please, just for a few minutes.

SOLLY. Oh well, if you insist, my son.

*He helps himself to another drink.*

Maybe I can help you, though I do want you to understand that my time is valuable.

MORRY. I'll make it worth your while. It's worth anything to me, just to get it all off my chest.

SOLLY. Alright then—just relax. Lie down.
*Using the method of a psychoanalyst, he makes* MORRY *lie flat on a settee.*
Tell me everything, confide in me, God is listening to you.

MORRY. I'm afraid of dying, I'm also afraid of living. Everyone fiddles. My accountant is a crook; so is my doctor and my solicitor. I don't trust my wife; she tries to look too beautiful—who for? Me? After all these years? So I hired a private detective to watch her and now I've had to hire another one to watch him.

SOLLY. That's right, tell me everything—unburden yourself.

MORRY. Yes, I can trust you. You radiate love and kindness. I'm a humble man, Rabbi. Not very intelligent, but a bit clever. You don't need brains to make money, you need knack. I don't believe in anything—what can I do? My son is a no-good snob, my wife nags, nags, grabs, grabs, and now I'm left with Romaine on my hands. Till the day I die I'll see her fat podgy fingers eating Turkish delight and marshmallow.

SOLLY. But surely anyone would marry her?

MORRY. You'd think money was good enough bait, but no, not with her—they fight shy of Romaine, and can you blame them?

SOLLY. But she's attractive! Lovely! A big girl, full of—

MORRY. Too bad you took that oath of chastity—still, once sworn never torn—besides, as you said, you loved your wife too much. You would have made a lovely husband for my Romaine. Too late now.

SOLLY. So what can I do for you?

MORRY. I'm useless, not going anywhere, not getting anywhere, except under the ground. I'm crippled with pain, so Rabbi, what can I do?

SOLLY. One minute! It just dawned on me—of course, now I remember you.

MORRY. Do the synagogue boys know me then? Am I that well known? Have I got a good name?
*He gets up.*

SOLLY. You started down the lane, didn't you, with a shoe stall?

MORRY. Yes, I started humble.

SOLLY. And you're still a humble man—God is pleased with you. Didn't you then start a small shoe shop in the Mile-end road?

MORRY. That's me.

SOLLY. Of course! And then you built up your shoe empire.

MORRY. Do you know, I'm shoemaker by appointment to the Queen of Tonga and the President of the U.S.A. But between you and me—I wouldn't be seen dead in my shoes.

SOLLY. My mother once brought me to your shop in Mile-end— you served me yourself, don't you remember?

MORRY. Does a prostitute remember all her customers?

SOLLY. You saw we were poor so you gave me the pair of shoes, for free. Providence has brought me to you to repay that debt —that wonderful gesture of a man with a soul, a man with such humanity—shush—don't talk—I'm trying to get in touch with the angels now. Marvellous things are going to happen to you.

MORRY. Rabbi, you're a wonderful man, I envy you. So you're an East End boy—like myself. Well, you made good, maybe there's still a chance for me.

SOLLY. I'll see what I can do. I'll put a word in.

MORRY. I know you. I know I do—as if I've known you for years. What did your father do?

SOLLY. He was a great composer and my mother was a ballerina, she used to dance at the Palaseum, didn't you ever hear of Bertha Goldskya?

MORRY. Not offhand.

SOLLY. Now, let's get down to hard facts—how much are you worth?

MORRY. Who knows? Between half a million and a million. It fluctuates. But what's the use? Has any single pound brought me a single ounce of happiness?

SOLLY. You could always give it away.

MORRY. You kidding? You're not married to my wife. Anyway, I don't really want to give it away. I mean I worked so hard for it. That's my dilemma.

*They have been drinking continuously and both are staggering around,* MORRY *more so than* SOLLY.

When I was a kid I was happy.

SOLLY *puts his arm around him.*

SOLLY. Tell me about it.

MORRY. Seven of us—happy kids, all sleeping in the same big bed.

*He takes some cushions and lays them on the floor.* SOLLY *does the same.*

The bedroom small, can't you see it? My father struggled and my mother worried and we played. I was rich then; caterpillars in boxes and conkers on strings and every day was an adventure. Mummeeeeeeee! Throw me down a peneneeeeeeee! And when the winter evening came we played hide-and-seek in a peasoup fog and went home to a bowl of peasoup. . . . And don't you remember the pillow fights and feathers everywhere?

SOLLY. On guard!

*He hits* MORRY *over the head with a pillow.* MORRY *is sent flying and feathers are flying everywhere.*

MORRY *gets up and hits* SOLLY *over the head. Soon they are fighting and laughing with everything they've got.*

MORRY. Hurray! Hurray! Charge! Confetti—Hiphip—Hip—Hoooray—

MILLIE *comes into the room followed by* ROMAINE *and* MR. *and* MRS. FINK.

MILLIE. Take no notice of him, Sadie, he never grew up.

*Pushing the others back into the room; trying to suppress her anger.*

Strange games you're teaching my husband, Rabbi.

SOLLY. I'm illustrating a theme from the Bible. We got carried away—such spirit your husband has.

MILLIE. Back inside, folks—he's a little unhinged tonight. The trouble I have with that man; never mind, there are worse fish in the sea, so they say.

MORRY. I wish you'd go fishing.
*They all laugh as they go back into the room but* MILLIE *turns on* MORRY.

MILLIE. You wait till I get you alone, I'll give you what-for, showing me up.
*She goes in with the others.*

MORRY. See what I mean? Who can I turn to? Child games are over. My mother and father died and everyone grew up.
*He starts to tidy the mess and* SOLLY *helps him.*
All the family have grown up and grown old—(*He groans*) Oh my back! It's like a knife. Everyone lives in Hendon and Hampstead Garden suburb—but there's no garden in the heart. We're all dead people in stuffy living rooms, now, but then it was paradise.

SOLLY. With my help you can become happy again.

MORRY. Come on, let's have another drink, let's eat, drink and be merry for tomorrow we die, please God.
*They drink again and* MORRY *dances and sings to the tune from* "Thieving Magpie" *by Rossini.*
   I am a lobos, I am a lobos
   I take the shicksers to pictures on shobos.
*He suddenly stops and becomes doubled up with pain.*
There it is—Oooooooohhhhhhh—I've overdone it. I'm finished. (*He gradually lies down*) Ohhhhhhhohohoh—I'm dying—I'm done for.

SOLLY. What can I get you?

MORRY. Stay here. Just speak to me, your voice soothes me. Will God forgive me? I'm dying. Will he forgive me, Rabbi?

SOLLY. He hasn't got much choice with me to help you. Don't speak now—you're doing alright.

MORRY. Oh my stomach, Oh my back, Oh my God.

SOLLY. Listen—I want you to stand up.

MORRY. You crazy! If I stand up I'll fall over.

SOLLY. Stand up!

MORRY. Oh go away from me. Leave me alone.

SOLLY. If you stand up you won't fall over. I have spoken.

MORRY. Leave me to die in peace.

SOLLY. Have faith in God! Stand up—He will heal you. Stand up. I promise you—you won't fall over.

MORRY. Alright, for His sake I'll chance it— Oooooohohohooo. (*He gradually gets to his feet*)

SOLLY. There you are—oh ye of little faith.
   At this MORRY *crumbles and falls over.*

MORRY. I told you—oh let me die. I'm suffering from an incurable disease.

SOLLY. Where's the pain now?

MORRY. Where isn't it! In my toes, in my head, in my fingers, in my neck, in my back. (*He slowly crawls to his feet by holding on to the settee*)

SOLLY. You'll be fine—I'll cure you. Nothing to worry about. Solly Gold will fix it.
   *Unintentionally* SOLLY *slaps the old man vigorously on the back.* MORRY *is hurled to the floor again.*

MORRY. Oh! You've killed me!
   *He writhes and moans and turns over and over in great agony but suddenly he stops and stands up.*
That's it! The pain's gone! You've done it!

SOLLY. Of course. What did I tell you?

MORRY. I'm cured! You don't understand—I can stand up straight with no pain! It's a miracle! A miracle!
   *He kisses* SOLLY *resoundingly on the forehead.*
For years I've suffered and now I'm well, thanks to you.

SOLLY. It's the work of God, I'm just His instrument.

MORRY. It's a miracle. And to think I doubted. He sent you to me—I can't believe it—how can I thank you? How can I repay you?

SOLLY. We'll find a way.

MORRY. Stay here with me—stay here for a time—for a few days. Please be my guest.

SOLLY. I told you my time is precious—there are others who need help . . . people starving. . . . I'm the best collector this side of the Thames.

MORRY. I'll make it worth your while—I'll give you more than you'll collect in a month. But you must stay, I need you. You can help me.

SOLLY. Alright, if this is the will of God, who am I to argue? I'll stay for a while. . . .

MORRY. Oh, we'll have a marvellous time, you and I together! I'm young again. I'm reborn. I can move, I walk, I can dance! It's a miracle. Thank you, thank you. Watch me dance— Kazatzka—I haven't done it for years.

> *He dances wildly to the music that comes from the other room.* SOLLY *claps his hands and they make a terrific noise. The family and the* FINKS *come in from the other room— stand around in amazement as* MORRY *dances into the other room followed by* SOLLY *clapping. The phone rings; everyone rushes for it but* MILLIE *gets there first.*

MILLIE. Hullo! Oh— It's them! They've just arrived—they're in the room.

MRS. FINK. What's it like?

MILLIE. What's the room like? Oh, it's all pink—and silver— overlooking the park. . . . They can see the speakers on speakers' corner . . . how thrilling—what's the weather like? Oh yes, of course.

ROMAINE. What's the food like?

MILLIE. Did you hear that? They haven't eaten yet—the waiter's just taken their order.

FINK. Tell them to behave themselves—I mean they can do what they like but tomorrow is another day.

MILLIE. Alan, your father sends his love. Wrap up warm, darling —the nights are drawing in. I'm so happy for you, you naughty girl.

MRS. FINK. Tell him to take his pills.

MILLIE. Take your pills, Alan.

> MORRY *comes dancing back into the room,* SOLLY *stops clapping.*

What's that, darling? How's Dad? Morry? Morry? Did you hear that? Haven't you got a message for your daughter?

MORRY. Tell them, God is good. I'm cured at last and Rabbi Solly Gold did it. (*Carries on dancing*)

MILLIE. How should I know, darling—he's round the bend—only more so. Says he's cured. Bye-bye—Dolly. Ring me later— Soon. If you want to know anything—I'm here all the time and don't forget. . . . Alan, look after her, and if you can't be good, be careful. . . .

> *She hangs up and they all once more turn to* MORRY *who continues his dance with* SOLLY *clapping his hands once more. They stand staring in amazement as*
> ## THE CURTAIN FALLS

# SCENE THREE

*The next day. The curtains are drawn and the lights are on. It seems like the middle of the night but in reality it is eleven thirty a.m.* SOLLY *enters in a very flamboyant-looking dressing gown, goes to the cocktail cabinet and drinks, goes to the peach mirror and smiles at himself.*

SOLLY. This is the life for me, I was born for luxury.

> *He takes another drink and* ROMAINE *comes on—also in dressing gown. She touches him on the shoulder, he jumps.*

ROMAINE. Talking to yourself, eh?

SOLLY. I was talking to God.

ROMAINE. Go away, you can't fool me. I'm not like my father.

SOLLY. Can I get you a drink?

ROMAINE. A bunny hug, please. (*He quickly hugs her*)

SOLLY. With pleasure.

ROMAINE (*Struggling free*). A bunny hug is Advocaat and cherry brandy.

SOLLY. Oh, I'm sorry, I'll get it. You must excuse me but I
want to make people happy and I thought that was what you
wanted.

ROMAINE. Wait till I tell my father.

SOLLY. Well, if you don't want it, at least you need it—that's
obvious.

ROMAINE. Wait till my mother comes down.
*She takes the drink and drinks it.*

SOLLY. Your father knows what he's doing—he understands the
intricacies of religion.

ROMAINE. He understands nothing, he's a fool.

SOLLY. He can't be a fool if he made a fortune.

ROMAINE. Most people who make money are mad—they're all a
bit touched.

SOLLY. My Aunt Sophie had a fortune and she was untouched.

ROMAINE. How long you staying?

SOLLY. How long do you want me?
*He pinches her cheek.*
I can help you.

ROMAINE. Don't need help.

SOLLY. We all need help. Come, my daughter, think of me as a
friend
*He puts his hands on her shoulders.*

ROMAINE. Not too close.

SOLLY. Confide in me. Tell me everything.

ROMAINE. There's nothing much to tell.

SOLLY. You're very deep, I can see it. I'm trained to search your
inner depths. You're a restless spirit, I can see great fires
raging in your soul. Oh, thou fairest of women—

ROMAINE. I'm starving.

SOLLY. Thine eyes are as a dove's.

ROMAINE. You been listening to Housewives' Choice?

SOLLY. Thy hair is a flock of goats.

ROMAINE. Cheek! I shampooed it last night.
*He tries to cuddle her but she keeps on retreating from him.*

SOLLY. Thy mouth is comely and thy breasts are like two fawns—

ROMAINE. How dare you! You're a dirty old man.

SOLLY. I'm not, that's in the Bible—here read!

ROMAINE. You're still a dirty old man.

SOLLY. I'm not old.

ROMAINE. Wait till I see my father, he'll throw you out— Man of God!

SOLLY. Wishful thinking, my daughter. I have not behaved improperly. I will admit though to being human. Under this habit is the same old habit—the desire for a beautiful girl like you.

ROMAINE. Wonder what's in the frig' for breakfast? How about some steak?

SOLLY. You know how to please a man. Why is it that you're not appreciated in this house? Why do they always leave you out?

ROMAINE. How do you know?

SOLLY. God knows everything, and I've come to tell you that you deserve better for you're the most beautiful woman I've ever seen.

ROMAINE. You trying to get round me?

SOLLY (*Soft*). That would be hard—the angels are doing their nut over you. I'm going to help you get what's coming to you, get what you deserve. Your body is a poem conceived by the love of God and my imagination.

ROMAINE. Come off it, you know I'm fat.

SOLLY. Not fat, well built, a big girl—a real woman, with everything in its place and plenty of it. A wonderful sight—paradise, the promise of bliss.

ROMAINE. Of course, I'm reducing. At least I'm trying—I'm going to cut down on potatoes tomorrow.

SOLLY. Don't! Stay as you are—you're lovely. Beauty is in the eyes of the beholder and behold thou art fantastic—colossal— a double feature—I'm here to show you how much you're wanted.

ROMAINE. Some boys whistled me last July.

SOLLY. Oh if I wasn't a rabbi—if I hadn't taken my vow! My wife! God rest her soul, would understand, I'm crazy about you.

ROMAINE. How would you like your steak?

SOLLY. Overdone—almost burnt to a cinder.

ROMAINE. I like the opposite—very rare—

SOLLY. Go quickly before I forget that I'm a holy man.
*She smiles and goes into the kitchen. He rubs his hands and looks at reflection in mirror.*
Careful, Solly my boy. Careful, go slowly or you'll spoil everything.
*He reads the Bible.*

ROMAINE (*Calls from kitchen*). Come and watch me cook!

SOLLY. You trying to lead me astray? (*He now fights with himself*) Careful, boy—take it easy. Oh, what's worth more to me? A fortune or a fat girl? Nothing's ever easy, is it? Just my luck. (*He still fights with himself*) No! Moneymoneymoney money! It all boils down to that in the end.

ROMAINE. Come on, come and watch me. I'm sorry I was cross with you before. I got you all wrong.

SOLLY. No, I can't come now, I'm reading.

ROMAINE. What?

SOLLY. The most stupendous, smashing, story of them all—rape, love, hate, war, sex, everything—the Bible.
*Now he flips through the book and gets really excited.*
Cooo, it's all here—everything. Now I know where everything comes from!
*Suddenly he gets wildly excited.*
This is it! Here it is! I've got it! Solly, you're marvellous! It's a cinch. A cinch, a winner! It's all here, in black and white— it can't fail.

*He can hardly contain his pleasure. He drinks to his reflection in the mirror.* MORRY *walks in briskly.*

MORRY. Wonderful morning.

SOLLY. How do you feel?

MORRY. On top of the world, thanks to you.
ROMAINE *comes in.*
Hello, darling. (*He kisses her*) How are you? Isn't it a lovely day?

ROMAINE. You feeling alright?

MORRY. Alright? I'm alive at last, aware—free! Make me some breakfast.

ROMAINE. But you never eat breakfast.

MORRY. This morning I feel hungry. Just something light, there's a good girl.

ROMAINE. Bit of toast?

MORRY. No, some grapefruit juice, some cereal and to follow, some fried kidneys and eggs.

ROMAINE. Something light? Oh, I see. Daddy, you kill me.

MORRY. Don't be saucy or I'll cut you off.

ROMAINE. Cut you off! Cut you off! That's all he knows. I feel like a water supply.

MORRY. Come on, there's a good girl—let's not argue anymore. I'll buy you a pound of marzipan whirls.

ROMAINE. With almonds inside? Daddy, I don't know what's come over you, but it makes a change.
*She goes into the kitchen.*

MORRY. I've got a good idea. Let's go to Brighton in my Rolls, lay on the sand, then maybe we'll go to the Wax Works. Or, I forgot—no sand at Brighton! How about coming to the East End and having a salt-beef sandwich?

SOLLY. No, there's important work to do. Now that you're healthy in body we've got to consolidate our position and then make you healthy in soul.

MORRY. But I'm happy now. I feel fine, thanks to you.

SOLLY. You only think you're happy, but the spiritual inertia will creep up on you if you're not careful and you'll have more than *angst* in your pants.

MORRY. Yes.

SOLLY. I want it louder than that—an affirmation, a total acceptance. Now listen, do you trust me?—Do you—place—yourself —in my—care?

MORRY. Absolutely! For some reason I trust you with my life. I dreamed and dreamed last night—wonderful dreams—you may be a stranger but you're not so strange as my own family.

SOLLY. Good! Now! Concentrate. I'm going to make a real mench of you. First I've got a message for you.

MORRY. From the Stock Exchange?

SOLLY. Somewhere more important.

MORRY (*Incredulous*). More important than the Stock Exchange?

SOLLY. I've got a message from God—for you. He spoke to me last night.

MORRY. Go on—you're a liar.

SOLLY. Would God talk to a liar?

MORRY. I'm sorry, I didn't mean it. A message for me?

SOLLY. When I knocked on the door I had a vision. And when I saw your face I saw a purple light, and when you spoke I knew my search was over.

MORRY. Search? Purple light?

SOLLY. How can I tell him I said to myself—how? How can I prepare this humble man for the news—for his mission. The Almighty said—"Speak, speak!"

MORRY. Don't leave me up in the air—for God's sake, spit it out.

SOLLY. All night I lay awake arguing with the angels telling them that you were not ready. There I was praying and weeping. All the stars in the sky burst into the room, a great halo covered the universe, and a golden rainbow stretched from Golders Green to Stamford Hill. Then, just at dawn, amongst a choir of assembled archangels the Holy One spoke again: "Behold—I send you Elijah the Prophet—"

    ROMAINE *comes in and* SOLLY *quickly stops gesticulating.*

ROMAINE. We haven't got any grapefruit juice.

MORRY. Grapefruit juice? What are you talking about? Go away!

ROMAINE. That's more like it. Now you're yourself again. (*She goes off*)

SOLLY (*Continues*). "And he shall turn the heart of the fathers to the children and the heart of the children to their fathers."

MORRY. What does it all boil down to?

SOLLY. "Behold nations shall come to thy light and kings to the brightness of thy rising . . . The fires—"

MORRY. Please tell me, don't beat about the burning bush.

SOLLY. I've come to proclaim you the messiah of the world.
*He kneels before him.*

MORRY. Me? Don't make me la— —ugh.

SOLLY. It's no laughing matter but a time for jubilation. For you and me and the whole world.
     ROMAINE *comes in to lay the table.* SOLLY *quickly gets up until she goes out again.*

MORRY. Would it be alright if I had a cigarette? (SOLLY *nods*) Like one?

SOLLY. What brand? (*Looks*) Alright.
*Takes one and strikes a match.*
You'll catch the whole world alight.
     *As he talks he forgets the lighted match and burns himself.*
It's hard to believe, I know, but you must believe.

MORRY. But Rabbi, you can't mean it. You're joking.

SOLLY. I never joke. Certainly not on matters like this. Would I jeopardise my immortal soul by such blasphemy?
     *He keeps his fingers crossed and offers up a silent prayer for himself.*

MORRY. Me? The messiah? Me? Little Morry Swartz? Go on, you're having me on. Me? The messiah?
     *He looks at himself in the mirror.*
I've got bloodshot eyes.

SOLLY. You should have seen Moses. Look at me—listen—I've come to help you, Morry. Look—I'm telling the truth, by **my** life. Tell you what I'll do—want another miracle? Alright. Will that please you? Ye of little faith, I'm surprised at you— and you all ready to be the messiah. Didn't I perform a miracle on you last night?

MORRY. Yes, you did—but—

SOLLY. That was the first sign—to make you stand up and believe in me.

MORRY. But why me? Why do they have to pick on me?

SOLLY. Why not you? Morry, listen. Do me a favour. Do your- self a favour. You are not the messiah yet— Oh no—not by a long chalk. Hahahah. Did you think—no, there's a long way to go and I've come to take you there—to prepare you.

MORRY. But I'm a hypocrite.

SOLLY. Who but a good man would admit that?

MORRY. When I pray my words are empty. I can't get through.

SOLLY. I've got a direct line.

MORRY. I have no real love or reverence for anything—

SOLLY. That's because you haven't been alive till now.

MORRY. Would you swear on the Bible? That what you've said is the truth, so help you God?

SOLLY. Of course I would.
        *Puts his hand on the Bible while crossing the fingers of
        the other hand.*
I swear on the Bible that you Morry Swartz are destined to be- come the messiah.

MORRY. It must be true—no one would swear like that without meaning it. I feel marvellous. Know what I'm going to do?

SOLLY. What? Pray?

MORRY. No, I'm going out in the garden—something I haven't done in years. (*He goes out*)

SOLLY. Please, God—you there? If you are there, forgive me, *feinlights*—I'm doing it for your good. You see—alright, so I'm a bad boy. To forgive is human—I'll make it up to you . . . I'll make a bit of cash and make myself happy, and if I'm happy

—well, we're all sailing— So listen, do me a favour—and if you're not there—and don't exist—what am I talking for anyway?
*ROMAINE comes in with MORRY's breakfast.*

ROMAINE. Where is he?

SOLLY. In the garden.

ROMAINE (*Shouts from door*). Dad! You're breakfast is ready!
*She puts it on table then brings SOLLY's breakfast and SOLLY starts eating. MORRY comes back in.*
This the way you like your kidneys, Dad?

MORRY. You mad? You know I never eat a big breakfast—who feels like eating anyway at a time like this? Now leave us alone, we're having a business discussion.

ROMAINE. Suppose I'll have to eat my steak in the kitchen. Business discussion! First he wants breakfast then he doesn't. Drives you mad, he does.
*She goes back into kitchen.*

MORRY. How we going to do this, Rabbi? How will we convince others?

SOLLY (*He furiously cuts into his meat*). You'll convince others not by magic but by logic, by example, by the lights that radiate from you—the light of wisdom, the light of knowledge. There, I will guide you. You'll bring people to God by your simplicity, by being humble. No miracles. Do they have to have miracles—disappearing tricks and rigmarole in order to believe? Oh, ye of little faith, you will say, isn't life a miracle?

MORRY. But why me? Surely there are others more worthy.

SOLLY. It happens that way sometimes. Look at Gautama Mohammed, and Izzy Totenspielgle. Listen, you are the new messiah—the everyday messiah—the ordinary fellow—the average bloke. Good common or garden messiah—a simple, humble, kind and worthy example—a heart of gold and an upholder of charity. This steak is tough, change your butcher—with you-being ordinary you become extraordinary. It is the specific, the specimen, that makes the generalisation pointed. The microcosm proves the macrocosm—simple! To cut a long story sideways, you are an honest man.

MORRY. Me? Honest? How do you suppose I made a fortune?

SOLLY. Silence. I cannot tolerate your scepticism—your self-criticism. You must learn to love yourself. It's not how you made your money that matters anymore—it's what you do with it! The millions you made in money we will now make in souls. Making money was an exercise God set you.

*He stands up and exclaims:*

The nation is ready—the Commonwealth is linked—the world is watching and with my help you'll come into your kingdom and heaven will reign on earth. Cats and dogs will lick your feet—people will be nice. God watched you from the start— He helped you make a fortune and found a shoe empire! And now it's no longer Morry Swartz the King of the Shoes, but Morry Saviour Swartz the King of the Jews!

*He sits down again and cuts more meat.*

MORRY (*Looks at mirror—gestures and poses*). Do you think it's possible? Why? But why not? Sure! I got a scholarship as a kid when nobody else did.

SOLLY. You'll follow me and I'll follow you.

*He walks round and round in a small circle and is followed by* MORRY.

    Morry Swartz the King of the Jews
    Have you heard the latest news?
    He saved the soles upon your feet
    And now He'll save your soul—complete.

I'll help you, Morry, don't worry.

MORRY. Who'll help you?

SOLLY. God help me, I mean God'll help me. Now get on with your breakfast, you need to build up your energy for the election campaign.

MORRY. Look at me—haha—the messiah! And I'm only a small man.

SOLLY. So was Napoleon.

MORRY. Look what happened to him.

SOLLY. Well, what about my father? Look what happened to him, and he was only a small man.

MORRY. What happened to him?

SOLLY. He was the first man to swim the Atlantic, wasn't he?

MORRY. You said he was a composer.

SOLLY. Can't a crazy composer go swimming?

MORRY. Rabbi, I only hope I prove worthy of my task. This is the happiest day of my life. I want to tell everyone. At last I've got something to live for.

SOLLY. Now listen, be a diplomat—not a word to anyone, not yet. It's too soon—they're not ready yet for the shock. They're not so spiritually advanced. This must stay our secret until God says otherwise—otherwise you'll be a laughing stock. You know how people are.

 ROMAINE *enters.*

ROMAINE. I've finished my breakfast. The steak was like butter.

SOLLY. Mine was like leather.

 MILLIE *enters in her dressing gown, looking like death.*

MILLIE. Did the phone ring?

ROMAINE. No!

MILLIE. Why not? What's the time?

ROMAINE. Getting on for twelve.

MILLIE. What? Why didn't someone call me? Why doesn't someone draw the curtains? I feel terrible. Oh, oh, what a night I had—and I've got such a day in front of me.

SOLLY. Maybe I can help you.

MILLIE. No one can help me—you can only help yourself. I didn't sleep a wink.

SOLLY. Is it the international situation that's worrying you, my daughter?

MILLIE. International? What? What are you going on about? And stop calling me your daughter—I'm old enough to be your mother. It's the servant situation that's worrying me. Other people's worries don't keep me awake, I've got enough of my own: my baby got married, my son's driving me to the grave and my husband to the workhouse—and she's (*Points at* ROMAINE) driving me to the madhouse.

SOLLY. If you go to all those places at once it should be very interesting.

ROMAINE. Would you like some breakfast, Mummy?

MILLIE. Couldn't touch a thing. I've got the shivers, and I've got daggers in my head, and my heart is pal—

ROMAINE. Made some lovely kidneys for Dad, who doesn't want them now.
*She puts the plate in front of her mother.*

MILLIE. No, I couldn't. Do me a favour, you know I never eat break . . .
*She sniffs plate and starts eating very ravenously.*
Such a day in front of me—an appointment with the hairdresser at two, the dressmaker at three, and the chiropodist at four, and the dentist at four thirty, and I told Sandra I'd go with her to a tea dance at five, and then this evening to the theatre with Estelle to see that wonderful play about homosexual-ality, and on top of all that I've got to find a new maid.

MORRY. What's wrong with the one we've got?

MILLIE. Nothing, except we haven't got her anymore. He didn't even notice she left.

MORRY. The German girl gone? Where?

MILLIE. Back to Germany. The German girl was three girls ago—we've had French, Italian and Irish since then.

ROMAINE. I'll have to do all the washing and the washing-up now, I suppose.

MORRY. About time you did something—it's all piling up in the kitchen. You can't blame the girls for not staying in this house. Who'd want to cope with us? But I'm going to change all that. From now on we're going to be a family again—all sitting down to meals at the same time. One happy family.
*The phone rings.* ROMAINE *and* MILLIE *dash for it.* ROMAINE *gets there first.*

ROMAINE. Sarah! Darling, how are you?

MILLIE. Give me that phone—I'm your mother! (*She snatches it away*) Hello, Dolly—Sweetheart. How are you darling? Did you sleep well? What? You poor girl, never mind, you'll get used to it. (*She turns to tell the others*) He likes to sleep with the window open. Had breakfast yet? Was it nice? Bed comfy? How's Alan? Send him my love. Tell him not to worry and remember this is your honeymoon. What's that? Oh, I'm so pleased. Bye-bye, Dolly, see you soon, then—see you—Tata—as quick as you like. Good-bye. (*She puts down the phone*) They're coming to lunch. She misses us.

MORRY. But she's only just left.

MILLIE. It was last night. She's homesick. Blood is thicker than water.

MELVIN *comes in dressed in blazer and white trousers.*

MELVIN. Lovely day. Seen the papers? What's it going to do?

MORRY. We're on the brink of another war.

MELVIN. I didn't mean that. Is it going to rain? What's the forecast?
*Takes a newspaper, reads the back page.*

MORRY. The back page—that's all he knows—and on the front page the world's doing its nut. Look at him, the English Sportsman, the Cricket Fixtures, the rugger scores—

MILLIE. You hungry, darling? Some nice fried fish in the frig'.

MORRY. I know what he needs, and I don't mean lockshen soup.

MELVIN. Think I'll have a bash in on the tennis court this morning, a nice brisk game to start the day. Has Derek phoned?

MORRY. Aren't you going to work?

MELVIN. Aren't you?

MORRY. How dare you talk to me that way—who paid for every-thing—who poured out his heart?

MILLIE. Melvin's not too strong, don't nag him.

MORRY. Look at him—the Sportsman. Tallyho Moishe. He's always on holiday. It's either winter sports or summer holidays. Climbing he goes, and all that horrible nonsense. What's wrong with Shoot-up Hill? All the year he's on holiday, and then he needs another year's rest to get over it.

MILLIE. How dare you chastise my child like that?

MORRY. He's a stuck-up snob, a delinquent with cash, a Teddy boy of the tennis court. Well, I'm telling you.

MELVIN. Really, this is all rather beneath me. He does go on. I'm going in the garden, can't stand the atmosphere here.
*He goes.*

SOLLY. Morry, remember all will change by your attitude—by love and understanding—don't excite yourself, let's go for a nice drive and look at trees.

MORRY. Yes, you're right, you're so right. Melvin, forgive me.

MILLIE. Now something is really up. Morry, I'm worried about you.

MORRY. I'm in good hands.

SOLLY. As I told your husband, you must learn to love everyone—or how will you love yourself and if you don't love yourself, who will love you?

MORRY. He's so right. Well, Rabbi, what about our drive?

MILLIE (*Fussing with breakfast things*). Come on, Romaine, don't leave it all to me.
    *She and* ROMAINE *go into kitchen.*

SOLLY. Morry, if only you could get rid of your family for a little while. They clutter up the place so—I can't concentrate.

MORRY. Now you know how I've suffered all these years.

SOLLY. Can't you send them on holiday? I must have peace to work. They inhibit me. I don't mind Melvin around—he's a fool—but the others must go.

MORRY. But how? How? If only I knew a way.

SOLLY. I'll fix it.

MORRY. You'll be lucky. She'll never leave me, never. Never let me out of her sight.

SOLLY. You leave it to me—I guarantee by tonight we'll have the place to ourselves. Let's go now and plan our campaign. (*He calls to* MILLIE) Don't worry, Mrs. Swartz, I'm taking care of your husband.
    *He and* MORRY *leave.* MELVIN *comes back in and then* MILLIE *and* ROMAINE *follow.*

ROMAINE. He's going mad.

MILLIE. Going? Going? He's gone. Went years ago.

ROMAINE. I don't trust that Rabbi.

MILLIE. Where was I? What was I doing? Must get a maid, number one. There's ice cream in the frig'. Melvin, have some

and be a good boy. I must get dressed.
*Doorbell rings.*
Oh, who can that be?
MELVIN *goes and voices are heard outside.*
It's them Finks again, they make me sick.
*The* FINKS *enter.*
Hello, Sadie, I was just speaking about you.

FINK. Only good I hope. You didn't mind us dropping in, did you, Millie? After all, we are related now.

MELVIN. Someone once said, "God gives us our relatives. Thank God we can choose our friends."

FINK. Heard from the children, Millie?
*He sits down, smokes one of* MORRY's *cigars and takes a lot of drink.*

MILLIE. They just phoned me.

MRS. FINK. How are they?

MILLIE. They sounded so happy.

MRS. FINK. I know, they were the same when they phoned me an hour ago.

MILLIE. They're coming to lunch.

MRS. FINK. What a coincidence, I'm dying to see them.

MR. FINK. It will be so nice—a happy family gathering! What's nice for lunch? Eh, Romaine?

MRS. FINK. Can I help, Millie?

MILLIE. Yes, get a chicken in the pressure cooker as quickly as possible. Now you must excuse me for a few moments—I must get dressed and I've got a thousand and one things to do. (*She goes*)

MR. FINK. Well, Romaine, it's your turn next. Who's going to be the lucky man—

ROMAINE. I'm not getting married—I like laying in bed in the morning. Anyway, men are all the same—only after one thing. . . .

FINK. Good thing, otherwise where would we be? Still, I don't know why you can't get off. Nice, well built girl like you. Wish I had my time again.

MRS. FINK. I'm sure she's going to make someone very happy; meanwhile come and help me make lunch.

ROMAINE. Lunch, lunch— We've only just had breakfast! That's all they think about in this house—food! food!
*She follows* MRS. FINK *into kitchen.*

MR. FINK. You're a sportsman, aren't you, Melvin? Do you ever shoot any nice wild—er birds, on your travels?

MELVIN. I've bagged some grouse, and a partridge once.

FINK. You're a dark horse, you know what I mean? You're a sport and I'm a sport—couldn't we go out together and perhaps you could show me some highlife in some low dives. Ain't that clever?

MELVIN. You're drunk.

FINK. I'm an outdoor type like you, but I love indoor sports. Anything between eighteen years and twenty-five, and female of course—

MELVIN. What do you take me for? Please, Mr. Fink, I think I've heard enough.

FINK (*Digs him in the ribs*). Come on, tell me, we're both men of the world—

MELVIN. You should be ashamed of yourself.

FINK. I'm only human, out for a bit of a skylark in the dark—

MELVIN. Have you no morals? What about your wedding vows? Play the game, for God's sake.

FINK. I was only kidding. I'm a sportsman like yourself—live only for dogs and horses. I love 'em. My wife's a girl in a million. What do you take me for? I've got a son as old as you! Never mind, Melvin—no offence, no harm meant—I won't hold it against you that you got me all wrong. I have these jokes. I understand you. Course I study a bit cycle-logy myself; what you need is a bit of this and that and one must never forget the other. Would you like to be a Mason? I'll propose you. Marvellous—the little case and the badge and the lovely apron— it's a brotherhood . . . a real brotherhood. . . .
*He almost slumps forward as he drinks and drinks.*
ALAN *and* SARAH *appear.*

ALAN. Hello, Dad, been celebrating?

FINK *jumps up, kisses* SARAH *and slaps his son on the back.*

FINK. Sadie! Sadie! They're here. Hello my boy. Yes! You've got that grown-up look.

MRS. FINK (*Rushing in*). Alan! How are you? Did you take your pills? Sarah darling, how are you?

SARAH. Ecstatic.

ROMAINE. Enjoying your honeymoon?

SARAH. Smashing! Where's Mum?

ROMAINE. Upstairs. Well, how's married life?

SARAH. Smashing. Where's Dad?

ROMAINE. Out. What's the hotel like?

SARAH. Smashing. Where's Dad gone?

ROMAINE. For a drive. What's the food like?

SARAH. Sma— Not so hot.

ALAN. She's marvellous to me, Mum—she thinks of everything. I married an angel.

SARAH. Oh isn't he lovely, I could eat him. (*Pinches his cheek*)

ROMAINE. Save your appetite, there's chicken for lunch.

MILLIE *enters dressed up with lots of very expensive but garish jewellery.*

MILLIE. You're here! And no one told me, darling! You look lovely.

MRS. FINK. They make such a lovely couple.

MILLIE. Taking care of her Alan? Good. Dolly, you look pale.

SARAH. I feel fabulous, Mummy. That hotel is out of this world.

MILLIE. You're thinner.

SARAH. Mummy, I only left yesterday.

MILLIE. I don't care, I've got eyes, haven't I? I'm so happy for you, you bad girl. It's not fair, you're only a baby. Oh darling, you looked lovely yesterday, now your worries will begin. I wish you every happiness. So, how do you like married life?

SARAH. Terrific.

MILLIE. Anyone seen my silver nail varnish? Can't find a thing
in this house. Look, I'm going mad—it's in my hand all the
time. Come over here, Dolly, and tell me all about it.

    SARAH *and the other women sit on the settee chattering
quietly while* MILLIE *paints her nails.*

FINK. Melvin, come here, have you got to know my boy yet? I
think you've got a lot in common. Have a chat—be friends—
it's nice to be happy. (*He drinks some more*)
Oh, this is the life for me . . . I'm so sleepy. (*Dozes off*)

MELVIN. Do you like sport?

ALAN. Who don't? Like a nice game of football, myself.

MELVIN. Cricket?

ALAN. No, it's a bit slow for me. Now football—

MELVIN. Rugger? No! Ever been yachting? Skiing?

ALAN. It's all a bit hard on the old calf muscles, ain't it? I have
a flutter on the pools each week.

MELVIN. Well, what do you play?

ALAN. I like a nice game of football, myself.

MELVIN. I loathe soccer; what about swimming?

ALAN. I'm afraid of water.

MELVIN. Do you ride?

ALAN. Sure, but only on buses, hate the underground, I like a nice
game of football, myself.

MELVIN. There must be some other sport you like. What about
running? Or tennis?

ALAN. I don't mind a game of ping-pong.

MELVIN. Ah! Table tennis, not a bad little game. As a matter
of fact, I'm the champion player of Hampstead Garden Suburb.
Care for a game?

ALAN. Well, I'm not so hot, you know—

MELVIN. Be a sport, come on—I have a table in the other room.
Don't worry, I shan't play my best game.

ALAN. You'll lick me hollow.

MELVIN. It's the spirit that matters—don't worry, just relax.
*MELVIN leads ALAN into the other room and now we can see them playing in there—ALAN wildly rushing to catch the ball with his bat and MELVIN being very calm.*

ROMAINE. The chicken must be ready; come and help me, Sarah. *Off they go.*

MILLIE. I wonder where that man is?

SADIE. They're all the same. I'll lay the table.
*She and MILLIE start laying the table.*

FINK (*In his sleep*). Come on, boy—come on—Silver Flash— Silver Flash—you're there, you're almost there—come on—all my money's on you.

SADIE. Wake up, Herbert. (*She shakes him*) Look, he's sweating. Wake up—you're dreaming.

FINK. Where am I? Where? What did you wake me up for? I had twenty-five on that dog! And he was winning—

SADIE. It was a nightmare. You look worried.

FINK. Hello, Millie, my ship was just coming in. Me worried? I never worry.
*In the other room, MELVIN is now frantic and rushing around while ALAN is calmly lobbing the balls. ROMAINE and SARAH enter the living room with the chicken and some vegetables, and everyone sits down. MELVIN comes in sadly followed by the beaming ALAN.*

MELVIN. I wasn't doing my best today, on purpose of course.

ALAN. I won, what about that, Sarah? I won. Can I join your club, Melvin?

MELVIN. I let you win, to encourage you. Who cares about stupid ping-pong anyway?

ALAN. I won! I won; since I've been married I feel like a new man. Did you see that, Dad? Did you see me win?
*MELVIN sits down.*

FINK. What? You won? Bravo! I'm proud of you! What did I tell you, Melvin?
*When he sees MELVIN's attitude he speaks more harshly to ALAN but much softer in tone.*

You bloody fool! Trust you, what did you go and win for? We don't want enemies in this house—now play him again, and lose next time.

*Now they are all seated and all are eating.* morry *and* solly *enter.*

solly *goes around inspecting the plates. He whistles.*

Did you have some birdseed for breakfast, Rabbi?

solly. Stop! All of you. Stop eating!
*Some are shocked and some splutter.*

millie. Oh my God—what's the matter?

solly. There must be no more flesh eaten in this house.

morry. That's right. No more meat.

solly. From now on this is a vegetarian house.
*He says a few words of gibberish—as if praying.*

millie. No more meat?

melvin. You gone potty?

sarah. Mummy, what's the matter with him?

solly. He has decided. No more steak, no more liver, no more fish, and no more chicken.

romaine. I'll die without meat.

millie. I don't mind you coming to this house—I don't even mind you hanging around for a few days—but when you tell me that I must become a vegetarian, that's the last straw.

fink. I'm sure there's some perfectly reasonable explanation.

romaine. But yesterday was Chicken Sunday, you said so yourself.

solly. Don't you people realise that we're in the last equinox of the solstice? We were just sitting near Highgate Pond contemplating the nature of things when suddenly it came to us in revelation—

morry. Honestly, by my life, a duck swam up to me and seemed to want to communicate. The Rabbi translated.

solly. It said, "The souls of innocent animals cry out in bondage. Save us from the knife; no longer must our blood be shed."
*He and* morry *seem to be enjoying themselves.*

MILLIE. A joke's a joke, but we've had enough. Eat up everyone, take no notice.

SOLLY. Don't move! This is God's word. The next one to eat flesh will be banished from this house.
    MILLIE *and* ROMAINE *eat.*
Alright, you brought this on yourself.

MILLIE. Isn't it time you were going, Rabbi?

MORRY. Show them a miracle—teach them a big lesson.

SOLLY. No, why should I waste miracles upon them? Would they believe it if they saw? Clear them all out of the room— all of them—they offend my eyes.

MILLIE. Right, now I've heard enough. I must ask you to leave. Mr. Fink, please help me—Alan, Melvin!

MELVIN. Be a good chap, go quietly.

FINK. Can't we talk this over quietly?

ALAN (*Hiding behind* SARAH). Sarah, what shall I do?

MILLIE. Call yourself men? Look at you!

MORRY. I'm the boss in this house, and I'm taking over. I'm wearing the trousers from now on and the Rabbi is my guest; if you don't like it you can lump it—and Mr. Fink, please don't come so often.

MILLIE. How can you talk to our guests in this way? What's come over you?

MORRY. For once I'm saying the things I believe.

SOLLY. You've all strayed from the path of righteousness, there must be a change before God can enter.

MELVIN. Yes, it is rather stuffy in here. Toodleloo, have fun.
    *He goes.*

MILLIE. Morry, shall I send for the doctor? Do you want a rest?

MORRY. I've had a rest too long. Carry on, Rabbi—the house is yours.

SOLLY. Let's all be calm, my children, and remember the wise words of the Karma Sutra. Now I want you all to go onto your knees, and think sensuously about life—become ecstatic, at one with the pulsing beat of the throbbing universe. The fast begins tomorrow.

MILLIE. Fast?

ROMAINE. I'll die.

MILLIE. Look, what do you want? Just tell us. For charity? A bit more money? Here you are—just take it and go—
   MILLIE *takes money from her purse.*

SOLLY. You don't understand. I'm staying until the new heaven on earth is proclaimed—but don't worry, we're preparing for it right away—for Morry Swartz is to be the first acolyte.

MILLIE. Morry, listen, this is me—Millie, your wife. This will break our marriage.

MORRY. This will make our marriage.

MILLIE. This man is dangerous.

SOLLY. Of course I am. Because I'm going to wipe out pride, to drive out greed and hate, and place in its place love. And then there'll be a new heaven on earth.

MILLIE. Oh, how much will it cost us? I can't have a Rabbi in the house—what will the neighbours say?

SOLLY. Halleluiah, eventually.

MORRY. Darling, don't upset yourself—don't cry. How lucky we are to have this illustrious saint in our own living room.

MILLIE. If he doesn't leave this house right now, I will.

MORRY. You can't leave me.

MILLIE. That's what you think.

MORRY. But I need you.

MILLIE. It's him or me.

MORRY. He must stay.

MILLIE (*Cries*). I've never been so insulted in my life. Romaine, pack your bags, we'll show him. I'm going as far away as possible.

SARAH. Where to, Mum?

MILLIE. Bournemouth! He'll see, he doesn't think I'll do it! Romaine, I said pack the bags.

MORRY. Good luck to you, my love—you deserve a holiday. We both need a rest from each other.

MILLIE. What? How could you? After all these years? That settles it. Romaine! Will you go and pack those bags?
*She punches her daughter.*
It's all your fault.

ROMAINE. It always is. Mummy, don't leave them alone, who knows what will happen.

MORRY. Millie, please don't go—I need you.

MILLIE. You just said—

MORRY. I've changed my mind.

MILLIE. Well I haven't. I'm going to teach you a lesson once and for all. Come!
*She is about to stomp out and she pushes* ROMAINE.
Sarah, don't stay in this house, it may be catching.
*She goes out.*

FINK. You're overwrought, Morry, I understand.

MORRY. Good-bye, Mr. Fink.
FINK *goes out after* MRS. FINK. MORRY *speaks to* SARAH *and* ALAN.
You going to Bournemouth with your mother?

SARAH. What, and break my honeymoon? Not on your life. We're going back to Marble Arch. Bye-bye, Daddy, I wish you better.
*She kisses her father and leaves with* ALAN.

SOLLY. Well, it worked. (*They shake hands*) Am I not a great psychologist? Now we're in business.
FINK *furtively appears as he puts on his coat.*

FINK. Did I hear someone mention business? Can you cut me in, gentlemen? I've got connections.

SOLLY. We're going to be a very limited company.

FINK. Too bad. I want you to understand, Morry, that I sympathise with you completely. We men should demand equality. I love the way you stood up to her.

SOLLY. Good-bye, you old hypocrite.

FINK. Good-bye, Rabbi, I love your sense of humour—they need putting in their place—they need a firm hand.

MRS. FINK (*Off*). Herbert? Where are you?

FINK. Coming, love. (*He hurries out*)

MORRY. Peace at last; all my life, for fifty years I've had screaming people around me, and you pulled it off.

SOLLY. But be careful, they'll try and turn you against me—people are afraid of purity.

MORRY. Just let them try. Oh well, I'll miss Millie, you know.

SOLLY. You won't have time. You'll be busy becoming the great messiah. Oh, I can see you now—virgins dancing around you and children, dressed in white, pelting you with rose petals.

MORRY. I don't want to show off, I want to be a quiet messiah. I don't want them to laugh at me.

SOLLY. They'll cry as you pass, cry for joy. I'll do all the talking and you do all the hand waving. (*Waves like an old queen*) You know, just like politicians at election time—
  MILLIE *comes in having hastily packed. She is followed by* ROMAINE.

MILLIE. Right, I'm all ready. I'll be staying at the Atlantic Hotel, Bournemouth. When you get rid of the Rabbi telephone me and I may consider coming home. You'll see, my boy, you'll learn.

MORRY. Get sunburnt and don't eat too much candy floss, and remember you're a vegetarian.

MILLIE. Right, that settles it. Good-bye! Come on, Romaine—what are you dawdling for?
  *She pulls* ROMAINE *off.*

MORRY. This calls for a celebration. I can't believe it! (*Looks out of window*) Yes, they're really going.

SOLLY. Now we must plan, prepare, organise.

MORRY. What can I do to help?

SOLLY. At the moment nothing but just give me a few hundred quid or so to start with, for petty cash.

MORRY. Sure. How much, exactly?

SOLLY. Eight hundred and fifty should see us through to the week-end.

MORRY. I'll get it for you.

*MORRY goes out of the room.*

SOLLY. Here's to Morry Swartz, the saviour—certainly saved me. Give us your money, we know what to do with it. Empty your pockets. Pop goes your sadness! Oh, I'll never go hungry again —not that I ever did. But this time I've hit the jackpot. (*To the mirror*) Well, and don't you deserve it? Ain't you working hard enough? Believe me, I like to see a Yiddisher feller getting on. You're looking well, take care of yourself. It does my heart good—so-long for now.

*He hears* MORRY *returning and returns to a pious posture.*
Give me the money.

*He snatches it and puts it away quickly.*
Shush! Don't move—hold your breath. (MORRY *obliges*) I'm getting a message. Turn off the light—I mean, pull the curtains. (MORRY *does so*) Ohyesohyesohyesohyes.

*He mumbles very fast some gibberish and moves backward and forward in typical Jewish praying style.*

MORRY. What is it?

SOLLY. A revelation. Shush—go on—I can hear you.

MORRY. Is it the Lord?

SOLLY. Shush! Yes sir, I've got that clear! We will do what you say—but my mother in the grave—yes sir. I understand— whatever you say. I've got the message and I'll pass it on! (*He turns to* MORRY) See them go? Radiant angels, look at them, what charm they have, did you ever. . . . Oh what do you think of those purple cloaks and those golden clouds like chariots—

(*Sings*) Bring me my bow of burning gold. . . .
Look!—just look at their halos— Good-bye. (*He waves at space*)

MORRY. Who are they?

SOLLY. Gabriel, Michael, and Raphael, of course. Didn't you see them?

MORRY. I'm not sure.

SOLLY. What, you didn't even see them?

MORRY. I—think I did.

SOLLY. I should think so too. Did you get the message? Surely you got the message—

MORRY. Almost—but it was a little blurred—please repeat it for me again.

SOLLY. It said that we must search for your throne—

MORRY. Yes, yes, I got that—where?

SOLLY. In the West End—it was plain enough. It once belonged to King Solomon and now it's going to be yours.

MORRY. What have I done to deserve all this? Why should I be chosen? I'm not worthy. How much will it be?

SOLLY. We must pay the earth if necessary. Don't worry, we'll beat them down. What's the matter, you worried about money all of a sudden?

MORRY. Of course not. Do you want it now? Shall we get it now?

SOLLY. No, plenty of time. We'll go tomorrow and we'll search all over Soho. That's where I'm sure it'll be, and do you know— I bet it won't cost more than three or four thousand.

MORRY. That cheap. What shall we do now?

SOLLY. Well, there's so much—lots of things, to buy—bills to get printed, clothes and everything, jewellery—ceremonial of course—but that can all wait till tomorrow. For the moment how about you and me going Morrie Bloom's and having some salt beef?

MORRY. But I thought we are vegetarians?

SOLLY. Don't be silly, that's for them, not for us. We must set the example but that doesn't mean we must follow it.

MORRY. I don't like that. I want to be pure. What's good for my Millie and everyone is good enough for me. Besides, I really feel now for the souls of little animals. It started as a joke but now I believe it.

SOLLY. Have it your own way but don't you see, how can we convert people to vegetables unless we go amongst the meat eaters? And where will we find meat eaters? Why, Bloom's, of course. And how can we go to Bloom's and not eat salt beef? Do me a favour. Use your head—don't worry—you'll lead the world, and I'll lead you.

*He puts* MORRY's *hat on and slaps him on the back and when* MORRY *smiles as if he understands,* SOLLY *leads him off.* MORRY *still seems slightly confused but* SOLLY's *smiling face seems finally to convince him.*

### THE CURTAIN FALLS

## SCENE FOUR

*A few days later. The contrast is amazing, for although it is the same room, all the furniture has been moved out. The room is completely transformed and now only contains a little table with a telephone on it, two chairs and a seductive couch. The peach mirrors remain. The interior, however, does not look bereft but rather like a throne room.* MELVIN *comes in, looks at himself in the mirrors, studies his nose, teeth and then starts exercising and then weight lifting. He is dressed in a swimming costume.* SOLLY *and* MORRY *enter, struggling under the weight of a grand looking throne.* MELVIN *doesn't notice them and carries on.* SOLLY *visually instructs* MORRY *of the exact place to centre the throne.*

SOLLY. There! Not bad for five thousand.

*He sits on it and smokes a cigar.* MORRY *sits on the floor.*

MORRY. Please let me smoke.

SOLLY. Please don't be so childish—you must practice frugality and economy. Self-denial is the way to sainthood.

MORRY (*Peers at the throne*). He said it was solid gold—I can't see it.

SOLLY. It's spirit gold. Can't you see the aura? It looks like wood but it has a spiritual inner tube.

MORRY. When is the coronation?

SOLLY. Be patient. Aren't you happy with the day drawing near?

MORRY. I miss Millie.

SOLLY. Look, sit down here and realise your true responsibilities.

MORRY (*Sits down*). I feel better now. It was a miracle the way you came into my life. Any message from your mother, Melvin?

MELVIN. No.

MORRY (*Rising*). I must phone her. I want her to know that I want her to be happy—that I want her to be Queen Millie.

SOLLY. No, sit down. She must come to you, in her own time.

MORRY. It's the first time we've been apart.

SOLLY. Now, listen. For a few days now you've been worried. Well, it just won't do. It's not easy being messiah. You've just got to grow up and stand on your own feet. You're not allowed to worry, you've got to radiate happiness and calm.

MORRY. Look, have a heart, I'm only just indentured, don't expect me to be a fully fledged graduate. You sure she didn't phone, Melvin?

MELVIN. Dad, leave me alone. I'm practising for the Maccabee games this evening.

SOLLY. I shall walk out on you if you continue like this.

MORRY. Please be patient with me. I'll be alright.

SOLLY. Now I must phone Rabbi Teitlebaum to tell him the latest news. You go to your room and stare at the sky. I want you to study cloud formations—add up the large ones, then add up the little ones and take one from the other and take away the first number you thought of.

MORRY. Thank you. There are moments when I lost heart. Thank you for being so firm and nice to me.

> He goes out counting on his fingers, trying to remember SOLLY's instructions. SOLLY picks up phone and dials.

SOLLY. Hello? International? Get me Washington, America— Central 19684. This is Speedwell 4756. Who? (*He looks at* MELVIN *and whispers*)
Joe Bloom— Yes, Joseph Bloom. What? Half an hour delay? What are you doing at that exchange? Exchanging dirty stories? Alright, you do that. (*He puts down phone*) They're going to ring back.

    MELVIN *is standing on his head.*
Isn't it a miracle? Do you know you can phone anywhere? Australia! Japan! Solomon Islands! I used to think they belonged to me. Who do I know in India? Good job I'm not rich, I'd spend it all on trunk calls. What are you doing standing like that? You hoping to become the Premier of Israel? Why do you waste all your time with muscle stuff?

MELVIN (*Stands upright*). Look, I don't tell you how to pray. So don't tell me how to play.

SOLLY. At your age you should be having a good time with girls.

MELVIN. Not interested.

SOLLY. All this sport is a cover up for the things you're really longing for.

MELVIN. Nice advice, coming from you.

SOLLY. Sex is nice, it's here to stay. You can't get away from it, it follows you everywhere. Don't swallow it, wallow in it— find yourself a nice girl, not too nice. When I was a young man I knew my onions.

MELVIN. *You?*

SOLLY. Girls were my downfall before I picked myself up. It was the fat girls—oh, fat girls were the ruin of me and the making of me. I still have a soft spot for them.

MELVIN. You surprise me.

SOLLY. Listen, a dog collar doesn't stop a man being a dirty dog. Mind you, I don't mean myself—I'm finished with all that now.

    *He puts on a record. The majestic choir of "The Messiah" by Handel is heard.*
Do yourself a favour—sow your wild oats on fertile feminine ground. Throw away your discus, take up the challenge.

MELVIN. But I'm shy—how do I start?

SOLLY. If you see a skirt, follow it. You're a man now—follow your natural instincts. Forget all about games, that sort of game—and play the game of life. A woman is the prey and you are the beast—and do they love it. Follow your natural inclinations—haven't you got any? You must have. Look at yourself—all them pimples; disgusting! Put some brilliantine on your hair, a smile on your face. (*He illustrates all this for* MELVIN) Then saunter amongst them, looking supercilious, debonaire, aggressive, like a lion, like a peacock—

MELVIN. All at the same time?

SOLLY. Like this: Inscrutable—slinky. Pout your nostril all the while and clench your jaw. (MELVIN *tries it*) And you'll be a wow. Go amongst them boy—there are masses of waiting virgins—go and break their . . . hearts.

*He puts up the volume of the record and he leads* MELVIN *out.*

Come, I'll help you choose the right suit.

*The music blares out.* ROMAINE *and* MILLIE *appear. They enter, gasp, and rush out of the room again after screaming. Then they stealthily creep back in again and* ROMAINE *turns the record off.*

MILLIE. It must be the wrong house.

ROMAINE. No, this is my record player but not my record. Oh, Mummy—

MILLIE. Oh, Dolly—what can we do? We're ruined! I'll kill him —kill him— Where's everything? (*She weeps*) I'm finished, finished.

ROMAINE. Mummy, don't cry, pull yourself togeth—(*She cries*) Ohohohohohohohohoho!

MILLIE. Romaine, I'm ashamed of you, always going to pieces in a crisis. Stop crying and be a big girl. (*She looks round the room*) Oh my lovely television set—where is it?

*She cries again and now they lean on each other and both weep.*

This is the end. I'll pull my hair out, I'll scream—I'll faint, I'll kill myself. Have you got a cigarette? (ROMAINE *gives her one*) Turn your back for five minutes—I'll kill him.

ROMAINE. I told you not to go. I warned you against that rabbi.

MILLIE. If we didn't go you'd have been head over heels in love with him.

ROMAINE. Me? Bloody cheek.

MILLIE. I saw you falling for that snake in the grass.

ROMAINE. *Me?* You think I'd throw myself away on that low-life?

MILLIE. That swine.

ROMAINE. A villain!

MILLIE. Crook. Rogue.

ROMAINE. Monster. Maybe it wasn't him.

MILLIE. Who else? Oh, we're ruined. My Sheraton! My cocktail cabinet, my virginals! He's taken everything, and your father's gone off his rocker. That's where you get it from.

ROMAINE. What are we going to do?

MILLIE (*Goes to phone*). The police, that's the only thing. (*Dials*)

ROMAINE (*Stopping her*). You out of your mind? Find out first who's taken the furniture. Who you going to accuse?

MILLIE. That terrible man! Don't you see, we've got to get him out. He's after our money.

ROMAINE. Who isn't? Listen, if you call the police, it will get into the papers and we'll be the laughing stock of the neighbourhood.

MILLIE. Better a laughing stock with money than being respectable and broke. Your father's mad—stone bonks. I must call the police.

ROMAINE. Alright, if he's mad they'll take him away, then there'll be a whole legal rigmarole. Meanwhile we'll all be starving.

MILLIE. Sometimes you use that stupid brain of yours. You're right. But I still say you've fallen for him.

ROMAINE. Fallen? May I drop down dead on this spot if I have! Oh, I feel wobbly at the knees—(*She collapses on the small settee*)

MILLIE. Darling, don't swear your life away, it's precious to me. Love is blind. You've done nothing else but talk about him since we left. I'm not a fool—you make me so mad. Feeling better, Dolly? My whole family's turning against me.

ROMAINE. Do you honestly think I'd fall for a rat like that?

MILLIE. Yes. Never mind, he's enticed you the way he has Morry. He's hypnotic—you know, like Rasputin.

ROMAINE. I never met him.

MILLIE. What have I done? Am I bad? Haven't I given to charity? Why should it happen to me?

MELVIN (*Breezes in*). Lo, Mum. Lo, Roroe. Back already?

MILLIE (*Falls on him*). Melvin! Darling! What's happening?

MELVIN (*Releasing himself*). You're smothering me.

MILLIE. What's been happening here?

MELVIN. Oh, I don't know. Something or other. Must dash now —I'm late as it is.

ROMAINE. But where's the furniture?

MELVIN. Oh yes, it's gone, isn't it? And about time too—it was simply gasters. Now, Mummy, please—later. I'll be late for the games.

MILLIE. Where's your father?

MELVIN. Your husband is contemplating or some such thing—

somewhere or other. Well, tata for now.
    *She won't let him go yet.*

MILLIE. And where's that snake of a Rabbi?

MELVIN. He's a very nice chap and I won't hear a word against him. Since he's been here the house has been tolerable.

MILLIE. What's he doing to your father?

MELVIN. I don't know and I don't care. I'm off now, please keep your fingers crossed for me. (*He goes*)

MILLIE. When I see that Morry I'll kill him.
    MORRY *wanders on, looking very happy and very far away. He sees* MILLIE *and kisses her.*

MORRY. Hello, Millie—how are you darling? Two weeks passed already?

MILLIE (*She stifles her anger*). I only stayed away two days. Do you think I'd trust you here any longer? Look what's happened already. What have you been doing?

MORRY. Looking at the clouds. I never knew they were so beautiful. Have you ever looked at clouds, Millie? Shall we both do it together now? And there are birds in London—and trees. I've never seen them before.

MILLIE. He's gone cuckoo. Listen Morry, come to your senses.

MORRY. All my senses are working overtime. I can smell and hear and see and touch.

MILLIE. This Rabbi is a phoney. Did you see his credentials?

MORRY. Do I ask for the credentials of God? He is honest and beautiful. The most trustworthy person I ever met.

MILLIE. How do you know?

MORRY. I know because I know.

MILLIE. How do you know you know?

MORRY. Because I'm happy. Really happy.

MILLIE. How do you know you're happy? You're not happy. You only think you are. He's taking you for a ride—I feel it in my water.

MORRY. It's a lovely journey and at the end of it I shall be the messiah.

ROMAINE. Messiah?

MILLIE. Messiah? Romaine, shut up—don't interfere. Listen Morry—carefully—take it easy. Did you say messiah?

MORRY. Yes, very soon now I shall be ready, when I reach perfection.

MILLIE. He won't make a messiah of you, you bloody fool. He'll make a mess of you. You're sinning—do you know you're sinning?

MORRY. Thought you didn't believe in God. Sinning against who?

MILLIE. Sinning against me—against you—against everything. Listen, Morry, look at me—I'm your wife, your other half. How

can you be a messiah? You're overwrought. I understand.
There ain't no such person as God and thank God there isn't,
because if he existed you'd really go to hell, and please God,
soon you realise all this and come to your senses.

MORRY. All I want is for you and everyone to be happy. Don't
get angry with me. I'm so happy.

MILLIE. I could ki—
> Turns to ROMAINE *as if to show her they must bear with
> him for the moment.*
It's just that you're getting old, Morry, old and scared.

MORRY. I'm not old. I'm as young as the world, and happy and
free. I must go now and see the new moon rise. (*He sails off*)

ROMAINE. Poor Daddy. Isn't it funny, he's happy and we're sorry
for him. Poor Daddy.

MILLIE. We'll have to humour him. I'll even become vegetarian
to please him now. How could he change so quick? He wouldn't
trust a fly till that Rabbi came along.

ROMAINE. Everybody believes what he wants to believe, believe me.

MILLIE. Oh shut up you! It's all your fault.

ROMAINE. But I told you I didn't trust him.

MILLIE. Now be quiet will you, and stop bickering. We've got
to think of a way. To make Daddy see, somehow. But we
musn't let the Rabbi know that we suspect he's a phoney.
> *The phone rings and they both dash for it but* SOLLY
> *enters the room briskly and while they are struggling for the
> receiver he takes it from them.*

SOLLY. If it's from America, it's for me. Would you mind, please?
This call is confidential—please leave the room.

MILLIE. From America? What do you think we are—millionaires?

ROMAINE. He wouldn't be far out.

SOLLY. Now leave the room, please. You shouldn't be here anyway, but in Bournemouth. This is urgent. Rabbi Teitlebaum!
> *They go but stand in the doorway. He is aware of this
> fact and has to modulate his conversation accordingly.
> Every time he looks at the door they pretend not to be
> there.*

'Lo! State Department? I want Joe Cohen in the visa section. Hurry, this is costing a bomb. (*Pretends now to pray*) I'll hold on, yes I'll hold on—oh God in heaven, give me the strength to hold on. Extension five-nine-one, so be it. Hurry up, for St. Peter's sake. Wrong testament? Sorry. Hurry up, oh Lord— Hello! Joe? You old bastard, this is me! Who, he says! Solly Gold— Don't hang up—listen! I've got money! M—o—honey— Money for a change. Listen, I need a visa urgently—I'm loaded, loaded man, and I'm all ready to blow. What's that? But I tell ya I've got loot. So make me a visa and be a sport. Who picked you up when you were on the floor? (*He sees the women coming closer*) Do you mind? No? Not you— GOooo— — For he will bring the wicked down to the ground! I'm loaded—would I lie? What do you mean? Gone respectable? Gone straight? Don't give me that! Joe, Joe—you can't do that to me. Listen! (*Sees the women again*) Thou shalt not covet thy neighbour's daughter nor his peach mirrors—Joe! Don't do this to me—remember the old days when we were both crooked and keep it holy. Joe, you're a lousy swine—you're my only hope! Joe! Joe! Joe. . . . (*Realises the women are there once more*) And Joseph brought the evil report of them unto his father (*Pretends to quote from Bible—then enraged again*) Oh, you rotten—lousy—stinking— good-for-nothing. . . . (*He sees the women again*) Bye-bye, Rabbi Teitlebaum . . . Let the wicked be no more. I'll let you know— He hung up! You can't trust no one. (*He puts the receiver down*) Hello, my daughters, how was Bournemouth? Still kosher and godless?

MILLIE. Hello, Rabbi, glad to see you looking so well, and I'm glad to see you looked after Morry.

SOLLY. Where is he?

ROMAINE. In the garden watching the moon.

SOLLY. Good. I'll find him. Well, welcome home. Are you thoroughly cleansed and vegetarian now?

ROMAINE *is about to protest when her mother shuts her up.*

MILLIE. What else? It's wonderful! Nuts and raisins for breakfast, turnips and lettuce for lunch, and carrots for supper.

SOLLY. Good! Good! You've got a glow in your face. (*He goes off*)

MILLIE. May he rot, may he burn—may he get run over and smashed—may he drown.

ROMAINE. And all at once.
MR. *and* MRS. FINK *and* ALAN *and* SARAH *enter.*

SARAH. Mummy! You're back.
*They kiss.*

ALAN. What's the matter, where's the furniture?

MILLIE. Sarah darling, we're in terrible trouble.

SARAH. I know, I've been having nightmares.

MILLIE. The Rabbi is a charlatan—what can we do?

ROMAINE. He's fleecing us—taking us for a ride.

FINK. I told you so.

MILLIE. No you didn't.

FINK. I could have told you so.

MRS. FINK. Shut up. It was a palace here, a real palace. Where's the furniture? Where?

FINK. The woodworm run away with it. (*Nobody laughs*) Ha-hahahahaha! I'm only trying to cheer everyone up.

ALAN. What's it all add up to?

MILLIE. My Morry thinks he's the new messiah no less. (*She weeps*)

ROMAINE. And that Solly Gold is getting all our money and Daddy won't hear a word against him.

FINK. I knew it. I can smell a crook a mile off.

MRS. FINK. What will the neighbours say?
*She cuddles* ALAN.
Oh my poor boy

SARAH. To hell with the neighbours—what about us?

FINK. Open and shut case. Leave it to me, let Fink think— Simple—the police!
*Goes to phone.*

MILLIE. What? And let my Morry be the laughing stock of all the world?

ROMAINE. They'll take him off in a strait jacket.

SARAH. And we'll be starving while the lawyers argue.

FINK. Poor Morry—what can we do?

ALAN. We must think of something.
  MORRY *wanders in.*

MORRY. Hello everyone. Lovely evening. I just saw Sirius and
  Orion, and heard the music of the spheres. I'm no longer just
  Morry Swartz of Golders Green—I'm Morris Swartz of the
  Universe. I'll see you all on the great day. Toodleloo.
    *Wanders out again and the women cry and the men shake
    their heads.*

SARAH. He overtaxed his brain.

MILLIE. He never had a brain—only an adding machine up there.

ALAN. Hold it—I've got an idea coming up! Shush. . . .

SARAH. Isn't he marvellous? I could eat him.

ROMAINE. Not yet, wait till he comes out with it.

ALAN. Got it! (*Claps his hand*) That Rabbi Whatyoumaycallit,
  must confess directly to your father, must say that he's a complete phoney, now how? How can we get him to confess?
    *They all walk backward and forward thinking.*
  Who would he tell the truth to? Who has he got a weakness
  for?
    ROMAINE *is somehow now in the centre of a circle of walk-
    ing people, they all stop together, turn and stare at her.*

ROMAINE. What's up? What have I done?

SARAH. It's not what you've done, it's what you're going to do.

ALAN. I've seen the way he stares at you. You'll have to do it.

ROMAINE. Do what? I'm getting out of here.
    *She tries to go but* MILLIE *stops her.*

MILLIE. Dolly, do you love me? Do you love your father? Do you
  love luxury? Well, then you'll have to help us all.

FINK. Only you could make him confess.

ROMAINE. But I don't trust him.

MRS. FINK. This time you don't need to.

SARAH. Lead him on a little, get him hot under the collar—

ALAN. Tell him you're passionately in love with him but unfortunately you couldn't give yourself to a Rabbi—

FINK. Tell him it's against your principles, and you could make love to a layman—

ROMAINE. Are you all mad or something? What do you take me for?

MILLIE. A good girl. And when he confesses that he isn't a rabbi, lead him on a bit more—tell him you don't like good boys—

ALAN. And when he confesses that he's a crook. . . . (*Thinks for the next move*)

SARAH. You'll switch on Melvin's tape recorder that we'll hide under the couch.

MILLIE. And when Daddy hears the tape, we'll be rid of that worm.

ROMAINE. I won't be left alone with him.

MILLIE. You'll be alright, don't worry.

ROMAINE. Do you think I'm gonna sacrifice my purity for rotten money?

FINK. You've got to lose it sooner or later.

MRS. FINK. Herbert, shut up. Listen, Romaine, we all have to take chances—

ROMAINE. You're all against me.

ALAN. Whatever happens, we'll sympathise and understand. We're depending on you. I expect you'll pull it off.

ROMAINE. Nobody cares for my feelings (*She almost weeps*) I'll be expecting, alright, with that snake in the grass. Mummy, look at me! I'm your daughter. Your own flesh and blood. Don't leave me alone with that monster.

MILLIE. Listen, your purity, my darling, is worth all the tea in China, all the gold in Hatton Garden. Don't worry, we won't let it go too far. If you scream we'll break the door down—but don't scream unless you can help it, they cost enough. He'll confess. After all aren't you a lovely girl? And why not, why be ashamed of what you've got?

ROMAINE. Oh go on then, go, leave me alone. What do I care? *She does a great tragedy act and falls on the sofa.*

MILLIE. Good luck, Dolly—a lot's at stake.

ROMAINE. Telling me!

FINK. We'll wait in there and be as quiet as little mice.

ROMAINE. Don't look through the keyholes—I'll be embarrassed. Promise?

ALL. Promise.

MILLIE. Where's the tape machine? Melvin's room?

SARAH. No, it's in here.
*SARAH gets it from the other room and brings it in and places it under the sofa.*
It's all ready. At the crucial moment just switch on, like this: *She demonstrates and then they all troop into the other room and shut the door.*

ROMAINE (*Overplaying*). What do they care? Do they consider my feelings? I shall run away!
*She overweeps and then stops as she sees herself in the mirror.*
How marvellous. I looked like Anna Magnani just then.
*She smiles and poses in front of the mirror as if to make herself look enticing, then she weeps again.*
Oh, what do they care—leaving me with that shark.
*She switches off the main lighting and the indirect lighting, now makes the room look seductive. She sprays perfume upon herself and then puts on a soft tango. She settles down and starts to eat Turkish delight but changes her mind and then, fixing her dress to look more sexy, she dances to the music seductively. Then we see SOLLY. He comes on like a furtive fly, in quick, sharp jerking angular movements, as if drawn by an irresistible impulse. He is about to go directly to her, but goes to the adjoining door, where the family are, and locks that door on this side. When she sees this she starts to get panicky, but carries on—dancing. Suavely he pours two drinks and goes to her. As she drinks, he pinches her on the bottom.*
Stop pinching me—I'll go black and blue.

SOLLY. I don't care what colour you go—I like you anyway. I don't hold with the colour bar.

ROMAINE. It's not nice, not decent, getting fresh like that.

SOLLY. I'm sorry but you see I'm homesick and my fingers twitch. Care for another drink?

ROMAINE. I'd like a bunny hug.
*He hugs her passionately. She struggles to get free.*

ROMAINE. I didn't mean that. I meant the drink. Cherry brandy and Advocaat.
*He pours her a vast glass full.*
Eh! When! When!

SOLLY. Anytime you want to.

ROMAINE. I didn't mean that! I meant—that's enough in the glass.
SOLLY *gives her the drink and then takes her arms and pushes her into a dance.*

SOLLY. May I have this dance? Do you come here often? What a smashing bit of overtime you are.

ROMAINE. I think you're crude.

SOLLY. Sorry, I get carried away by your beauty—what I mean is, God worked overtime when he created you.

ROMAINE. Never knew that rabbis drink, and dance, and pinch girls.

SOLLY. What else? All work and no play makes Jacob a very miserable geezer. Haven't you read the Songs of Solomon? But anyway—you are so marvellous I could even leave my religious world for you. Let's sit down. I want to give you some spiritual instruction.

ROMAINE. No, no, I'm afraid.

SOLLY. Foolish lady, I'll look after you. Sit down, I'll make it worth your while.

ROMAINE. I shouldn't really.
*She sits down.*

SOLLY. Doing what we shouldn't is one way of finding out the mysteries of creation.
*She leans down to switch on the machine and as she does*

*so he kisses her. First she struggles but then she subsides into his arms and while doing so, she switches off the machine again.*

ROMAINE. You're free with your kisses. But what about your dead wife and your vow of chastity?

SOLLY. I know Sophie wouldn't mind.

ROMAINE. You said her name was Miriam.

SOLLY. Don't change the subject, I'm doing my nut over you. When the ape is king dance before him—and desire is ruling my soul right now. Shall we dance?

ROMAINE. Please come down to earth, I've got something to tell you.

SOLLY. You are as pure as the moon, as passionate as the sun, my dove.

ROMAINE. Make up your mind.

SOLLY. My undefiled one.

ROMAINE. And I intend to stay that way. Now listen! I don't know who you are or what you're after, but I'm giving you a chance to get away.

SOLLY. How beautiful are thy feet in sandals—

ROMAINE. I've got corns.

SOLLY. The joints of thy thighs are like jewels.

ROMAINE. And they're staying in the safe because you're a thief. But I like you, so I'm giving you a chance to run. Run, before you're caught.

SOLLY. What are you talking about? I've got nothing to be ashamed of.

ROMAINE. I don't know why I'm telling you, but I don't trust you, so don't try and get round me. You're a bad boy and you know it.

SOLLY. Me? I'm a—angel, a saint. Ask anyone.

ROMAINE. Listen, you can trust me. There's no time to lose.

SOLLY. Enough of this.

ROMAINE. You're no good.

SOLLY. What's good? What's bad? Relative terms, my daughter. Thy navel is like a round goblet.

ROMAINE. Cheek! How dare you, you've never seen me! Oh don't you see I'm on to your game? You're a fraud.

SOLLY. Enough of this, let's get down to something serious—let me kiss you, let me love you!
*He tries furiously to embrace her, but she keeps freeing herself. It's almost a chase.*

ROMAINE. It's because I like you that I won't go along with them —let them do their own dirty work.

SOLLY. Thy belly is like a heap of wheat.

ROMAINE. That's the last straw.

SOLLY. Forgive me, I get carried away. I was only quoting from the Bible.

ROMAINE. Then it should be banned.

SOLLY. Nonsense, it's beautiful—have you ever read it?

ROMAINE. No, but I've seen the film. Please, listen, there's no time to waste.

SOLLY. Alright, spit it out, what's it all about?

ROMAINE. Now he hears. Solly, my family are on to your game, they are trying to get me to make you confess. I'm the decoy.

SOLLY. On to my game? Confess? Confess to what?

ROMAINE. You can trust me, I'm on your side. I must be mad, but I am.

SOLLY. Why should I trust you all of a sudden?

ROMAINE. Because here's the tape machine that I was supposed to switch on when you started confessing.

SOLLY (*As she shows him the machine*). Tape machine? What are you talking about? I'm a servant of the Lord.

ROMAINE. I must be mad—I'm out of my little mind. Fancy telling you, but you've turned my head—turned it against my own family. I'll never live it down. I'm no good.

SOLLY (*Embracing her*). We make a fine pair.

ROMAINE. So you own up that you're a crook?

SOLLY. Not on your life. I'm straight—straight up—strait as a jacket.

ROMAINE. Solly, Solly, oh Solly boy, you can trust me.
*She cuddles him.*

SOLLY. Why should I?

ROMAINE. Cos I want to see you get away—I don't want them to catch you. Because you're romantic. Take what you want and go.

SOLLY. I want you. But why are you doing this for me? I can't believe it.

ROMAINE. Look! They're waiting in there, waiting for me to entice a confession out of you—I swear on my soul, on my purity, that I'm on your side and speaking the truth. By my Aunt Sadie's life.

SOLLY. Alright then, if that's the case I'll be on my merry way. Good-bye, maybe we'll meet in the desert.

ROMAINE. Not so fast. Just one little thing before you go. Please tell me everything—tell me why a nice boy like you should be such a bad boy.

SOLLY. Why? You want to redeem me? Sorry, I pawned myself ages ago and lost the ticket.

ROMAINE. Oh Solly, what can I do? I've fallen for you, for a tyke like you. My mum always told me I was no class. I've fallen right down.

SOLLY. Don't believe you. (*She kisses him*) Well, maybe I believe you a bit—kiss me again (*She does*) Yeah! Oh, Romaine—I could feel your whole heart pouring into that kiss.

ROMAINE. I want to help you. Can't you see that? Tell me about yourself.

SOLLY. Alright, I admit I'm not a Rabbi. I'm a liar, a lobos, a gonif. You know—I take things from people who can afford to do without. But I'm the best con man in the business—the world's not much to write home about is it?

ROMAINE. Maybe, but fancy doing your tricks on my father, he's such a good man.

SOLLY. Alright, so now you know. Happy? I'm a lowlife. I'm a thief. That let's me out. . . .
> *He turns his back and is about to go when he turns back and smiles.*

Run away with me.

ROMAINE. Where?

SOLLY. Anywhere.

ROMAINE. Run away? No, I couldn't.

SOLLY. Why not?

ROMAINE. Why not? Why not? I love my luxury.

SOLLY. Now's your chance to really live.

ROMAINE. I couldn't run fast enough to keep up with you. Besides I'm too selfish—I've got so much to give that I need a lot in return. . .

MILLIE (*Off*). You alright, Dolly?

ROMAINE. Fine—fine! Hurry, hurry—Solly, Solly, time is pressing.

SOLLY. Nobody here understands you—how deeply romantic you are. Just like me. Chasing the stars, looking for kicks and only getting kicked in the teeth. Look at you—you're a child of the sun, a victim of circumstance holding on to your chastity—saving it all for a rainy day. But why be a pessimist? No one can love you like me. You're fat and I love you that way.

ROMAINE. I'm not fat, I'm well built. Besides, I'm starting to diet tomorrow.

SOLLY. No! No! No! You musn't do that. I'm crazy about you the way you are. I'll take you to the life of luxury you dream about—a life of romance in the best hotels, as much Turkish Delight as you want, we'll go to Rome, Miami, Glasgow.

ROMAINE. But you're a liar, Solly, how can I believe you?

SOLLY. What's truth? Ask philosophers, they're all in the dark—

ROMAINE. But you've committed crimes, I know it. You're on the run.

SOLLY. Who isn't on the run? I'm not bad darling, I'm just not good.

ROMAINE. How can I do this to my family after all they did for me?

SOLLY. Such as?

ROMAINE. Offhand I can't remember.

SOLLY. With me you'll come first—after me. No more dull life. I'm your man from now on and you'll hide with me. Hiding and flying—romance on the run. Snatched hours of passion in hotel bedrooms; different places, different faces. Romaine, your humdrum life is almost over for Solly Gold is taking over. Give me another kiss. (*They kiss*) There's plenty more in store where that came from, and so much more—oh so much more. Why have I told you everything? You know more than anyone now! It's the first time I've told anyone anything. I must love you—I must really love.

ROMAINE. That settles it. I'll get my things.

SOLLY. Don't bother, I'll buy you everything new on Broadway next week.

ROMAINE. With what? On peanuts and prayers?

SOLLY. With the money I've got from your father already and the money I'm getting from him in a minute or two.

ROMAINE. Oh Solly, I was forgetting that. It's so dishonest.

SOLLY. Is it dishonest to make him happy for the first time in years? You'll help me.

ROMAINE. I'll never forgive myself.

SOLLY. You don't have to—Good will. We'll fill a suitcase full of fivers and be on our merry way.

ROMAINE. It is true, he *is* much happier. That can't be bad, can it? What about the police?

SOLLY (*He jumps*). Please, I don't like bad language. That word makes my blood run cold. We'll go to the docks tonight and get a boat. Let's call your father now.

ROMAINE. One minute, I'm not coming with you unless you marry me.

SOLLY. Don't you relish sin? Silly girl—alright! I'll marry you, on the other side.

ROMAINE. Other side of where?

SOLLY. Tell you when we get there.

ROMAINE. Just one thing more—are you sure you're not married?

SOLLY. Absolutely, definitely not—I cross my heart, that's the truth so help me God. Come on—

ROMAINE. There's just one other thing—

SOLLY. I love the way you're so concise. What is it?

ROMAINE. Where did you get the Rabbi's clothes?

SOLLY. From an old lady in the East End.

ROMAINE. You must take them back, I'm superstitious.

SOLLY. Let me burn then, let me chuck them away.

ROMAINE. No! We'll take them back to her on our way to the docks.

SOLLY. It's too risky.

ROMAINE. If you love me you'll do it—just this once, for me.

SOLLY. I must learn the art of blackmail from you. Alright, and now I'll find your father. Wait here for me.
*He pretends to go but hides and watches* ROMAINE.

MILLIE (*Off*). You alright, Dolly?

ROMAINE. Sure.

MILLIE (*Off*). How's it going?

ROMAINE. Perfect.

SARAH (*Off*). Got the recording yet?

ROMAINE. Not yet, be patient.
SOLLY *is obviously satisfied with her, and goes before she sees him. Now she poses herself in front of the mirror, and obviously she thinks she is stunningly beautiful.*
Oh God forgive me, but I must grab the opportunity. Why not? Eh? Oh romance, Romaine—romance at last!
SOLLY *brings* MORRY *on.*

SOLLY. Well Morry, the great day approacheth and verily I say unto you that a purple light surrounds you. Sit on your throne.

MORRY. How we doing, Solly? What's the score?

SOLLY. Great news. We're almost there—I saw half a dozen angels at Golders Green Station today—they're assembling and all roads converge here and now rejoice even more so, for your blessed daughter Romaine has become an acolyte. She is our very latest and brightest disciple. She has repented from her evil ways and stands before us, devoting herself to the cause.

MORRY. About time too.

ROMAINE. Daddy darling, how you feeling?

MORRY. Never felt better in my life.

ROMAINE. Solly, let's go now.

SOLLY. Yes. Now listen Morry, Romaine and I are going on a pilgrimage

MORRY. I want to come with you.

SOLLY. I'm afraid that's impossible.

MORRY. It's so lonely becoming the messiah sometimes. Please!

SOLLY. Not tonight. We must go to sordid places to spread the word, to the docks to get love and give love. You must be unsullied—think only of higher things. And then we're going to Westcliffe-on-the-Sea where we'll distribute charities to the Jewish Society for the prevention of cruelty to dead poets and to the Sisters of Nathaniel Greenbaum. We'll need a little money for this purpose.

MORRY. How much?

SOLLY. Don't want to bother you with sordid details, tell me the combination of the safe and I'll save you the trouble.

MORRY. No, no, the secret of the combination dies with me. Not that I don't trust you. How much will you need?

SOLLY. Not too much, a few to begin with—about—erm—forty thousand?

MORRY. That's a lot of money.

SOLLY. It's to help the needy, the lonely, the sick, the lost, the sad dreamers and happy destitutes.

MORRY. Well that includes practically everyone alive. I'll get it. You going to give all this away tonight?

SOLLY. If I can. That's why I'm taking Romaine with me.

MORRY. Good. Money must go to those who need it. As for me, what else is it but bits of metal and paper around an idea? Forty thousand. Hope I've got that much loose laying around. . . .

    MORRY *goes off.*

ROMAINE. I don't like it; Daddy's out of his mind.

SOLLY. We've burnt our boats now and we're in this together—sink or swim. Don't worry. (*He calls out*) Morry! There'll be plaques up to you all over London "Morry Swartz, the saviour, saved our hospital"—"Morry Swartz, the messiah, got us out of a mess"—"Morry Swartz lived here"—"Morry Swartz ate here"—

    MORRY *enters with some packets of money and tosses them to* SOLLY.

MOLLY. Don't want no plaques, just a plain bit of marble when I die, saying: "He tried to do good." Hope that keeps you busy.

    As SOLLY *stuffs it into the suitcase.*

ROMAINE. Daddy, Daddy, are you happy giving this away?

MORRY. The more that goes the happier I am.

ROMAINE. What about your life's work? You worked so hard?

MORRY. My life's work is just beginning. Listen darling, in this world you own nothing but your bones and even they let you down in the end. You come in with nothing and go out with nothing—and you're nothing unless you realise this, at least, now and again.

ROMAINE. Come on, Solly, time's getting on.

SOLLY. Rest now, Morry. Contemplate. Count the stars and lose yourself in the cosmos. Pray for us all, especially me, just in case—with all this money. We'll see you in the morning.

ROMAINE. Forgive me for everything.

MORRY. There's nothing to forgive. Go in peace. The way you both look so lovely, I could kiss you. As a matter of fact I will. (*He does so*) I'm so happy because before I only thought I was rich, now I know I am. Goodbye.

ROMAINE. Good-bye, come, Solly.

SOLLY. Good-bye, Morry—you're a lucky man. I'm carrying all your worries from now on.

> *He holds up the case and follows* ROMAINE *off.*
> MORRY *picks up the Bible that* SOLLY *has left behind, sits down and reads from it.*

MILLIE (*Off*). Romaine! You ready yet? Romaine? Are you there?

SARAH (*Off*). Romaine? Did you do it? Why don't she answer?
> *The door is tried and they furiously push it from the other side.*

MILLIE (*Off*). Romaine! Stop playing about. It's locked on the other side. Romaine! You alright? Darling where are you?

FINK (*Off*). I'll have to break the door down.
> MORRY *goes to the door and unlocks it just as* FINK *has flung himself against it. They all fall into the room.* MORRY *goes from them and sits on his throne.*

MILLIE. What are you doing?

MORRY. Isn't it obvious? Just sitting down.

SARAH. Where's Romaine?

MORRY. Gone with the Rabbi.

ALAN. Gone?

SARAH. Gone where?

MILLIE. What do you mean? Oh my poor baby.

MORRY. They've gone on a pilgrimage. She's in safe hands. Don't worry.

SARAH. Daddy, don't you realise, he's a crook! A no-good good-for-nothing. He's not a Rabbi!

FINK. I'm afraid you've been taken for a ride, Morry; it happens to the best of us.

MORRY. Don't worry about me, Fink. Go home and settle your own problems.

MILLIE. Take no notice, Herbert. Morry, you ought to be ashamed of yourself. Listen! Just listen to his confession.
> *She switches on the tape recorder and "The Messiah" blares out.*

MORRY. They're playing my music again.
> MILLIE *switches it off.*

MILLIE. Oh, my daughter! He's carried her off.

SARAH. That would have been difficult—

MILLIE. What's going to happen to her? I knew it.

MRS. FINK. Call the police, Millie, call the police.

MILLIE. What? And have her dragged through the Sunday papers? I'll never live through it.

MORRY (*Reads from the Bible*). Praise him with the sound of trumpets, with the stringed instruments and the pipe. Praise him upon the loud cymbals—
> MILLIE *crashes two metal trays together. Everyone jumps except* MORRY. MILLIE *also jumps.*

MILLIE. Will you shut up! He reads the Bible. Will that bring your sanity back? Don't you see? He's taken your furniture, your sanity, your money and your daughter. I suppose you won't be happy till he takes me!

MORRY. That's an interesting thought. (*Returns to the Bible*)

MILLIE. I knew all along, I knew it.

SARAH. What?

MILLIE. That he was a crook and she was no good. I knew it.

FINK. I knew you knew. So did I.

MRS. FINK. What did you know?

FINK. I knew that I knew. You didn't know—but I did. I told you so.

ALAN. I knew all along—he couldn't kid me.

SARAH. I didn't know then that I knew, but now I do.

MRS. FINK. I knew. I don't say much but I see all. I could tell from his face. I knew. Mark my words, I said, he's up to no good.

MILLIE. I knew it. I knew it. Serves them right. They deserve each other. What do you think of it, eh? Your own daughter. Please God, she should be safe, the lousy bitch. I knew it. I knew it would happen. I knew it.

MORRY *sits quietly reading and they all walk around his throne. Round and around they go, talking to themselves and trying to convince each other. Then suddenly they all come into one group and carry on with the above dialogue all over again and far more quickly. It seems they are about to come to blows, when*

## THE CURTAIN FALLS


## SCENE FIVE


*We are back in the East End. Scene is exactly the same as in the Prologue. It is early morning. The tailor is seen working away in his house, sewing frantically; he reacts— looks up, and soon we realise he has heard something.* SOLLY *comes on followed by* ROMAINE *who carries lots of cases. She seems all in.* SOLLY *is dressed in very American-looking clothes and he carries the Rabbi's clothes in a small bundle. The tailor comes to the window and hides as soon as he sees* SOLLY *but watches them all the time.*

ROMAINE. Why did we have to get up so early?

SOLLY. The boat leaves in an hour.

ROMAINE. I'm still asleep.

SOLLY. Here's the house. I'll dump it on the doorstep.

ROMAINE. Oh no you're not. You're giving it to the lady in person and apologise.

SOLLY. She won't be up this early.

ROMAINE. We'll wake her up.

SOLLY. You're very cruel. Look, the door's open. Obviously she still trusts people . . . let's go inside. (*He calls*) Yoohoo— yoohoo—
　　　*Soon they are inside and now we cannot see them.*
　　　JOE, *the tailor, jumps up and goes to a door in his house and calls his wife.*

JOE. Rita! Rita! Get up—get up quick! Rita, for God's sake get up—

> RITA *rushes in in her nightclothes, she is distraught and almost panicking.*

RITA. Joe, what is it? Is it bombs?

> *She tries to dress hurriedly and gets everything in the wrong place.*

JOE. Shush! That blaggard who got that money from us and the lady next door has returned.

RITA. Thank the lord. I thought the world had come to an end.

JOE. And guess what?—he's got with him that missing heiress, what's her name— —Rona Swarb or something—

RITA. Missing heiress?

JOE. Wake up. The one who was in the papers. The one that reward's for. You phone her mother quickly while I keep them here. The number's in the paper.

RITA. All night he works. All night. I just want to get some sleep. I'm fed up with you and the whole business.

JOE. Do as I say. We'll make a few hundred and I'll take you on a cruise. Quick!

> *She quickly runs for the newspaper and then goes into a backroom.* JOE *comes out of his house and creeps towards the next house just as* SOLLY *comes running out with* ROMAINE; *they are chased by the old woman who is throwing things at them.*

WOMAN. A fire on you! Get out of my sight!

SOLLY. I've come to pay you back—to make it worth your while.

WOMAN. What do you take me for? Think you can buy me after what you did?

> *She hits him with a stick and he takes shelter under his coat. He brings out several pound notes and waves them about.*

SOLLY. Truce! Truce! Is this flag the right colour?

WOMAN. Thief! Liar! Rogue! Crook—police . . .

> *She suddenly stops and takes the money.*

Get out of my sight! (*She is about to go inside*)

SOLLY (*To* ROMAINE). See darling, anything can be bought with money, especially people. When pound notes flash, principles crash.

WOMAN. I can't afford principles. They won't buy my husband's tombstone.
> *She is about to go in and* SOLLY *is about to go off with* ROMAINE *when he sees* JOE. *He is about to run when the*

SOLLY. Must you be so passionate?

JOE. So, you've returned to the scene of the crime?

SOLLY. Can't we talk this over like English gentlemen?

ROMAINE. Leave my Solly alone or I'll murder you.
> *As* JOE *gets off him* SOLLY *gets up.*

SOLLY. I'll explain and settle everything.

JOE. Wish there was a copper about; they're never around when you want one.

SOLLY. I agree with you. And it all comes out of the taxpayer's pocket.
> RITA *comes out*

JOE. Well, what have you got to say for yourself?

SOLLY. Help.

JOE. You're a lousy rat.

SOLLY. Let me go and I'll make it worth your while.

JOE. You can't buy me.

SOLLY. I actually came to give you your money back.

RITA. There you are, Joe—I knew he was an honest feller.

SOLLY. Look, here's the money. I'll give you twice as much.

JOE. Nothing doing, I won't be bought. I demand justice.

SOLLY. You're living in the wrong world.
> *The* PROSTITUTE *comes from her room.*

PROSTITUTE. What's all the noise? Can't a nightworker get some decent sleep?
> JOE *is holding* SOLLY *by the arm and* ROMAINE *is trying to*

*pull him in the other direction. The* PROSTITUTE *walks around* SOLLY.
Haven't we met before?

SOLLY. Perhaps in some previous incarnation.

PROSTITUTE. I've heard it called some things. Why are you holding him?

JOE. He owes me money.

SOLLY. I've offered to pay him back, twofold.

ROMAINE. It's the truth, honestly it is.

JOE. I don't want to be paid back, I want justice.

SOLLY. There he goes again, using horrible words, makes me shudder. Just think of that poor old bitch, Justice—blind, deaf, dumb, crippled, and no hands.

WOMAN. He's a thief. He got money out of me, my poor husband's clothes, and chickens.

PROSTITUTE. Come on, Joe, let the poor blighter go, the law will be around if you're not careful.

RITA. Let him go, Joe, we don't want no trouble.

SOLLY. Lady, I admire your common sense. Joe, do what your wife says.

JOE. I'm thinking about this poor girl here. He's a deceiver, leading her up the garden.

SOLLY. It ain't half pretty.

JOE. Don't you see he's no good? (*To* ROMAINE) How can you fall for a type like this?

SOLLY. I'm not a type, I'm a specie.

ROMAINE. Soll's a good boy, I've changed him. Leave him alone.

RITA. Come on, Joe, let's go to bed. Poor girl, I pity her running off with a type like that.

JOE. I'm not going to let this happen. I'm going to save her.

RITA. I know what you're after—the reward.

JOE. Shush. Yesyesyes, yes. Quite, for her own good.

PROSTITUTE. Go on, let them go. You were young once.

RITA. Never. He never was young.

JOE. Will you shut up?

SOLLY (*As they argue*). I think you're all marvellous and here's
a token of my appreciation—
*He throws a small packet of pound notes in the air. Every-
one starts scrambling for them; at this* SOLLY *pulls* ROMAINE
*and starts to rush off. The attaché case, however, comes
undone and pound notes are flying everywhere.* SOLLY
*rushes about like a madman and* ROMAINE *sits down and
cries. Everyone else desperately fights each other for the
money.*

JOE. He's robbed the bank of England.

SOLLY. Have you no respect for private property?

PROSTITUTE. Someone's been working overtime.

RITA. Joe, Joe, come inside.
*As she pulls* JOE *she is stuffing pound notes into her
dressing gown.*

WOMAN. Now my husband can have a marvellous memorial.

POLICEMAN (*Enters*). Hello, hello, what's all the fuss?
*They all try to shield* SOLLY *but* POLICEMAN *walks into the
centre and sees him.*
SOLLY *is sitting on the pound notes now like a chicken sits
on an egg.*

SOLLY. We're discussing the political situation.

POLICEMAN. Looks like a mother's meeting—what's it all in aid
of? Eh? I remember you. Didn't I run you in? Wasn't your
mug in the *Police Gazette*?

SOLLY. The only *Gazette* I was in was the London *Gazette* when
I was mentioned in despatches, and the Hackney *Gazette* when
I was born.

POLICEMAN. I remember you now. You're the loud-mouth spiv I
spoke to last week. What are you sitting on?

SOLLY. Lettuce leaves.
POLICEMAN *tries to drag him up.*

ROMAINE. Leave him alone.

SOLLY (*In a gibberish codding way*). Lettuce alone—leave us alone—they're my lettuce leaves.

POLICEMAN. Stand up.

SOLLY. Oh alright. Bloody law has to interfere.

POLICEMAN. Where did you half-inch these from? Whew! Quite a fortune—talk yourself out of this!

SOLLY. I talked myself into this. This is my personal fortune. I can explain. I won it.

POLICEMAN. What? On tiddlewinks?

SOLLY. No, on Pontoon.

WOMAN. He's a liar. He's a villain.

POLICEMAN. Alright, come along with me. We'll sort it out down at the station.

SOLLY. Come on, Romaine. Whither I goest thou must go.

ROMAINE. I've never been in a police station before.

SOLLY. Better get used to it.

JOE. One minute, Officer, may I have a word with you?

ROMAINE. Solly, tell him the truth. The fact is we're running away, we're madly in love.

POLICEMAN. Just you two wait there and don't move (*To* JOE) Now what is it?

JOE. Don't you recognise her? She's the missing heiress. Don't you read your Express?

POLICEMAN. What do you mean—heiress?

JOE. Listen, just keep them here for a while. Her old man's on his way to claim his daughter and to pay me the reward.

POLICEMAN (*Loudly to all*). I've got my duty to perform. There's some dirty business going on with all this money. I'm taking them into custody.

PROSTITUTE. What's the matter with you this morning, George? Why are you so narked? Didn't you get your dropsy from the girls last night?

POLICEMAN. Now you shut up—or I'll run you in also.

SOLLY. Please, Constable—a word in your ear.
*He leads* POLICEMAN *to one side.*
This is not a bribe, it's just a present or a loan. Just turn the other way, will you? I've got a boat to catch.
SOLLY *offers him a wad.*

POLICEMAN. Right! Bribery and corruption as well! You're for it, my lad.
*The* POLICEMAN *takes the money, puts it in his pocket and takes* SOLLY *by the scruff of his neck.*

SOLLY. In that case give me my money back.

POLICEMAN. What money?
MORRY, MILLIE, SARAH, ALAN, MR. *and* MRS. FINK *and* MELVIN *enter hurriedly.*

MILLIE. Oh darling! (*She rushes to* ROMAINE) How are you? Where have you been, you bad girl? I could murder you. You alright darling?

ROMAINE. I'm so pleased to see you, Mummy.

MORRY. Hello, Solly. How's tricks?

SOLLY. Complicated.

MILLIE. Fancy running away like that, where have you been?

ROMAINE. Lying low.

MILLIE. Naughty girl.

SOLLY. You said it.

ROMAINE (*Sings*). "Ah, sweet mystery of life, at last I found you."
*She kisses all the family on the cheek.*

MILLIE. You'll have to marry him now. You're ruined otherwise. (*To* SOLLY) You'll have to marry her.
SOLLY *kisses* MILLIE, *who smiles.*

SOLLY. Who's disagreeing? Mother.

MORRY. Congratulations.
*General back slapping.*

ALAN. Wish you joy.

FINK. Please God, by you.

MRS. FINK. May we only meet on holidays.

SARAH. I'm so happy for both of you.

MILLIE. Isn't it wonderful?

PROSTITUTE. Here comes the bride. . . .

WOMAN. I love a wedding!
*Everyone is joyful except the* POLICEMAN.

SOLLY. Ladies and gentlemen: I'm delighted to announce my betrothal to Romaine and I'm going to make it all worth your while. I'm marrying a fortune—I mean I'm so fortunate. A priceless beauty. A jewel. A gem.
*Everyone cheers and* JOE *brings out some drinks and everyone drinks.*

POLICEMAN. Hold on! What is all this? Is all that money his legal property? Didn't he steal it from you?

MORRY. Steal from me? He'd have a hard job.

POLICEMAN. There's something fishy here.

SOLLY. Probably your socks.

POLICEMAN. I'm not letting you get away with this. There's some conspiracy somewhere—abduction, seduction, larceny—Come on, I'll get to the bottom of this if it kills me.

SOLLY. Now listen, what have you got against me?

POLICEMAN. You're guilty. You're a common crook. Society ain't safe with you around.

SOLLY. We'll hear what society has to say. Nobody has anything against me. Now listen folks (*He addresses the people around him*) You judge me dispassionately. I'll make it worth your while. You stick by me and I'll stick by you. Be my tribunal. Roll up, roll up one and all—am I guilty or not guilty?

WOMAN. Not guilty—a nice boy. Look at his eyes, so kind.

RITA. Not guilty. I hope you'll come and visit us sometime.

JOE. Not guilty. I'll make you a nice suit. Saville Row cut—Mile-end Road cost.

FINK. Not guilty. A potential Mason of the highest order—an influential custodian of property.

MRS. FINK. Not guilty—a nice boy. Thoughtful.

ALAN. Not guilty. Blood is thicker than water.

SARAH. Not guilty. He makes my sister happy.

MELVIN. Not guilty. He's a sportsman.

MILLIE. Not guilty. How could he be? He's my future son-in-law.

MORRY. Not guilty. Officer, you haven't a leg to stand on.

SOLLY. You're wasting your time, Constable. Back to your beat now, my good man.

POLICEMAN. Alright, but I'm keeping my eye on you.
*He goes off and everyone cheers.*

SOLLY. Whenever you want to get the better of them call them Constable or my good man. (*To* MORRY) How can you forgive me?

MORRY. You showed me the way.

SOLLY. But I must confess to you now, I'm not a rabbi.

MORRY. I've known that for days now.

SOLLY. You know?

MORRY. Suddenly I came to my senses but in such a way that I see more clearly now than ever before.

SOLLY. But you did believe that I was a rabbi, admit it. I'm a bloody marvellous actor.

MORRY. Yes, I believed. You see, I'm a simple man and you swore on the Bible.

SOLLY. Aren't you disappointed that you're not the messiah?

MORRY. In a way; I just wanted to make people happy. But now maybe I can be a saviour in another way. I was bored with life until you came, but now I can feel a miracle working inside me. I'm going to travel and relax from now on and try and do some good with my money.

SOLLY. And what about my money? This money?

MORRY. It's yours. Call it my dowry for Romaine. Besides, you earned it. You cured my backache. Hundreds of doctors treated me for years and fleeced me blind and still I suffered. You worked a miracle.

SARAH. It was an accident.

MORRY. Call it what you like. The point is the pain is gone.

SOLLY. But I must admit, Morry—I've been a bad boy. Can you forgive me for my past?

MORRY. Easily. What about my financial advisers? My solicitor and accountant? And my branch managers? They've been diddling me for years. You're an amateur compared to them.

SOLLY. I'm not an amateur—I won't have you say that.

MILLIE. Relax, Solly, let's all be friends. You're one of the family now.
*She kisses him.*

SOLLY. I'm so glad you like me now. You had me worried at first.

MILLIE. No, I admit that I didn't understand you but I feel so much better since you came into our lives. I'm a vegetarian now—on your advice, and it's working wonders. I've lost two pounds in three days—I look so young, don't I? Besides you've got such a big dowry from Morry, we must keep it in the family—so welcome.

SOLLY. Mother! At last I've got a Mum of my own. My Mum took one look at me and run away.

MILLIE. No more lies now. We want you to look after the business—to take complete charge.

SOLLY. What?

MORRY. It's true. If you can't lick them, make them join you. With you in the business nothing can stop us.

SOLLY. You said it. You're very smart. I'll make it the greatest shoe concern in the universe! I can sell anything, even your shoes. "Swartzes everlasting immortal soles." I can sell binoculars to a blind man, roller skates to a cripple. Romaine, Romaine, I'm the happiest guy in the world.
*He cuddles her but she doesn't react.*

SARAH. Solly, you're as good as gold.
*Everyone slaps him on the back.*

MELVIN. I would like to thank you, Solly, for helping me so much.

SOLLY. You as well? I'm so glad I helped. But tell me how?

MELVIN. I took your advice. The other evening at the Maccabee games I took the plunge and spoke to a girl, and now we're mad about each other. We're going to Israel next week—going to get married. And then we're going to start a new Kibbutz—devoted entirely to the propagation of sports and English sportsmanship. You know, cricket, polo, and badminton. She's lovely. What a figure, and can she throw the discus!

MORRY. Come on then, let's all go home and prepare for more weddings.

SOLLY. I feel like dancing.

*He dances with* MILLIE *and soon everyone is dancing round and round as* JOE *plays the mouth organ.*

Come on Romaine, back to Golders Green, back to a life of luxury and love.

*She was the only one not dancing.*

ROMAINE. I'm not going back.

SOLLY *leaves* MILLIE. *He wonders if he heard right. Meanwhile the rest of the cast dances around—in and out of the houses—where they drink and eat.*

SOLLY. What do you mean, not going back?

ROMAINE. I love you, Solly. I want to go forward with you.

SOLLY. But everything's arranged, everything's marvellous. Your family approve of me.

ROMAINE. Well, I don't approve of them. I want us to start afresh—without their lousy money. For you and I to go off into the world with nothing except our love.

SOLLY. Oh God, you've been reading *True Romances*.

ROMAINE. Darling, I want us to start from scratch.

SOLLY. I've been scratching all my life. Sweetheart, I want us to have a little money to start with.

ROMAINE. I want you to work for me—to prove you love me.

SOLLY. Work? That's something I've done without for thirty years and I'm damned if I'm going to start now. You're mad. I agree let's not go back with them—we'll just go as we are—take the money and ourselves, that's all.

ROMAINE. It's the money or me.

SOLLY. Why do you see everything in black or white?

ROMAINE. What do you want—the money or me?

SOLLY. I want both. Don't you see I was born for luxury?

ROMAINE. Well I've had enough of it.

SOLLY. Come on, darling, I love you, you know I do.

ROMAINE. You work so hard at not working, you may as well work and have a holiday. It's goodbye then.

SOLLY. Goodbye? What? What about last night and the night before? What about the things you whispered in the Three Nuns Hotel?

ROMAINE. No! No! No! I don't trust you—I never should. I should have listened to my Mum.

SOLLY. Alright darling, come with me, now.

ROMAINE. No, it's too late, you're hoping to get that money later on. I don't want you any more.

SOLLY. Alright then, I'll take the money.
*The family have now stopped dancing.*

ROMAINE. I'm not going with him.

SOLLY. She's mad.

ROMAINE. He doesn't love me for myself.

MILLIE. Oh darling, you sure?

ROMAINE. Oh Mummy, I don't want a life of poverty, I want to come home with you—(*She weeps*) He just wanted, that was all—after he ruined me.

MILLIE. I don't like my Dolly unhappy, and on such a happy day.

SOLLY. But it's all crazy. I do want her! Morry, please try and persuade her—

MORRY. Do you want him, Romaine? Make up your mind.

ROMAINE. No! I never want to see him again. I don't want him or any man—you can't trust them.

SOLLY. Morry, as her father it's your duty to make her see sense. You know I'm right for her.

MORRY. Sorry, my boy. She must make her own decisions—I'm

not going to interfere. I learned from you how to be tolerant. Thanks.

SOLLY. Alright then, I'll go—I'll take my money and go.

MILLIE. Oh no you don't! That's my money—Romaine's money, for her dowry, and as she's not getting married, I'll keep it for her.

ROMAINE. I don't want it.

SOLLY. Well I do. I earned it, you said so.

MILLIE. Well, it's mine now.

SOLLY. But I made you all so happy—you said so.

MORRY. I know, but women—what can you do with them? Tell you what I'll do—to save any arguments—I'll send it to Israel when Melvin goes, and with it, maybe they'll plant avenues of orange trees. I might even live to see them grow—the way they work out there. Well, that's that. Goodbye, my boy—thanks for everything. If you're ever passing, drop in for a chat.

SOLLY. A chat! A chat! I say, can you lend me a fiver?

MORRY. Sorry, I don't keep any loose change on me. Come on, everyone. Come on, Fink.
      *They start to move off.*

FINK. I told you, Morry, never to trust that man.

MRS. FINK. Herbert, shut up.

MILLIE. Feeling better, darling?

ROMAINE. Smashing; what's for lunch?

SARAH. Chicken, casserolled, and Neapolitan ice cream to follow.

MELVIN. Goodbye, Solly. If you ever want to become a pioneer— and play hockey in the Holy Land, look me up.

MORRY. Come on, everyone—liven up. Goodbye, Solly—all the best. . . . (*They are gone and now the other people go in*)

SOLLY (*Forlorn. Looks around, picks up a cigar butt*). I made them all happy and I didn't earn a bean and I let a fortune and a fat girl slip through my fingers at the same time. What am I going to do for cash? There you are, you try and help and that's the thanks you get. What a life. The world's nothing to write home about. Believe me, if we can't help ourselves how are we going to help others? One thing I'm sure of, I'm not going to work. No, work's too much like an occupation—work's alright for the working class, but for me—it's got to be something better. I must think of something—something really spectacular this time. . . . I've got it! No, no— (*He walks around the stage*) One minute— No. I'm bloody fed up. You can't con an honest coin these days. . . .

*He sits down, picks up some fag ends, rolls a cigarette and becomes deep in thought as*

## THE CURTAIN FALLS